BOGEY NECK ROAD
"The Roots Are Still Growing"

by
Mary Jones Day

A fourth generation descendant compiles the history of African American families in a rural community of the Northern Neck of Virginia.

Printed in the United States of America

ISBN: 1491248963
ISBN-13: 9781491248966

Contents

To my sons,
Robert Eugene Day, Jr., and Timothy Alan Day

To my grandchildren
Ryan Alexander Day, Rachel Michelle Day,
Andrew Sterrett Day, and Emmanuel Timothy Day

I dedicate this book to you. Continue to record the history of our family to be passed on to future generations.

Acknowledgments

A special thanks to the Northumberland County Historical Society (NCHS) and Margaret Forrester for the many hours of research; George Hopkins for assistance with digital image editing and cover; Bettye Fennell and Blondell Hunter for assistance with editing; Warren Jones for the community photos; William T. Jones for his original sketches and hours of telephone consultation; my husband, Robert E. Day, Sr.; and my children, Rob and Tim, for their support and patience. My deepest appreciation to the following Bogey Neck descendants for coordinating their family history:

Heads of Household	Descendants/Coordinators
William Ball, Sr.	James Ball
Joseph W. Jones	William Jones, Hortense Walters Jones, Elwood Jones, Barbara Jones, Deloris Gordon, and Warren Jones
Lombard Jones	Ceddra Yerby Jones, Leonard Jones, Carolyn Jones Matthews, Beatrice Jones Moody, and Gwendolyn Jones
Raleigh Jones	Mary E. Jones and Kim Jones
Adolphus Wallace	Sarah Wallace Brassfield and Anthony Wood
Sylvester Warner, Sr.	Lloyd Warner, William Warner Jr., and Clifford Landon
John Walters	Emma Smith Jones, Douglas Norris, Clara Walters Priester, Helen Norris Ball, Joyce Norris Wilson, Lori Ball Fenner, Fannie Mae Kennedy, and Carroll Smith
Washington Walters	Barbara Jones, Sarah Walters Harcum, Lillie Mae Walters Kearney, and Hortense Walters Jones
William Wilson	Joyce Norris Wilson and Doris Yerby

PREFACE

When I published my first book, *My Father's Journey,* in 2009, never in my wildest dream did I think that I would travel down this road again. It all began on the second Saturday in August 2012, at an annual community picnic on Bogey Neck Road in Northumberland County, VA. For the last thirty-two years, the descendants and friends of Bogey Neck have gathered in the field next to my family home to meet, greet, and eat. I suppose this occasion could be called the "Bogey Neck Family Reunion."

On the second Saturday in August 1981, a group of us were sitting on the porch, reminiscing about our childhood and how much we looked forward to returning to our roots. Subsequently, I have heard year after year, "Somebody should write a story on Bogey Neck because there is a lot of history here that will never be told." The next day after the 2012 picnic, my cousin Mark Alonzo Jones and I stood in front of his family home on the side of the road talking and revisited the idea of getting something on paper about Bogey Neck. As we chatted, we looked down the road at the old oak tree that we have seen all our lives. We recalled that it had served as our official school bus stop and provided shelter for us on rainy days. This tree was a gathering place for us after school and on weekends because there wasn't much else to do. Mark and I agreed that the tree could really be the official landmark for Bogey Neck. My response to him was "OK, Mark, I think I might draft something." Mark responded with his familiar grin, "Sister (my 'Bogey Neck' name), if you write a story about Bogey Neck, you will be doing such a wonderful thing—something that can be passed on to generations. It is so amazing that when I start to think about my childhood, wonderful memories just start to flood my mind."

I left Mark to return to my house. Instead of taking the usual shortcut across the field, I walked down the road toward the tree. The sunset behind the tree cast a large shadow that reached east across the road on the front lawn of my family's home and covered the front yards of the Ball and Taylor homes, which sat west of the tree. As I approached the tree, I became mesmerized by the enormous size of its trunk and the roots extending around it. The roots seemed to be bursting out everywhere above the ground. Some roots seemed like anchors that extended from the base of the trunk straight down into the ground.

This was the first time that I had been so interested in observing a tree. I wondered, *How old is this tree?* Maybe a hundred years old. *Did the tree begin growing before the road was constructed?* Maybe, this road was once a trail or path. *When did African Americans start living on this road?* They may have been slaves on the plantation and stopped under this tree to rest their horses after working in the fields. *How did "Bogey Neck" get its name and when? Was there a Bogey Man around?* I remembered that this place was called "Buggy Neck" because of the horse and buggies that used to travel here. I thought, *If these roots keep growing, they may continue to grow and extend across the road.* I crossed the road, headed to my house, and looked back at the big old oak tree. The leaves were waving back and forth as if saying "good-bye." The tree and the roots reminded me of the Bogey Neck families and how they are still growing.

Riding back to Columbia, MD, I felt a rush of excitement as I began thinking of what I could possibly write about an oak tree, a country road, and the families who lived there. *What will be the title?* Maybe *The Roots Are Still Growing.* There certainly couldn't be much on the Internet or in books about these families. Most of the sources have passed, and my generation was the oldest of those that remained. Still curious about the tree, I called my older brother, William, to find out what he knew about the tree. He promised to write a few notes about what he remembered, and here's his brief story:

THE OAK TREE by William T. Jones[1]

In April 1933, my father, Daniel Olin Jones, and mother, Vera Sebree Jones, moved to our home in "Buggy Neck." This was a trip from Mila Neck (my grandfather Sebree's home on Mila Road). Their mode of transportation at that time was walking, with me in tow, on this two-mile trip along a wooded trail and across a swamp. As we approached the house, there was a big tree on the other side of the narrow dirt road—almost directly in front of the house. In later years, my mother often worried that a strong wind could blow the tree down into our yard. That old tree, like the community, has withstood the worst of times. No one knows its exact age, but it was as tall as our two-story house when we settled there. Judging from its size now, it is at least one hundred years old.

Over eighty years have passed since I first saw that tree. As we approach our next "Bogey Neck Day Celebration," I often think about

---

1   William T. Jones, great-grandson of Stafford B. Jones, native of Bogey Neck, resides in Jacksonville, FL, 2012.

the many hardships our ancestors endured—slavery, wars, segregation, illnesses, and the Depression. There have been many changes and improvements since the first group of families settled there. Other families have moved to Bogey Neck, and their descendants now live there. That old oak tree seems to symbolize the history of Bogey Neck. The strong and deep roots represent our ancestors, their endurance, and their many outstanding contributions to the community and the nation. The many spreading branches represent us—the generations that have followed.

CHAPTER I—BOGEY NECK COMMUNITY

"The life of the individual is first and foremost an accommodation
to the patterns and standards traditionally handed down in his
community."—Ruth Benedict

Bogey Neck is a small community located east central of Northumberland County, VA, south of the Great Wicomico River.[2] It is located in the Wicomico Church district, one of four districts in Northumberland County.[3] Known to be the "mother" of many counties, Northumberland was officially formed in 1648 and divided to form *Lancaster County* (1652) and *Westmoreland County* (1653). Other counties were later formed from Lancaster (*Middlesex* 1673 and *Rappahannock* 1656–92); and Westmoreland County (Stafford 1664 divided to form *Loudoun* and *Fairfax* counties). *Richmond* and *Essex* counties were formed from Rappahanock and a division extended into *Dickenson County* (1880).[4]

---

2 Miller, Mary R. *Place Names of the Northern Neck of Virginia*–from John Smith's 1606 map to the present. Virginia State Library, Richmond, VA, 1963, p.13.
3 Ibid, p.171.
4 Northumberland County Chamber of Commerce, Northumberland County Directory, March 1971.

Snowden Park

Snowden Park, originally a 1,545-acre farm with a dwelling and storehouse owned by Cyrus Harding, is located east of Wicomico Church, VA on Route 607. It was Harding's wish that the land be divided among his children, and the land was divided in 1873. The tract of land currently known as Snowden Park (where Bogey Neck is located) was a 330-acre tract valued at eleven dollars an acre (or $3,639) and was divided into two shares.[5]

What was probably once a trail through Snowden Park became a dirt road, dividing the east and west of Snowden Park. The name of this road was known to some as "Buggy Neck" and to others as "Boogy Neck" until it was officially named "Bogey Neck" in 1998. The horse and buggy was the mode of transportation for some, and others traveled on foot. I recall that in the 1940s, the road was all dirt that was dragged by horses pulling a flat piece of wood to make the road smooth. In later years, a tractor was used with a flat board hooked to the back to smooth out the rough spots. The road was often sprinkled to keep down the dust. Sarah Harcum, a descendant of the Washington Walters family of Bogey Neck, reminded me that, as children, we called it "Washboard Road" because it was so bumpy when we would ride on it in a car.

Land in Snowden Park was sold to the first African American families on the east side of Bogey Neck Road between 1900 and 1913, starting at the corner of Route 607 and going north on the road toward Barrett's Creek but stopping at what was known as "the hill."[6] Later in

---

5 Deed Book E, Northumberland County, VA, pp. 443-448.
6 Land Records of Wicomico District in Northumberland County, VA, 1900-1913.

the 1900s, African American families were able to buy land at the lower end of the road on the west side, starting at "the hill" and heading south on Route 607.

Currently, the upper part of the west side of Snowden Park starting at the corner of Route 607 is a development with its entrance off of Route 200 in Wicomico Church. The barrier was broken, and African Americans own property in this development.

Homes–Early 1900s[7]

The first African American families in Bogey Neck lived in two-story houses on five or more acres of land surrounded by big shade trees and a fruit orchard, garden, hog pen, outhouse, hen house, horse stable, well, smokehouse, woodpile, and clothesline. There were vegetable and flower gardens in the front and back of the houses. Many of the families farmed fields of crops, such as corn, hay, tomatoes, greens, and potatoes. Mounds in the field were used to preserve potatoes. Fruits, vegetables, and hog meat were put in glass jars and stored in a closet or smokehouse to be preserved for the winter. (See Chapter VIII, Recipes from Bogey Neck's Kitchens.)

---

7   Oral history.

Floor Plan[8]

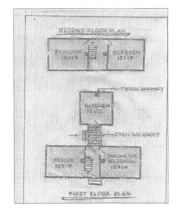

Though slightly different in each house, the basic floor plan in the original homes consisted of a hallway that extended front to back with a door at each end, a kitchen/dining area, and a parlor downstairs. One or two bedrooms and a hallway were upstairs. Some of the most striking features about these old houses were the high (and sometimes slanted) ceilings and two to three windows in a room. The wooden floors were often covered with linoleum.

Whenever my mother wanted to change the floor covering, she would put the new linoleum over what was already on the floor. When I pulled up the linoleum a few years ago in what was my old bedroom, there were five layers of linoleum covering a beautiful wood floor. The layers of linoleum were left purposefully to help keep the room warm.

Kitchen. Some kitchens were set off from the main house by an open walkway and a back door leading to the outside. Locating the kitchen outside of the main house was considered to be a safety feature in case of fire from the wood-burning cookstove. A wooden icebox was placed in the corner of the kitchen, with a pan underneath to hold the water from the melting ice. The oak table was usually rectangular with benches on both sides and an oak chair at each end, and a kerosene lamp sat in

8 Sketch by William T. Jones, great-grandson of Stafford B. Jones, native of Bogey Neck, resides in Jacksonville, FL, 2012.

4

the middle. A painted wooden cupboard with two doors and shelves for dishes and "dry goods" sat on an open wall. The cookstove was a flat-top with an oven and enclosure above (called "the warmer") to keep the food warm as well as to heat the room. A kettle filled with water was often on top of the stove, and a pot of beans or vegetables (greens, cabbage) would most likely be boiling for dinner. A box was next to the stove—or in a corner near the stove—and was stocked with wood. Somewhere in the corner would be a water bucket, a basin, and towel for hand washing and cooking. After dinner, the children would gather around the kitchen table to do homework around the kerosene lamp.

Living room. The living room was on the opposite side of the hall from the kitchen and was used for special occasions. A beautiful "settee," draped with an afghan or doilies, was placed on the longest wall and sometimes in front of a window. There were one or two side chairs, a kerosene lamp on an end table, and a potbelly stove in the center of the room, in front of the chimney. Framed pictures of Jesus, the Lord's Supper, ancestors, and family members hung around the walls. Shades and lace curtains covered the windows. It was where the guests often slept. A tradition in my family was to gather in the parlor on Sunday morning for "family prayer" before breakfast. The Family Bible was visible on the coffee table in front of the sofa or somewhere in the room. In the early days and even today, the Bible served as a safe place for important documents—birth certificates marriage certificate, and receipts—and important dates, such as deaths and births.

Kerosene lamps and lanterns were the sources of light for the homes on Bogey Neck Road until the early fifties, when electric poles were installed. Electricity was provided to white families living on the lower end of Bogey Neck (on Barrett's Creek) from electric wires extending from Route 200 across the Great Wicomico River to the residents. Wood was the source of heat for cooking and heating. The heater used to warm the room(s) was the potbelly stove.

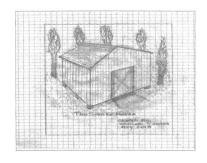

The "smokehouse" in the backyard was about an eight-foot by eight-foot structure.[9] It was used to store food items, such as hog meat, canned fruit, and vegetables from the garden. Also, nonfood items, such as chicken and hog feed, and tools were kept in this little house. When the hogs were slaughtered, usually around November or as soon as it was cold, the meat was cut up, cured, and stored in this house for the winter. As kids, we were eager to get the pig's bladder, blow it up like a balloon, and hang it in the smokehouse until Christmas morning, when we took turns pounding it with the broom handle until it popped.

The "outhouse" was located a distance from the back of the house, with the door always to the side or back.[10] A washbowl and pitcher with water, soap, towel, and toilet

9   Sketch by William T. Jones, great-grandson of Stafford B. Jones, native of Bogey Neck, resides in Jacksonville, FL, 2012.
10   Ibid.

paper (or old catalog) were provided. Indoor plumbing for most houses was added in the early sixties.

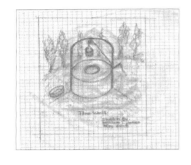

Some of the best water I ever had was from the hand-dug well in the backyard.[11] Water was pulled from the well by lowering a bucket down a fifty- or sixty-foot well. Once the bucket was pulled up with water, it was transferred to a bucket that stayed in the kitchen. Also, water from the well was used for the livestock. One of the well diggers was James Ball, a native of Bogey Neck.

Every household raised chickens for food and sometimes for sale. The chickens were ordered and delivered in a box to the post office. When fully grown, the chickens were used for food, and some were placed in a crate and placed at the end of the lane for a special truck that picked up the crate of chickens to be shipped.

On one of my visits to Bogey Neck, I stopped in to chat with my eighty-four-year-old cousin, Lloyd Warner, the last living of his siblings. Lloyd died less than a year after my visit with him. I am grateful that I was able to spend the time with him. He was the grandson of Fredrick and Sophronia Warner and son of Sylvester and Cornelia Warner. Lloyd and his twin sister, Laura, were the youngest of eight children and the last of the siblings to leave home. When asked, "What was it like growing up in your family?" he responded with a sense of pride as he talked:

11   Sketch by William T. Jones, great-grandson of Stafford B. Jones, native of Bogey Neck, resides in Jacksonville, FL, 2012..

"I had a good life. Papa and Mama didn't have to buy much for us to survive. We were "self–sufficient." When it came to eating, we had meat from the hogs and chickens, milk from the cow, eggs from the chickens, canned fruit and jellies or preserves from the orchards, vegetables from the garden, and water from the well. We cut our own wood to heat the house and cook the food. Mama and Papa worked hard to provide for us children, and we worked too. My father died when I was twelve, and I was the last boy to leave home. I got up early and made the fire so that the house would be warm for Mama when she got up. Before going to school, I had to milk the cow. Mama would say, "Get to that cow before he gets to the onions." You knew that if the cow got to the onions, that's what the milk would taste like. Then I had to pick the fruit before the birds got to it; that was one of my after-school chores. I cut wood for the stove in the winter and tended the garden in the spring and summer using our horse and plow. Yes, we owned a horse, too. I worked and always gave Mama money to help out with whatever bills she had. I did this until she died, that is helping her out financially."

Lloyd's description of his family was similar to other Bogey Neck families during this time. The heads of the households (husbands/fathers) did seasonal work, such as watermen, loggers, carpenters, laborers, or cooks. The wives/mothers worked in the home and often outside of the home as washwomen, servants, or cooks for the white families. The children worked on the farms at home and as laborers for the white farmers. Many left school at the end of seventh grade or earlier to work or attended school for a half day in order to work.

Map of First African American Homes in Bogey Neck[12]

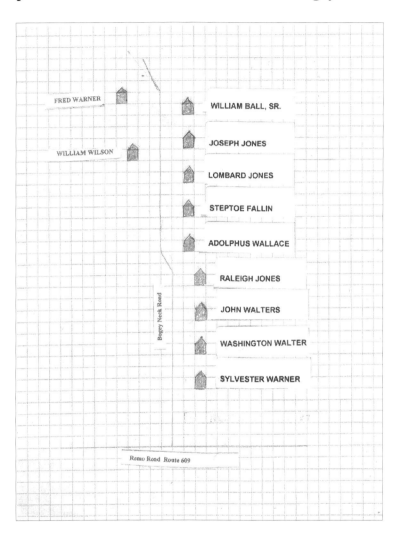

FRED WARNER

WILLIAM BALL, SR.

WILLIAM WILSON

JOSEPH JONES

LOMBARD JONES

STEPTOE FALLIN

ADOLPHUS WALLACE

RALEIGH JONES

Bogey Neck Road

JOHN WALTERS

WASHINGTON WALTER

SYLVESTER WARNER

Remo Road Route 609

12 Sketch by William T. Jones, great-grandson of Stafford B. Jones, native of Bogey Neck, resides in Jacksonville, FL, 2012.

Landmarks and Trails[13]

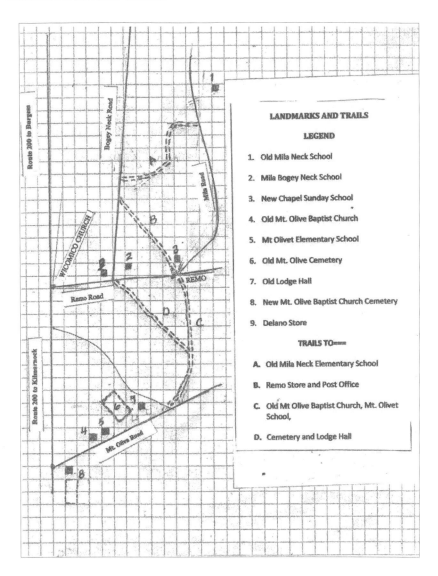

---

13 Sketch by William T. Jones, great-grandson of Stafford B. Jones, native of Bogey Neck, resides in Jacksonville, FL, 2012

General Merchandise Stores[14]

Two main general stores—Remo and Delano—were located within less than two miles from Bogey Neck. These stores stocked a variety of items: dry goods, furnishings, shoes, clothing, hardware, toiletries, food, etc.

Remo General Store and Post Office. The Remo General Store and Post Office, located two miles east of Wicomico Post Office, opened in 1913 as a post office, with Joseph P. Delano serving as the first postmaster, followed by Albert Hank in 1918. A. G. W. Christopher (ca. 1898–1974) was appointed postmaster in 1928 and operated the store and post office. I was unable to find the official opening date of the store; however, copies of ledger sheets dated 1915 for purchases made at Remo Store by Walter Kennard Jones, Lombard Coleman Jones, Adolphus Wallace, Raleigh Doleman Jones, and William H. Ball of Bogey Neck were provided by the NCHS. (See Appendix E: Ledger Sheets.)[15] Before automobiles, the customers accessed the store by way of trails or the Remo Road (Route 609). In the early days, the store served as a gathering place for the people to socialize. It was once said that the men gathered after work and sat around the potbelly stove to catch up on the news and weather report. The stove served as a divider between whites and blacks,

---

14 Northern Neck of Virginia Historical Magazine, *"Northumberland Post Office,"* Vol. XLVIII, The Northern Neck of Virginia Historical Society; Montross, Westmoreland County, VA, December 1998.

15 Northumberland County Historical Society, Remo General Store, A. G. W. Christopher's ledger pages; Remo, VA, 1915.

who sat on different sides of the stove when they talked. Years after the post office and store closed, it served as a landmark—especially when giving directions for how to get to Mila or Harvest Neck from Wicomico Church. (Photo taken by William T. Jones, 2010.)

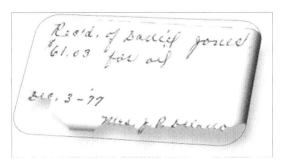

Delano General Store. The Delano General Store, located on the corner of Remo Road (Route 609) and Bogey Neck Road (Route 607), was owned and operated by Joseph P. Delano (ca. 1888–ca. 1949). According to the federal census, the store was operating in 1920.[16] My memory of Mr. Delano is that he was a very dear friend of my family and very nice to me. When I was about five or six years old, I often walked to the store in the evening with my dad, and I always had a penny to spend. I would tell Mr. Delano what I wanted to buy with my penny—Mary Jane candy or gingersnaps—and he always put more than a penny's worth in my bag. Daddy made his purchase of groceries and sometimes kerosene, and Mr. Delano would record the amount of the purchase in his ledger, and Dad would pay it at the end of the week or when he got paid. After Mr. Delano's death, his family continued to operate the store for several years and maintained an oil delivery service. After the store closed, the doors stayed open. Eliot Earl Delano (J. P. Delano's youngest son) sold crabs and oysters. They had an oil delivery service and provided heating oil for the community.

---

16 Federal Census 1920.

In 2010, I visited the store and had a chat with Eliot Earl about the history of the store. He was kind enough to give me a quick tour of the store as he talked about its history: 1) prior to Delano, Harding's store was located on same property, 2) Delano clerked with the Anderson brothers and then opened his own store, and 3) Sam Conley (a nephew) clerked with Delano and later opened a store in Wicomico on the corner of Routes 200 and 609. Even without merchandise on the shelves, in many ways, the store looked the same—counters, shelves, office, storage room, and a stove in the center of the store used for heating. He pointed to where various items were shelved. I recalled the corner where the shoes were kept and the counters where the jars of candy and cookies were stored. Eliot Earl shared a few invoices from the old file cabinet and gave me two, dated September 1937, to take with me. I did some Internet shopping and compared the prices of the items today with those in 1937. Today, some of the items or even the containers are collectibles. For example, listed as a collectible was a used "Sweet Pea talc cardboard container with metal ends" that was selling for $9.99 on eBay.[17] Another example is oyster tongs shafts that are manufactured in just a few places. The following are two invoices for merchandise shipped to Delano's in 1937:

---

17 www.ebay.com

INVOICE: Wholesale and Importing Druggist–Baltimore, MD
September 9, 1937

Qty	Description		1937	2013[18]
1 doz.	Rubbing alcohol Adde	1.50	1.50	$1.89 ea.
1/2 doz.	Pts. Crude Carbolic Acid	1.75	0.88	
1 doz	Colgate D, Cr,		0.85	
1 doz,	Listerine T. Oaste		0.91	$4.79 4.2 oz.
1 doz.	Tubes Zonite Paste		4.00	
1 doz.	Listerine 10		0.91	$6.29 1 L.
1/2 doz.	Mex, W, Oil Lint.	2.25	1.13	$4.39 pt.
1 doz.	Tooth Ache Drops		0.85	$6.99 14 oz.
1/2 doz.	Lapactic Pills	3.00	1.50	
1 doz.	Ground cloves		0.40	$6.99 0.6 oz.
5 lbs.	White Butter Paper	0.22	1.10	$4.72 30 ft. roll
3 doz.	Sweet Pea Talcum[19]	0.85	2.55	$35.00 4.5 oz.
2 doz.	Perfecto Vanilla	0.75	1.50	$6.50 1 oz. bot
1 doz	Murray's Hair Dressing		2.00	$3.99 3 oz.
1 doz.	Griffins All White		0.85	$16.00 bottle 2.ozs
		Frt	0.69	

---

18 www.Drugstore.com
19 eBay

INVOICE: Oyster and Butcher Tools, Shipped from Crisfield, MD

September 15, 1937

Quantity	Description	1937 Unit Cost	Total Cost	2013[20] Cost
1 pair	#880–18 ft. Fine Oyster Tong Shafts pr.	$2.60	$2.60	
2 pairs	#880–16 ft. Pine Oyster Tong Shafts pr.	$3.50	$7.00	$175
1 pair	#880–20 ft. Fine Oyster Tong Shafts pr.	$5.25	$5.25	
2 pairs	#820–16 tooth Eel Pot Oyster Tongs pr.	$5.50	$11.00	
1 pair	#856–4 & 5 Nippers pr.	1.25	1.25	$27.95

Chapter II — First African American Family Homeowners In Bogey Neck

"You don't choose your family. They are God's gift to you, as you are to them." —Desmond Tutu

Head of Households — Generation 1[21]

The heads of households born in slavery and parents of the first families to move in Bogey Neck have been identified as "Generation I" for the purpose of tracing the genealogy for this project. The heads of families were: Frederick Warner (b. ca. 1847), William Walters (b. ca. 1845), Stafford B. Jones (b. ca. 1826), Betsey Ball (b. ca. 1826), William "Willie" T. Wilson (b. ca. 1849), and Robert Wallace (b. ca. 1840).[22] Unable to locate land records of ownership during the periods 1865–1900 for African Americans in Bogey Neck, federal censuses place the residence of the first generation in the Wicomico Church district of Northumberland County, VA. However, it is possible that some in this generation lived in Bogey Neck on plantations as "free and slave Negros" in Snowden Park—later referred to as Bogey Neck.

---

21 Federal Census 1850, 1870.
22 Federal Census, 1850, 1870, 1880.

Land Records and Personal Property Records[23]

The following are eleven second-generation families who became land owners in Bogey Neck in the 1900s. These properties were located on the east side of Snowden Park about a two-and-a-half-mile span north of Route 609 on Route 607, called Bogey Neck Road. Land records show that these eleven families purchased approximately 125 acres and ten families lived in Bogey Neck all of their lives. In addition to owning property, they were taxed on their "personal property" by categories. After 1930, "tangible personal property" (TPP) categories were condensed into one category: "tangible personal property."[24]

1. **William Ball** (b. ca. 1872)—son of Betsey Ball

   Land: 20¼ acres and building, $171.00, seller unknown, (1900)

1912	Sold 1 acre to Sylvester Warner
1912	19¼ acres listed
1913	Sold ¾ acre to Wm. Beal (Ball)
1913	18½ acres listed
1913	Conveyed tract of land in "Boogy" Neck to John Bale (Ball), Sr., son–6 acres for $60
1914	Owned 10½ acres listed
1923	Owned land and building; value: $13.00
1926	Land value: $414 (increase of $101 in three years)
1948	10½ acres listed

23   Northumberland County VA Land Records, 1900-1913; Land Tax Books 1900-1930; Personal Property Books 1920-1950.

24   Northumberland County Personal Property Tax Records, Northumberland County, VA, 1930–1950.

1949–50 10½ acres and 2 acres; no building assessed

1953   10½ acres and 2 acres; value: $150, no building

1960   10½ acres, value: $80 (land only)

1966   Listed as William Ball estate, 10½ acres, value: $240, no building

Personal Property: Total taxes owed–$140

1910   1 male inhabitant over 21; 1 mule, 2 cows; 2 wagons or family carriages; 2 farming implements; household furnishing value: $10; 1 firearm

1920   1 male inhabitant over 21; tangible property valued at $325; 2 horses; 3 carriages or wagons; farm implements valued at $10; household furnishing value: $30; 1 boat; weapons value: $10

1930   No personal property listed in William Ball's name; tax records recorded until 1966

2. **John Walters** (ca. 1870–ca. 1930)—son of William and Ann V. Walters

Land: 10 acres purchased from Sam Walker's estate by C. H. Walker, $171.50 (1904)

1957   Recorded as John Walters estate through 1994–10 acres

1995   Recorded as John Walters estate through 2004–10 acres

2005   Recorded as John Walters estate through 2010

2010   Recorded in John Walters's name with Spencer Norris, c/o H. Ball

2012   No will found

Personal Property

1890	No records
1900	1 male inhabitant over 21; 1 family carriage
1910	1 male inhabitant over 21; 1 horse, 2 hogs; 1 family carriage; 2 farming implements; household and kitchen furniture
1920	1 male inhabitant over 21; 1 horse, 1 cattle, 1 hog; farming implements; 2 carriages; 1 watch; mechanic tools; 2 musical instruments (organ and other); household and kitchen furniture
1930	No records
1940	No records

3. **Washington Walters** (b. ca. 1880)—son of William and Ann V. Walters

Land

1904	10½ acres forest land purchased from Samuel Walker's estate by C. H. Walker
1906	Owned 8¾ acres previously owned by W. W. Walters near Harcum Wharf; sold to George Walters (1908)
2012	No will found

Personal Property

1890	No records
1900	1 inhabitant over 21; 2 horses, 4 hogs; 1 family carriage; farming implements; household and kitchen furniture
1910	1 inhabitant over 21; 1 horse; 1 family carriage; farming implements; household and kitchen furniture

1920   1 inhabitant over 21; 1 horse, 1 cattle, 2 hogs; 2 family carriages; farming implements; 1 piano or organ; 2 shotguns; household and kitchen furniture

1930   1 inhabitant over 21; TPP value: $135

1940   No records

4. **Joseph Warren Jones** (ca. 1867–ca. 1940)—son of Stafford B. and Susan Warner Jones

Land

1906   9$^1/_8$ acres in Snowden Park

1908   Sold 4 acres to Steptoe Fallin

1908   Recorded: Snowden Park—5¼ through 1989

1990   Note on record: 5¼ acres, c/o Ellis Jones

Note: Owned another tract of land in Bogey Neck (record not available)

2012   No will

Personal Property

1890   1 inhabitant over 21; no other items

1900   1 inhabitant over 21; 1 horse; 1 family carriage; household and kitchen furniture

1910   1 inhabitant over 21; 1 horse; 1 family carriage; 1 piano; household and kitchen furniture

1920   1 inhabitant over 21; 2 horses, 1 cattle, 2 hogs; 3 family carriages; mechanic tools, farming implements; 1 watch; 1 piano; household and kitchen furniture

1930   1 inhabitant over 21; all TPP value: $91

1940   1 inhabitant over 21; all TPP value: $34

1941–1945 Joseph W. Jones estate, TPP values varied

5. **Lombard Coleman Jones** (b. ca. 1873)—son of Stafford B. and Susan Warner Jones

 Land

1906	5 acres in Snowden Park
1906	1 tract–5 acres through 1955
1955	"By will" to Louis Thomas Jones[25]

House occupied by William and Mary Coursey; property later sold to James Ball.[26]

 Personal Property

1890	No records
1900	No records
1910	1 inhabitant over 21; 1 hog; household and kitchen furniture
1920	1 inhabitant over 21; 1 horse, 2 hogs; 1 family carriage; farming implements; 1 watch, 1 clock; household and kitchen furniture
1930	1 inhabitant over 21; TPP value: $122
1940	1 inhabitant over 21; no TPP listed
1944	No inhabitant listed, TPP value: $24
1950	No records

6. **Steptoe Fallin** (ca. 1863–ca. 1925)—son of James and Betsy Taylor Fallin

 Land

| 1908 | 4 acres purchased from Joseph Jones (1908) |
| 1925 | Land left to sole heir, "Nancy Johns," recorded[27] |

---

25 Will Book E, p. 505.
26 Oral history and deed book, p. 109.
27 Will Book C., p. 672.

Personal Property: aggregate value of tangible personal property: $72

1910–1920 1 male inhabitant taxed $1.50; 1 horse; 2 family carriages or wagons; 2 farming implements; household items and furnishings value: $10

7. **William "Willie" Wilson** (b. ca. 1879)—son of James and Clara Wilson, Westmoreland County, VA

Land

1920   36 acres purchased from Julia V. Harding and Julia A. Harding: $900; no building, Snowden Park

1923   No listing

1924–1931 26 acres–part Snowden Park

1966   William Wilson estate; 36 acres–land and building, value: $128

1973   35.01 acres divided among 6 children–5.85 acres each

Personal Property: aggregate value: $333

1920   1 male in home over 21; 1 horse; 2 wagons; 2 farm implements; musical instruments; household items value: $50; 1 weapon

1930   1 male in home over 21; $136 value of property

1940   1 male in home; tangible property value: $14

8. **John Ball, Sr.** (ca. 1870–ca. 1928)—son of Betsey Ball (widow)

   Land

1913	6 acres purchased from William Ball, Sr., $60
1939	6 acres sold to Dennis Yerby by J. P. Delano

   Personal Property

1890	No records
1900	1 inhabitant over 21; 1 horse; 1 clock; household and kitchen furniture
1910	1 inhabitant over 21; 1 horse, 1 hog; 2 farming implements; household and kitchen furniture
1920	1 inhabitant over 21; 1 horse, 1 hog; 2 family carriages; 1 musical instrument; 2 farming implements; 1 watch; household and kitchen furniture
1930	No records
1940	No records

9. **Adolphus Wallace** (ca. 1879-1930)—son of Robert and Ellen Wallace

   Land

1912–1913	5 acres and building purchased (1912), listed in Adolphus Wallace's name through 1990
1923–1948	$450 value, land and building
1949	$450 value, land and building
1950–1959	$1,210 value, land and building
1960	Forest land, 5 acres, value: $1,060
1966	$1,380 land value
1970	$2,000 land value
1980–1985	Forest land, 5 acres

1990   Adolphus Wallace, c/o Anthony Wood
No will found

Personal Property

1910   1 male over 21; 1 watch; 1 weapon

1920   1 male over 21; household and kitchen furniture; weapon; value: $52

1930 $30 value

1940   No personal property

10. **Sylvester Warner** (ca. 1887–1937)—son of Fredrick and Sophronia Warner

Land: 6 acres, owned 2 tracts–Snowden Park

1912   1 acre purchased from William and Addie Ball; 5 acres purchased from Fred Wiggins

1924   Added 1 tract–4½ acres; purchased tract woodland from T. M. Wright

1957   Sylvester Warner estate: 1½ acres to W i l l i a m Warner by heirs

1961   Sylvester Warner estate to T. E., Sr., or Irene B. Turner (Plat Bk 2–55)

2012   No will found

Personal Property

1890   No records

1900   No records

1910   1 male inhabitant over 21; 1 cow

1920   1 male inhabitant over 21; 1 horse; 2 family carriages; farming implements; 1 clock; household and kitchen furniture

1930	1 male inhabitant over 21; TPP: $179; Cornelia Warner (female) listed; no TPP
1940	Sylvester Warner estate; no male inhabitant over 21; TPP: 1½, $24 Cornelia Warner (female) listed; no TPP
1950	1 female; TPP value: $134; lists William Warner and Julia Warner; TPP value: $134

11. Raleigh Doleman Jones (ca. 1867-1944)—son of Stafford B. and Susan Warner Jones

Land

1913	6 4/5 acres, purchased from C. H. Walker
1921	1 tract–Dividing Creek–19 35/100 acres, purchased from "N. J. Whaley extux," sold to J. P. Delano thru C. S. Towles, trustee, and the 6¾ acres on part of Snowden Park was sold to Noble J. Whaley through C. S. Towles, trustee
1929	No listing through 1942
2012	No will was found

Personal Property

1890	1 inhabitant over 21; no other personal property listed
1900	1 inhabitant over 21; household and kitchen furniture
1910	1 inhabitant over 21; 1 horse, 2 hogs; 2 family carriages; mechanic tools; 1 piano; household and kitchen furniture

1920	1 inhabitant over 21; 1 horse, 1 cow, 1 hog; 2 family carriages; farming implements; 1 piano; household and kitchen furniture
1930	1 inhabitant over 21; TPP value: $50
1940	1 inhabitant over 21; TPP value: $10
1944	1 inhabitant over 21; no TPP listed
1945	No records

Over forty additional acres of land were sold to the second, third, and fourth generations of African Americans between 1930 and 1974 on the east and west sides of Bogey Neck Road.[28]

1. **Joseph Russell and Sarah Jones**—5 acres and building, purchased from Mamie J. Haynie, $200 (1930); property sold to J. P. Haynie at public auction in front of Remo Post Office (1939), $150. (Grandson of Stafford Jones, son of Joseph Warren Jones)

2. **Arthur Reid and Elmira Corbin Jones**—Note: No records found for land and house located on property adjacent to father, Raleigh Doleman Jones. Several families lived in this house, including father Raleigh Doleman until his death in 1944. After Raleigh's death, other families who lived there were Miria and Boson Taylor and Hannah and Alonzo Norris.

3. **Daniel Olin and Vera Sebree Jones**—5 acres and building, purchased from Stuart and Imogene Blackwell, $550 (deed dated 1943). Note: The house was originally occupied by his brother,

---

28 Northumberland County, VA, Land Records and Deed Books, 1930–1945.

Clarence Jones, who returned from WWI. When Clarence could not make payments, his brother Daniel purchased the house and moved in with his wife and son in 1933; they paid the balance owed on the house to Stuart and Imogene Blackwell in 1943. (Grandson of Stafford B. Jones, son of Joseph Warren Jones)

4. **Grace Cornelia Walters and Emerson Norris**—6 acres and building, purchased from Mary Alice Whaley, $225 (1938).

5. **Cecil Taylor**—5 acres and building, purchased from J. P. Haynie for taxes and levies (1939); previously owned by Joseph R. Jones and auctioned in 1939. Records remained the same through 1970. In 1970, land listed valued at $240 with no building to 1980. (No relation to original families)

6. **Alice Wilson and Dennis Yerby**—6 acres, purchased from J. P. and Nellie K. Delano, $150 (1939). (Granddaughter of William Wilson, daughter of William "Willie" J. Wilson)

7. **Ellis Dubois and Hortense Walters Jones**—5 acres purchased from J. P. and Nellie K. Delano, $275 (1943). (Grandson of Stafford B. Jones, son of Joseph Warren Jones, and great-granddaughter of William Walters)

8. **Heirs of William "Willie" Wilson**—36 acres divided equally among Alice Wilson Yerby, David Wilson, William Corbin Wilson, Maud R. Norris, Robert H. Wilson, Frederick Wilson, Sarah L. Wilson (1945). (Children of William "Willie" and Julia Corbin Wilson)

9. **John and Mable Taylor**—2 acres, purchased from Julia V. Harding, $175 (1944). (No relation to original families)

10. **William Gilbert and Lois Ball**—2 acres, purchased from Julia V. Harding, $10 (1946). (Great-grandson of Betsey Ball; grandson of William Ball, Sr.; son of William W. Ball)

11. **Beatrice Walters and Samuel Brown**—2 acres, purchased from Julia V. Harding. (Great-granddaughter of William Walters, granddaughter of Washington Walters, daughter of Solomon Walters)

12. **James Edward and Ceddra Jones**—2 acres, purchased from Julia V. Harding, $230 (1951); 2 acres purchased from estate of Julia V. Harding by F. Warren Haynie, administrator, $250 (1974). (Great-grandson of Stafford Jones, grandson of Lombard Jones, son of Louis T. Jones)

13. **Onard "Sanny" Jackson Jones**—2 acres purchased from Julia V. Harding, $10 (1968). (Grandson of Stafford B. Jones, son of Joseph W. Jones)

Chapter III — Schools Serving Bogey Neck Community

"Education is the key to unlock the golden door of freedom."
—George Washington Carver

There is very little recorded about the early schooling for African American children in Bogey Neck or the Wicomico district. The federal census records indicate that the first generation could read and write, and they passed their knowledge and skills on to their children. The four oldest descendants of Bogey Neck (with whom I had the opportunity to interview regarding the earliest schools) were descendants from the fourth generation: Hortense Walters Jones (1922–2013), great-granddaughter of William and Ann V. Walters; Lloyd Warner (1928–1913), great-grandson of Frederick and Sophronia Warner; William Thomas Jones (b. 1928), great-grandson of Stafford B. and Susan Warner Jones; and Ceddra Yerby Jones, wife of James Edward Jones, who was the great-grandson of Stafford B. and Susan Warner Jones.

In two articles, "Three Hundred Years of Education" (in the Northumberland Echo and The Bulletin of the Northumberland County Historical Society), Carolyn H. Jett gives a historical sketch of schools in Northumberland County, VA.[29] One of the earliest schools for the children of Bogey Neck was the Mt. Olivet School, located next to the old Mt. Olive Church on Mt. Olive Road. It was in existence for sixty years (ca. 1882–1942).[30] Although I found no student school records, Mt. Olivet was probably the only school available to the second generation of children in Bogey Neck: William Ball, Sr. (b. ca. 1872), Raleigh Doleman. Jones, Sr. (ca. 1867–1944), Joseph Warren. Jones (ca. 1869–1940), Lombard Coleman Jones (b. ca. 1873), John Walters (b. ca. 1877), Adolphus Wallace (b. ca.1879), Washington Walters (b. ca. 1880), and Sylvester Warner (ca. 1884–1937). Considering the birth dates of Washington Walters and Sylvester Warner and the fact that Mila Neck School opened in1888, it is possible that they could have attended. If they attended the Mt. Olivet School, it was about a five-mile walk from the Wicomico/Remo area to the school, following a trail along Stuart Blackwell's property line in Remo through a swamp to the Cross Hills Road and walking right up the hill to the school on Mt. Olive Road. Federal census records indicate that this generation could read and write. Although I found no record of their formal education, it may be assumed that they acquired their skills from parents and on the job.

Following the Mt. Olivet School, three other schools served the Bogey Neck community: Old Mila School, Mila Neck (1888–1939), New Mila School, Bogey Neck (1939–1949), and Anna T. Jeanes, which opened in 1942; the name was later changed to Rehoboth Elementary

---

29   Jett, Carolyn H., *Northumberland Echo,* March 1, 1984.
       Jett, Carolyn H., "Three Hundred Years of Education," *Bulletin of the Northumberland County Historical Society.* Vol. XLVII, 2010.
30   Ibid.

School. Anna T. Jeanes closed after the Northumberland County schools were integrated. Like the typical classroom of the early 1900s, Mila Neck had two rooms, and Mila–Bogey Neck was a one-room school. The enrollment in these schools varied between forty and fifty children, with the basic subjects and grade levels first through seventh grades. When Anna T. Jeanes opened in 1942, Mila–Bogey Neck school went up to grade four. Grades five, six, and seven attended Anna T. Jeanes or Hygeia in Burgess. A few students who went to school beyond grade seven, prior to the opening of Northumberland Training School in 1916, attended the Northern Neck Industrial Academy in Richmond County, VA. Gladys Theresa Jones, daughter of Joseph Warren and Mary L Jackson Jones, was one student who studied at the academy. Northumberland County Training School opened in 1916 (renamed Julius Rosenwald in 1919), and Central High School became the high school for African American students in the Wicomico Church district when the school closed in 1958. There was a high school in Wicomico Church for white students; however, the district high schools remained segregated in Northumberland County until the closing of Central High School.

Before school buses were provided on Bogey Neck Road, the children walked to school. The high schoolers walked to Wicomico on Route 200 or to J. P. Delano's store on the corner of Routes 607 and 609 to catch the bus. Currently, integrated public schools serving African American students in Northumberland County are Northumberland Elementary, Middle, and High Schools, and buses are provided for children on Bogey Neck Road.

The only living Bogey Neck student who attended Hygeia before going to Rosenwald is ninety-one-year-old Hortense Walters Jones. She still resides in the home that she and her husband, Ellis Jones, bought in 1943 in Bogey Neck. Hortense, though bedridden, has an excellent memory of her school days and willingly shared memories with me through my many telephone conversations with her. Sometimes her daughter, Barbara, would ask Aunt Hortense the question and then relay her response to me while we were on the phone—the *who*, *what*, *when*, and *why*. Aunt Hortense would quickly respond, and Barbara would then share the answer with me. When I visited Aunt Hortense, I sat at her bedside and talked about the history of Bogey Neck, the schools, the church, the people, and the community. If Aunt Hortense did not hear from me, she often asked her daughter, "Is Sister (my Bogey Neck name) still working on that book?"

Following is a sketch of the earliest schools located in the Wicomico area serving African American children: Mt. Olivet School (1882–1942), grades one through five; Mila School–Mila Neck (1888–1939), grades one through seven; Mila School–Bogey Neck (1939–1949), grades one through seven, until Anna T. Jeanes opened in 1942, serving children in grades one through seven.[31] Beginning in 1942, Mila–Bogey Neck housed grades one through three until it closed in 1949.

Mt. Olivet School (1882–1942)

The one acre of land adjacent to Mt. Olive Church was purchased from Warner Hurst to build Mt. Olivet School for African American children. Mrs. Betty E. Gray served as the principal in 1922, and Daisey

---

31   *The Bulletin of Northumberland County Historical Society*, Vol. XLVII, 2010, "Three Hundred Years of Education." Carolyn H. Jett.

E. Moore was the assistant. Rev. D. H. Chamberlyn, pastor of Mt. Olive Baptist Church, was a teacher between 1900 and 1908.[32]

Mrs. Elizabeth Savoy, who grew up in the Mt. Olivet School community, started first grade at Mt. Olivet in 1934. She has close ties to Bogey Neck through her work at Mt. Olive Baptist Church and her personal affiliation with families. Mrs. Savoy is the mother-in-law of Elwood Jones, who is a native of Bogey Neck. Mrs. Grace Walters Norris, daughter of John Walters (a native of Bogey Neck), was married to Mrs. Savoy's uncle, Emerson Norris, who also resided in Bogey Neck. Mrs. Savoy shared the following memories of her school days:

> *"My principal was Mr. James Moss from Richmond, VA, who boarded with Mrs. Sarah Gray. Mrs. Laura Taylor of the Wicomico community and Mrs. Evelyn Williams from Richmond were teachers. Mrs. Williams boarded with Mrs. Mary Adeline Norris. Grades one through five were taught. We studied English, arithmetic, geography, history, and physical education, which was our recess. Children walked from Remo, Mila, and Harvest Neck. I remember Henry Washington and John and James Parker (raised by Mr. Noble and Lizzie Parker), and there were*

---

32   *The One Hundredth Anniversary, Mt. Olive Baptist Church;*Wicomico, VA, 1973.

several others who attended the school. The bus driver was Mr. Elmore Edwards, and the cooks were Mrs. Sally Taylor and Mrs. Eliza Holmes. I went to Anna T. Jeans (1939–1941) and Julius Rosenwald (1941–1945). Later, Mt. Olivet and Jones Run Schools were consolidated, and the school name was changed to Jones Run School.[33]

Teacher Profiles

Memories of teachers are lasting. The children of Bogey Neck were fortunate to have caring teachers who were involved with the home and community. Parental support was the norm, and there was truly a home and school partnership. Teachers modeled professionalism and were our parents when we were away from home. They brought the world to the classroom because field trips were minimal. The one field trip that I will never forget was my seventh grade visit to the White House during Easter vacation, wearing my Easter outfit: black patent shoes, white socks, blue skirt, white blouse, and a pink topper. When I spoke with various people who attended the schools in the Bogey Neck district, I asked two questions. First, I asked, "Who was your favorite teacher?" The response was unanimous: "Most of them." Then I asked, "What one thing do you remember about your teacher(s)?" Some responses were: *"Tough and didn't play"; "Visited my house on Sunday"; "Kept my parents abreast of what was going on in school"; "Didn't tolerate nonsense"; "Did not spare the rod"; "Would give you a whipping at school and then take you home, where you got another one"; and "Looked out for me and helped me because I was slow to catch on sometimes."*

---

33 A telephone interview with Mrs. Elizabeth Savoy who resides in Ditchely, VA.

Thanks to memories, obituaries, and church and federal census records, I am able to present a profile of some of the outstanding teachers who taught the children in the Bogey Neck school district.

Rev. Daniel H. Chamberlayne (ca.1877–1957), born in Virginia; college graduate; fourth pastor of Mt. Olive Baptist Church (1900–1908); known as a community leader who facilitated a partnership between the school and community; and taught at the Mt. Olivet School while pastoring at Mt. Olive Church. From the 1910 census: wife was Bertha K. Chamberlayne; children: Annie (6), Dubois (5), and Irma (1); 1920 census: wife was Oral L. Chamberlayne; Dubois (14), Irma (10), and Graham (1); resided on Route 200 between Kilmarnock and Wicomico Church; after resignation from Mt. Olive, founded the New Saint John's Baptist Church in Kilmarnock, VA.[34]

Mrs. Betty Gray (b. ca. 1865), born in Washington, DC; married Shadrick Gray of Wicomico Church, VA (1887); resided in Harvest Neck; public school teacher; served as principal of Mt. Olivet School (1922);[35] known as community leader, an advocate for children who often took children in her home; active in Mt. Olive Baptist Church (member of choir, representative to the Northern Neck Women's

---

34 *The One Hundredth Anniversary, Mt. Olive Baptist Church*; Wicomico Church, VA. 1973, p. 8.

35 Jett, Carolyn., *"Three Hundred Years of Education,"* Northern Neck of Virginia Historical Society, Vol. XLVII, 2010 p, 75.

Education Convention [1912]);[36] family home in Harvest Neck was left to Mrs. Dorothy Taylor and remains in the Taylor family.

Mrs. Maggie Wiggins (b. ca. 1874), married Ely Wiggins of Wicomico, Harvest Neck.[37] Hortense Walters Jones recalled:

> *"Miss Maggie rode to Mila Neck School in a horse and buggy. Mott Wiggins used to bring her from Harvest Neck every day. She was my first teacher in 1928. I walked with the other children on the path from Bogey Neck to Mila. It was so cold in the winter, but 'Miss Maggie' came every day in that wagon. The school was where Grace Taylor lived on Mila Neck Road. It's torn down now. Miss Maggie could teach. She wasn't from around here."*

Mrs. Catherine Payne Taylor (b. ca. 1912), born in Philadelphia, PA; daughter of John and Margarite Moore Payne of Northumberland County, VA; granddaughter of Martha Payne Day; great-granddaughter of Rev. Daniel Payne, founder of First Baptist Church, Heathsville, VA; grew up and attended public schools in Philadelphia; graduate of Virginia Union University, Richmond, VA; served in the military and worked with Red Cross; taught at Howland, Mila Neck, and Mila–Bogey Neck schools in Northumberland County, VA; while teaching in the Mila schools, boarded with Mrs. Eliza Brown in Remo and Eliot and Emaline Waters in Mila; married William Taylor of Remo; shortly thereafter, returned to Philadelphia and taught in the public schools there until retirement.

---

36   *The One Hundredth Anniversary, Mt. Olive Baptist Church*; Wicomico, VA. 1973, p. 24.
37   Federal census 1910, 1930.

Source: Catherine Day Harris Flyght, native of Heathsville, VA, resides in Philadelphia, PA.

Mrs. Lillian Pollard Sebree (ca. 1889–1994), a native of Gloucester County, VA; attended Purton Elementary School (Gloucester, VA), Cappahasic Agricultural Industrial Institute (Cappahasic, VA), Hampton Institute (Hampton, VA), Virginia Union (Richmond, VA), and Virginia State College (Petersburg, VA); resided in Mila Neck with her husband, Rev. William Sebree, who often substituted  for teachers at the school. Mrs. Sebree taught at the "Broun" Store School (1917), currently located on Route 610 in Browns Store.[38] Her forty-two-year teaching career in Virginia included more than thirty years at the Old Mila School in Remo, VA, and the New Mila School in Bogey Neck; known for her penmanship and high expectations for all students; favorite memory was a note left by a second grader that read: *"We love Mrs. Seabreeze. She teaches us so many goode things."*[39] Douglas Norris shared these memories of Mrs. Sebree:

> *"Mrs. Sebree was one of my favorite teachers. She had pretty handwriting. She taught me how to write in cursive. She put letters, the ABCs, on the blackboard to show us how the letters should be written. She had a thing with strokes on the blackboard—writing all the way across the board, which helped us form the letters in cursive."*

---

38 Jett, Carolyn. *The Northumberland Echo Newspaper*, History...Education, Thursday, March 1, 1984.

39 Obituary–Funeral Service, "Final Triumph," Mrs. Lillian P. Sebree, 1889-1974, Mt. Olive Baptist Church, Wicomico Church, VA; Saturday, May 25, 1974.

Mrs. Sebree, my great aunt, was always interested in how I was doing in school. She taught my parents and siblings at the Mila Neck School and my siblings at Mila School–Bogey Neck and Anna T. Jeanes School. My father, Daniel Jones, the guest speaker at a dedication ceremony for The Lillian Pollard Sebree Community Center in Baltimore, MD, made the following comments in his tribute to her:

> *"I applaud Mrs. Sebree, not just for what she did for me, but for her dedication to all the children that she taught over the years. It was Mrs. Sebree who planted my feet on the sea of time and laid the foundation for my appreciation of the importance of education."*

Rev. William W. Sebree (ca. 1879–1968), born in Mila Neck, Wicomico Church District, VA; grandson of John Sebree and Peggy Pride, slaves on the Sebree plantation, Tidewater, VA (Northumberland County, VA); one of eight children born to John and Sally Ball Sebree; married to Lillian Pollard Sebree, who was also a teacher in Northumberland; four children: Charles Sebree, John Sebree, Alice Sebree Handy, and Vashti Sebree Bates; raised family on part of the waterfront property left by his father in Mila Neck; graduate of Hampton Institute and Lynchburg Theological School; a forty-year teaching career included Mila Neck, Mila–Bogey Neck, Lottsburg Graded School, and a school in Laurel, MD;[40] served as a full-time

---

40 Ervin, Evon Handy. "Five generations of Sebree family remember their slave roots," *Washington Post.*

and substitute teacher in schools throughout Northumberland County; in addition to his teaching career, Rev. Sebree was pastor of Lively Hope Church, Hyacinth, VA, in 1918.[41]

Mrs. Jemima Elizabeth Pinn Burton Carter  (ca. 1899–1989), born in Wicomico Church, VA; only daughter of Samuel E. and Sallie Lawson Pinn; attended the old Mt. Olivet School, Northern Neck Academy (Richmond County, VA), and Virginia State University (Petersburg, VA); married Garfield Burton (1926) and Raleigh W. Carter (1942); she and Mr. Carter lived next door to Anna T. Jeanes, where the children frequently went for after-school snacks; taught for forty-seven years (1921–1968): twenty-two years at Hygeia (Burgess, VA), Old Mila School, Adult Education (Edwardsville, VA), and twenty-five years at Anna T. Jeanes (Wicomico, VA).[42]

Mrs. Carter was very active in Mt. Olive Baptist Church in the Sunday school, Missionary Society, Architect and Planning Committee, One Hundredth Anniversary Committee as chair of the souvenir program; wrote a poem, "A Hundred Years Ago," that was published in the One Hundredth Anniversary Bulletin.[43]

41 Ancestry.com, Draft registration, 1918.
42 Obituary, "*In Loving Memory of Jemima Elizabeth Burton Carter,* Sunday, February 19, 1989, Mt. Olive Baptist Church, Wicomico Church, VA.
43 *The One Hundredth Anniversary*, Mt. Olive Baptist Church; Wicomico, VA, 1973.

Grace Sophronia Norris Carter (1915–1977), born in Wicomico Church, VA.; daughter of Charles, Sr., and Mary Norris; attended Northumberland public schools, Dunbar High School in Washington, DC, DC Teachers College, and Virginia State College in Petersburg, VA; full-time and substitute teacher in Northumberland County schools, including Mila Neck, Mila–Bogey Neck; worked as a secretary in the Northumberland school system; married Cyrus Carter of Mila Neck in 1939; active member of Mt. Olive Baptist Church and active in the service club; children: Cyrus Jr., Grace Delores, and Constance Elizabeth.[44]

Mrs. Alma Ann Benns Butler (b. 1921), one of four daughters of Reilley V. and Georgia S. Benns; reared in Beverlyville, VA; graduate of Julius Rosenwald High School in Northumberland County and St. Paul's College in Lawrenceville, VA; married to the late Cobren Butler of Heathsville; the mother of Cobren, Jr. (wife, Queen), grandmother of Cheryl B. Jones (husband, James Jones), great-grandmother of Jarae E. Jones.

---

44 Eulogistic Services, Mt. Olive Baptist Church, Wicomico Church, VA; September 1, 1977.

In addition to being my first teacher, she touched the lives of hundreds of other children at four Northumberland County Schools, namely: Booker T. Washington, Mila (Bogey Neck), Anna T. Jeanes, Reedville, and Fairfield; soft-spoken and nurturing, knew how to motivate students to learn; teaching in a one-room school, she individualized instruction and kept students on task in a large group setting.

I am often reminded of my experience in the one-room school during my teaching experience in the model school program, using individualized instruction at Wilde Lake High School in Howard County, MD. I attribute my decision to pursue a career in education to Mrs. Butler; even in retirement, Mrs. Butler continued to share her talents with children at her home church, Shiloh Baptist Church through the preschool program in Reedville, VA; positions held in the church included: Sunday school teacher, Usher Board president, and member of Deacon's ministry; "Teacher Butler, you are our living Legend, and we are your legacy" was a tribute from her former students on the program honoring her in 2010.[45]

Hiram Nathan Taylor (1922–1987), son of Nathan and Martha E. Taylor of Heathsville, VA; member of Macedonia Baptist Church, sang in junior choir, chair of deacon board, superintendent of Sunday school; resided in Heathsville until his death; first marriage, Alice M. Brooks (1949) and had three

---

45 Program—"Our Living Legend, Teacher Alma Ann Benns Butler," Northern Neck HELP Center, Reedville, VA; September 11, 2010.

children; second marriage to Maxine Redmond (1974) and preceded her in death.

Mr. Taylor was educated in Northumberland County Public Schools, earned a Bachelor of Science degree from St. Paul's College (Lawrenceville, VA), pursued advanced studies at Virginia Union University (Richmond, VA) and Washburn University (Topeka, KS); taught in the public schools of Northumberland for thirty-three years, one of which was at Anna T. Jeanes.

Upon retirement, Mr. Taylor worked diligently in the church, in the community, with the Interfaith Council, and at the Masonic Lodge No. 220.[46]

Mrs. Margaret Jones Zarif (1924–1983) and her husband, Principal Walter Jones, brought the world to the children of Anna T. Jeanes through their collection of pictures and slides of their travel. Upon retirement from education, Mrs. Jones Zarif opened a travel agency to help finance her passion for traveling. In 1983, she was one of the passengers killed on the Korean Air Lines Flight 007 that went down as it flew thirty-three thousand feet over the Sea of Japan. Mrs. Zarif sat in seat twenty-seven. She and five of her close friends were among the passengers on a sixteen-day Asian trip to Japan, Taiwan, and Hong Kong.[47]

---

46 Obituary, June 20, 1987.

47 Peter Carlson and William Plummer, *People*, "Faces of Flight 007," reported by correspondents in New York, Atlanta, Washington, DC, Detroit, Philadelphia, and Tokyo; September 19, 1983.

Mrs. Clarissa Dorothy Parker Jackson Banks (1917–2006), native of Washington, DC; daughter of Benjamin Parker and Georgiana Jackson; educated in Washington, DC, public schools; married Lewis Banks in 1939); one son, Jerold Rodgers Banks; joined Shiloh Baptist Church, Burgess, VA (1947).

Post-secondary training: Bachelor of Science degree in elementary education from Minor Teachers College (Washington, DC), Master of Science degree in reading (State University of New York at Potsdam), Master of Education in special education and Doctor of Education at age sixty-seven from the College of William and Mary (Williamsburg, VA); further studies at Hampton Institute, New York University, and University of Minnesota.

Professional career: Over a span of fifty years, taught reading in Georgia (1938–1942), Lancaster and Northumberland Counties in VA, including Anna T. Jeanes (1947–1969); assistant professor at Hampton University (1968–1985); after retirement, remained connected with Hampton University as adjunct professor (1982), deputy dean in the School of Education; served as adjunct professor in early childhood education at Norfolk State University (Norfolk, VA).[48]

---

48 *Celebration of Life of Dr. Clarissa Dorothy Parker Jackson Banks,* Hampton University Memorial Chapel, Hampton, VA, August 21, 2006.

Mr. Lewis Elmer Banks (1912–1979), born in Salem, VA; received a Bachelor of Arts degree in mathematics from Morris Brown College in Atlanta and Master of Science degree in biology from Hampton Institute (currently Hampton University) in Hampton, VA; further studies at New York University, Michigan State University, Macalester College, and Indiana University; pursued additional studies in educational media with emphasis on photography; married Clarissa Banks, also a teacher; extensive professional career brought him to Northumberland and Lancaster counties as a principal (1969–1975) and also principal at Anna T. Jeanes school during this period; known in Northumberland County community as a promoter/organizer; held numerous leadership positions: Boy Scouts of America, human relations, Voters League, NAACP (president), Omega Psi Phi Fraternity, and various committees throughout the Northern Neck.[49]

Miss Virginia Addison (1939), born in St. Stephens, SC; daughter of Saul and Eloise Addison; two siblings: brother passed away in 1999, and sister passed away in 2010; attended public schools in St. Stephens, SC; Bachelor of Science degree from Benedict College (Columbia, SC) in social studies and elementary education; Master of Education from Bowie State College (Bowie, MD) in

---

49 "Obsequies" for Lewis Elmer Banks, The Memorial Church, Hampton Institute, Hampton, VA, October 30, 1979.

special education; first teaching assignment in Northumberland County, VA, Anna T. Jeanes Elementary School, (1961–1966); lived with Emma and Ernest Walters in Wicomico Church and Ellis and Hortense Jones in Bogey Neck while teaching at Anna T. Jeanes; moved to Prince Georges County, MD (1966); taught elementary education in Clinton, MD, and Oxon Hill, MD; recalls other staff members at Anna T. Jeanes: teachers (Evelyn Treakle, Lewis Banks, Ruth Nickens, Elizabeth Burton Carter, and Pamela Charlton), principals (Charles Wade, Frances Crockrell Howlett, and Lewis Banks), cafeteria worker (Merita Pope); memory of children: *"The children were very nice and eager to learn."* (Source: *Virginia Addison, interview*)

Mila School–Mila Neck (1888-1939)[50]

Mila School was a two-room structure erected on one acre of land purchased from Sadie Butler. My grandfather, Joseph Jones, was one of the carpenters. It was located on the east side of what is currently Route 665 in Mila Neck, about one mile from Remo and after Sandy Point Road on the east side. There were seven grades, and the school year varied for the students to coincide with the farming season, which was normally between April and October. The school closed in 1939, and the land was sold in 1945.[51] For several years, the school was used as a dwelling until it was torn down.

---

50 Sketch by William T. Jones, native of Bogey Neck; great-grandson of Stafford Jones, resides in Jacksonville, FL.
51 *The Bulletin of the Northumberland County Historical Society*, Vol. XLVII.

<u>Teachers:</u> Grevious W. Ross, Lottie Beane, Maggie Wiggins, Lillian P. Sebree, Rev. William Sebree, Catherine Payne Taylor, Betty Gray, and Nora Walker.

Mila Neck School students and teachers, taken in early 1900. Contributed by Hortense Walters Jones.

<u>The Trail.</u> Gladys Norris Cockrell remembers the trail as "a long cold walk through the woods to Mila Neck School." William T. Jones described the trail that he and other children walked from Bogey Neck to Mila Neck School:

> *"I started in the first grade at Mila School in 1934, and Mrs. Nora Walker was my teacher. I have vivid memories of the walk from our grandpapa's house in Bogey Neck to the school in Mila Neck. We followed a wooded trail from*

Bogey Neck to Mila Neck to get to school. Starting at the old road between the homes of Joseph Jones and William Ball, we passed the Jones graveyard on the right of the road and proceeded to walk the logs across the swamp behind the Ball's property. Logs were placed across the running water swamp, which was about four feet wide and about one foot deep to serve as a foot bridge. Once across the swamp, we crossed a field near what use to be "Bo" Washington's house, crossed the former "Peer" Delano's field onto Mila Road (currently Route 665), walked left, and continued about one-quarter mile past Sandy Point Road to Mila School, sitting on the east side of the road."

My father, the late Daniel Olin Jones, started first grade at Mila School in 1914. He often talked about his school days and his walk to school. As he described the walk, he remembered the number of times somebody fell in the running water swamp en route to school when some of the logs that provided the walkway had been washed downstream. Daniel said:

"Many days I had to walk to school in rain, hail, and snow. Never missed a day. It was about a two-mile walk from home to school. In the winter, we would almost freeze. Sometimes we fell in the swamp while trying to walk on the moving logs; our clothes would be frozen in the winter when we got to school. Mrs. Sebree had a bucket of warm water waiting for us to warm our hands. If our clothes were wet, then Mrs. Sebree would give us a change of old clothes while our clothes dried on a chair at the "potbelly" stove that sat in

the front of the room. Mrs. Sebree would always let us stand
by the stove to get warm before we started our work."

School rosters have been generated for the two Mila schools. The students who possibly attended Mila Neck and Mila School Bogey Neck have been identified by the first-generation head of household and birth year. Students possibly started school at age six or seven, depending upon the date of birth and family circumstances. Likewise, students left school sometimes before seventh grade, due to family circumstances.

Mila School–Bogey Neck (1939-1949)[52]

As a result of the league (parents) petitioning the school board to build a new school, three acres of land located on the corner of Bogey Neck Road and Route 609 were purchased by the school board from heirs of Homer Walters in 1938 for $370. Douglas Norris, great grandson of John Walters, recalls that his mother, Grace Walters Norris, who was an heir to the property, said that her share of the land sale was $3.46. In order to get the school built, the parents had to agree to reimburse the school board. This school, one of the Work Projects Administration projects (WPA), was built by my grandfather, Joseph W. Jones, and other local carpenters. My uncle, Lombard Jones, was the cement man.[53]

I started first grade at Mila–Bogey Neck one month before my seventh birthday in 1947. I had to wait a year because my birthday was after October 8. October 1 was the cutoff date to enter school. Mrs. Alma Benns

---

52   Jett, Carolyn. The *Northumberland Echo* Newspaper, History...Education", Thursday, March 1, 1984; oral history.
53   Jett, Carolyn. *The Northumberland Echo* Newspaper, "History...Education Thursday, March 1, 1984.

Butler from Browns Store taught all three grades in this one-room school. Students sat in rows by grade level. The school day started with devotion. Someone was designated to lead a song, which was a hymn, followed by the "Lord's Prayer" and pledge to the flag. Douglas Norris, one of the devotion leaders, would often lead us in singing "I'm rolling; I'm rolling; I'm rolling on to Kingdom land" when it was his turn, or others would lead their favorite church hymn or "My Country 'Tis of Thee." Next came "the inspection," when someone was designated to check fingernails and teeth and confirm that your face was washed and your hair combed.

The black slate board was on the east wall. Mrs. Butler rotated our instruction. While she was working with one class, the other two grades were assigned "seat work." If we finished our work and the teacher was working with a higher group, we were allowed to sit near the grade receiving direct instruction. It was always an incentive for me to finish quickly so that I could listen to what was being taught in the next grade level. Mrs. Butler, a kind and lovely person whom I enjoyed seeing when I returned to Virginia or talking with on the phone, resides in Browns Store, VA.

Transportation was not available for us in Bogey Neck and surrounding communities. I recall the bus passing us every morning on our way to school and the white children yelling out the windows, "N—, get out of the road." Of course, we found a few choice words to yell back. There was a ditch between the road and embankment; so when we heard the bus coming behind us, we hopped up on the embankment because we knew the driver was not going to give us an inch of walkway. It soon became a game. Someone would yell, "Here comes the bus," and almost in unison we yelled, "Hop!" One day I got a bright idea and waited on the embankment for the bus to pass, and as soon as I heard the children yell, "Get out of the road, n—," I responded with a 1947 "shake your booty," which then became our daily retaliation at the white children on the bus. Did our parents ever find out? Of course not, because I am alive to tell about it. Did we ever think of the danger and that one of us could have slipped while playing "Hop and shake your booty," as the bus was passing close enough to us that we could touch it? Of course not.

Like most of the schools during this period, Mila served as a place for community activities, including the various holiday programs, ice cream dips, and meetings. My brother William recalls the boys transporting the piano from our grandparents' house on a wagon to the school for the various functions.

Douglas Norris remembers his years at Mila–Bogey Neck School:

"Mrs. Sebree was my first teacher and then Mrs. Butler. I remember the spelling bees, singing, and the big boys having to cut wood. Also, somebody was assigned to the cloak room at the end of the day to hand out coats."

Parents played a major role in the school—from making sure there was wood for the stove to cleaning the school daily and lobbying for whatever was needed to make it better for their children. Parents bought used books as well as supplies from the white parents for a small fee. When the school board told the parents that they had to buy desks and chairs for the classsroom, my father paid a surprise visit to the school board meeting and demanded that the county pay for the seats and made it clear that "no" was not an option. Soon thereafter, the school board approved the money, and seats were provided.

Superintendents: The first superintendent was Mr. William Brent followed by Mr. R. E. Brann.[54]

Supervisor: Mrs. L. B. Cheatham Taylor worked many years as the coordinator of activities of the "black" schools in Northumberland County. She was responsible for the dental clinic.[55] Also, she was instrumental in getting funds to hire the first paid cook, Mrs. Ceddra Yerby Jones of Bogey Neck. Mrs. Cheatham (as we knew her) visited Mila–Bogey Neck school frequently and often with superintendent R. E. Brann during the years I was there. The students were expected to stand and greet guests and in unison say, "Good morning, Mrs. Cheatham and Mr. Brann," if Brann was with her. She would respond with "Good morning, children," and then signal us to sit.

Teachers: Mrs. Catherine Payne Taylor, Mrs. Lillian Pollard Sebree, and Mrs. Alma Benns Butler. Mrs. Butler also prepared lunches with the help of students who took turns working in the kitchen.

Substitute teachers: Mrs. Grace Sophronia Norris Carter and Rev. William Sebree.

Cooks: Mrs. Ceddra Yerby Jones, Mrs. Maggie Sebree Carter, and Mrs. Harriett Washington Milton.

---

54 Program: "Avalon School Day, June 26, 1982, Northumberland Middle School, Heathsville, VA.
55 Ibid.

The school closed in 1949, and the property was sold to Mrs. Gertrude (Gertie) Sebree and James Johnson, sister of Cornelia Warner Sebree. Subsequently, different families have lived in the one-room school on Bogey Neck Road; it is still a family dwelling.

Student roster by descendants and birth date for Mila Neck School (1888–1939)[56]

Descendants of Betsey Ball—Helen Ball (1900), William Ball, Jr. (1903), Essie L. Ball (1905), Edmund Ball (1906), Etta Ball (1908), Bernice Ball (1909), Connie Ball (1910), Addie Ball (1918), William Gilbert Ball (1930), Essolene Ball (1932).

Descendants of Mary Davenport—Addison Davenport (ca. 1898), Ethel Davenport (1901), William Davenport (1903), Leroy Davenport (1904), Estelle Davenport (1907), Florence Davenport (1909).

Descendants of Stafford B. Jones—Paul Jones (1894), Clarence Jones (1895), Eula Jones (1897), Walter Kennard Jones (1898), Glesner Jones (1901), Gladys Theresa Jones (1903), Joseph Russell Jones (1905), Daniel Olin Jones (1907), Onard Jackson Jones (1909), Miriam Telitha Jones (1914), Logan Aster Jones (1912), Mertice Elaine Jones (1920), Coolidge Jones (1929), Arthur Reid Jones (1892), Julia Ann Jones (1893), William Scott Jones (1896), Raleigh Dolman Jones, Jr. (1901), Martin Luther Jones (1903), James Edward Jones (1925), Louis Thomas Jones,

---

56 Birth dates from Federal census 1880, 1900, 1910, 1930, 1940.

Jr. (1926), Grafton Jones (1927), William Thomas Jones (1928), Coolidge Jones (1929), Beatrice Jones (1931).

Descendants of Robert Wallace—Elizabeth Wallace (1902), Robert Wallace (1903), George Otha Wallace (1908), Hilda Modelle Wallace (1912), Alonzo Wallace (1914), Beatrice Hazel Wallace (1916).

Descendants of William Walters—Edward Walters (1900), Elvin Walters (1903), Emily B. Walters (1904), John C. Walters (1906), George F. Walters (1909), Grace Cornelia Walters (1911), Julia G. Walters (1913), Stewart C. Walters (1916), Harold Walters (1918), Annie Walters (1920), Ernest Walters (1900), Lena Walters (1903), Henry Walters (1905), Washington Walters, Jr. (1907), Sarah Walters (1908), Solomon Walters (1909), Luther Walters (1912), Gertrude Walters (1917), Gladys Norris Cottrell (1930).

Descendants of Frederick Warner—Reva Warner (1912), John Warner (1914), Rosie Warner (1915), Sylvester Warner (1916), William Warner (1925), Lloyd Warner (1928), Laura Warner (1928).

Descendants of James Wilson—Maude Wilson (1909), William Corbin Wilson (1911), Robert Henry Wilson (1914), Frederick Lucius Wilson (1914), David Carroll Wilson (1916), Mary Alice Wilson (1919), Sarah Wilson (1923).

Student roster by ancestor and birth date for Mila School–Bogey Neck (b. 1939–1942)[57]

Descendants of Betsey Ball—James Linwood Ball (1935), Stanley Burnell Ball (1940).

Descendants of Stafford Jones—Coolidge Jones (1929), William Thomas Jones (1928), David Samuel Jones (1935), Daniel Rudolph Jones (1935), Mary Mahalia Jones (1940), Barbara Mastine Jones (1941), Milfret Williams (1940), Deloris Williams (1941).

Descendants of William Walters—Gladys Norris (1930), Janise P. Norris (1932), Violet J. Norris (1933), Emerson W. Norris, Jr. (1934), Randolph Norris (1936), Douglas Norris (1937), Helen Norris (1938), Otis Norris (1940), Joyce Norris (1941).

Descendants of Frederick Warner—Lloyd Warner (1928), Laura Warner (1928).

Descendants of James Wilson—Ernest Wilson (1935), Leon Yerby (1937)

Other neighborhood children—Roosevelt Taylor (1935), Lola Taylor (1937), Julia Taylor (1940), Christine Taylor (1941), Earl Edwards, Wilbert Taylor.

---

57 Dates from Federal Census 1930 and 1940, and family history provided by Bogey Neck descendants.

Anna T. Jeanes School (1942)[58]

Located on Route 200 between Wicomico Church and Rehoboth, Anna T. Jeanes School opened its doors to students in 1942 as a result of the decision to consolidate Mt. Olivet and Jones Run Schools. The facility

was built on land purchased by the school board from Eolinea Ball Jesse, Crickett Hill Estates, and the use of Work Progress Administration (WPA) project funds. It was agreed that the league would purchase a minimum of four acres; thus, the additional land was purchased in 1946 from Jesse. Anna T. Jeanes was renamed Rehoboth School after integration. The consolidation was supported by Mt. Olive Baptist Church in Wicomico by securing teachers, buses, and bus drivers. The school was closed after school integration in Northumberland County and sold to Lighthouse Baptist Church in 1983. Following is a partial listing of staff, provided by former students:

Principals: Samuel T. Jones, Walter "Pete" Jones, Lewis Banks, Frances Cockrell Howlett, and Charles Wade.

Teachers: Jemima Elizabeth Burton Carter, Laura Taylor, Christine Ruffin Waller, Margaret Jones, Virginia Addison, Hiram Nathan Taylor, Lillian Pollard. Sebree, Elizabeth Benns, and Evelyn Treakle.

---

58   Jett, Carolyn. The *Northumberland Echo* Newspaper, "History...Education", Thursday, March 1, 1984.

Substitutes: Rev. Oliver Brinkley, Rev. William W. Sebree, Rev. French, and Hortense Walters Jones.

Cooks: Sally Taylor, Mirah Cain, Mary L. Jackson Jones, Ruth Campbell, and Tina Taylor.

When students finished seventh grade at Mila Neck School, some went to work, and a few attended the Northern Neck Industrial Academy, a boarding school in Richmond County, VA, and the Northumberland Training School (renamed Rosenwald High School in 1932). When the Mila Neck School closed in 1939, students attended the new Mila School at the corner of Bogey Neck Road and Route 609 or Mt. Olivet School, Anna T. Jeanes, Hygeia, or boarding school—or dropped out.

Teachers at Anna T. Jeanes

Left to right: *Mrs. Laura Taylor, Mrs. Clarissa Banks, Mr. Walter Jones (Principal), Mrs. Margaret Jones, and Mrs. Elizabeth Burton Pinn Carter.*

Bogey Neck students at Anna T. Jeanes School (1954)

Standing on school grounds, from left to right: *Barbara Mastine Jones*, *Joyce Norris, Christine Taylor, and Miriam Deloris Williams.*

CHAPTER IV—MEDICAL SERVICES
FOR BOGEY NECK

"The greatest wealth is health." —Unknown

The first settlers in the Bogey Neck community relied primarily on home remedies as a form of treatment for illnesses. Because of the lack of access to doctors and other medical services, many died because of a lack of medical treatment. A midwife delivered the babies because there were no clinics or hospitals for the mothers.

Midwives in the Wicomico Church area whose names were passed on through oral history were: Mrs. Addie Saul, Mrs. Reddy, Mrs. Jessup, Mrs. Luvenia Ball Carter Lewis, and Mrs. Claudine Smith. Mrs. Luvenia Ball Lewis ("Aunt Lou") walked through ice and snow from Harvest Neck to Bogey Neck (about five miles) to deliver babies, even before she had the luxury of the horse and buggy. In the late 1930s, Aunt Lou could be heard traveling in her Model-T Ford on the bumpy dirt road of Bogey Neck.

Dr. Morgan E. Norris was a great support to the midwives upon his arrival in the area in 1917. According to Ceddra Jones, Aunt Lou was in the office with Dr. Norris when he did a tonsillectomy on her son, Alfred. I remember vividly my tonsillectomy in his office and when it was over, Dr. Norris telling my mother to give me some ice cream. The thought of getting ice cream took away any discomfort I had from having my tonsils removed.

A TRIBUTE TO DR. MORGAN E. NORRIS (1888–1966)

Dr. Morgan E. Norris, born in Lancaster County around the turn of the nineteenth century, completed medical school and returned home to Kilmarnock, VA, to open a medical practice (1917).[59] African Americans in Bogey Neck, as well as people all over the northern neck, were grateful for and highly respectful of Dr. Norris for what he brought to the community. He often traveled to Bogey Neck, a two-mile isolated road, in the middle of the night to see a patient. My father and grandmother, who were both asthmatic, were two of his regulars and always seemed to have an attack around midnight. Before there were telephones, my uncle, Ellis, would set out to locate Dr. Norris when there was an emergency. Sometimes it meant going to "Doc's" home to find out his schedule and then track him down. It did not matter that it was midnight. Dr. Norris would send a message with instructions until he could get there. If Dr. Norris had to treat my father and it was after midnight, Mom had a cup of tea and a snack for him if he wanted it. In 1937, he was my brother's doctor when his eye was put out while playing

---

59 www.ssentinel.com

with a stick. I believe everybody in Bogey Neck and elsewhere has a positive story to tell of this great man's contribution to the community.

Dr. Norris went beyond his medical practice and reached out into the community not just for medical needs, but he tackled social and political needs as well. He was an advocate and role model for young people. Elwood Jones recalled that Dr. Norris gave him the tools that he needed when he enrolled in Virginia State's automotive program in 1963.

Dr. Norris worked unselfishly for decades to make his community a better place for all. A proclamation, signed by the mayor, B. B. Edmonds, Jr., was issued in Kilmarnock, VA, proclaiming July 22, 1971, as "Morgan E. Norris Day."

A tribute to Dr. Norris was made by his son, Dr. James Norris, who published a book about his father's life, *Fight On, My Soul*.

Here are just a few of Dr. Norris's accomplishments:

- Led the building of an elementary school for African American students.
- Organized a bus boycott in Lancaster County, VA.
- Organized an African American fair on the grounds north of Kilmarnock, which was said to be as successful as any in the Commonwealth.
- Worked diligently in his church as well as churches all over the Northern Neck of Virginia; served as a deacon at his church, Calvary Baptist Church, Kilmarnock, VA.

All in all, Dr. Norris spent his entire adult life in Lancaster County, providing health care services for people who didn't have them, enhancing educational opportunities, and standing up for fairness and justice. He was a man respected by people of all races.

Dr. Jaehn Benjamin Charlton

Dr. Jaehn Benjamin Charlton opened an office in Northumberland County in 1947 and practiced family medicine for nearly forty-seven years.[60] Having an African American doctor locate in the area was welcomed by people—especially north of the Great Wicomico River. Dr. Charlton, like Dr. Norris, had office hours but also made house calls. When his office was located on the lower level of his home in Burgess, he would return to his office to see patients. During the latter years, his practice was located in Wicomico Church until he retired.

---

60 James E. C. Norris, M.D. *Fight On, My Soul,* 2009, p.110.

Chapter V — Mt. Olive Baptist Church

"Upon this rock I will build my church." —Matthew 16:18 (KJV)

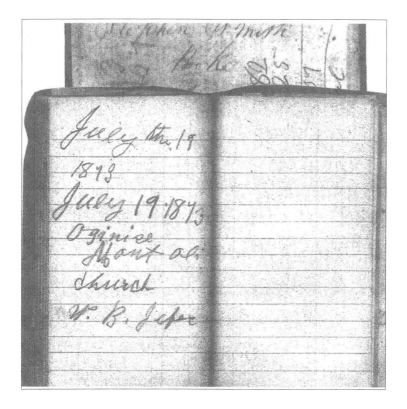

A page from a book byStephen Smith (b. ca. 1838–1909) of Wicomico Church, VA.[61]

---

61 Contributed by Benjamin Rudolph Caster, a native of Ditchley, VA, and the great-grandson of Stephen Smith.

In 1873, Rev. Nelson Lee and a small group of men received letters from Old St. John Church in Kilmarnock and met to organize a new "colored church" in the Wicomico area. They were: Walter Johnson, Osborne Taylor, Frederick Warner of Bogey Neck, and others. Prior to this time, the worshippers met in backyards or homes, while some met at churches in Kilmarnock, VA: Old St. John Church, Union Chapel Church, Morattico Baptist Church (white church), and First Baptist Church in Heathsville, VA.[62]

The first place of worship for Mt. Olive's congregation was a "brush arbor." The first structure was in an old mill house located on one acre on Ingrams' farm. This structure was later purchased and moved to a new site on Mt. Olive Road.[63]

Ten years later (1883), the congregation had exceeded the capacity of the mill house, and a committee was formed to develop plans to build a new facility, referred to as the "Old Mt. Olive Church." The church was completed in about 1884. (*Sketch above left by William T. Jones.*) For several years, services were held on the second and fourth Sundays because the minister served two churches. On the Sundays when there was no church service, Sunday school was held in the various communities. Bogey Neck families attended New Chapel Sunday

---

62 Souvenir Booklet. Mt. Olive Baptist Church, 133rd Anniversary, 53rd Homecoming, September 24, 2006.
63 Ibid.

School, held on the first floor of a lodge hall in Remo. The residents of Bogey walked on a trail that led to the Remo post office and the lodge hall, which was located across the road on Route 625.[64]

Because of the increase in membership and the age of the Old Mt. Olive Church building, the congregation began plans for a new facility. Bogey Neck members serving on the committee to find land for the new church were Ellis Jones and Emerson Norris. In 1967, the congregation marched up the road to the "New Mt. Olive Church" site on the corner of Route 200 and Mt. Olive Road. The Old Mt. Olive Church was hit by lightning and burned down in 1982. Remaining on that site are a monument and cemeteries.[65]

Mt. Olive had a partnership with community schools in support of the educational programs for African American children. As an affiliate of the Northern Neck Baptist Association, Mt. Olive was involved in the building of the Northern Neck Industrial Academy. Another of the memorable contributions was Mt. Olive's influence in the consolidation of two community schools (Anna T. Jeanes and Jones Run). Additionally, the church provided assistance in securing teachers, buses, and bus drivers for the early schools.[66]

The members from Bogey Neck were very active in the development and growth of the church. They were represented in all of the ministries

---

64 Souvenir Booklet. Mt. Olive Baptist Church, 133rd Anniversary, 53rd Homecoming, September 24, 2006.
65 Ibid.
66 Ibid.

and organizations of the church: namely, deacons and deaconesses, trustees, ushers, Sunday school, Missionary Society, Boy Scouts of America, music, food bank, Church Aid Society, Pulpit Committee, Cemetery Committee, and Kitchen Committee. When members moved from the church community, the "Mt. Olive Helping Hand Club" was formed in Baltimore, Philadelphia, New York, Richmond, and the District of Columbia for the purpose of providing financial support to the church. Bogey Neck members continue to be active members of the church for the over 140 years of its existence. (See Appendix C: DESCENDANTS' CHURCH PARTICIPATION.)

Ministers: Rev. Nelson Lee, pastor and organizer (1873), Rev. Robert Hayne (1881), Rev. John R. Walker (1882), Rev. D. H. Chamberlayne (1900), Rev. John Amos Nickens (1908), Rev. John J. Nickens (1928), Rev. B. L. Robinson (1958), Rev. Milton Foster (1969), Rev. Ronald Turner, Rev. Todd Gray, and Rev. Dwight Seawood.[67]

---

67 Souvenir Booklet. Mt. Olive Baptist Church, 133rd Anniversary, 53rd Homecoming, September 24, 2006.

NEW MT. OLIVE BAPTIST CHURCH

Chapter VI — Postal Services[68]

"For centuries, our universal mail system has strengthened the bonds of friendship, family, and community." —John E. Potter, postmaster general[69]

The first centralized post office serving the Wicomico district opened in 1813, thirty-eight years after the United States postal services began in 1775.[70] The post offices that served Bogey Neck were located in Remo and Browns Store. The Wicomico post office continues to serve this district.

Wicomico Church post office. The Wicomico Church post office, one of the first post offices in Northumberland County, is located at the intersection of Route 609 in Wicomico Church and Route 200. The first postmaster was Thomas Brown. This post office served Bogey Neck

---

68 *Northern Neck of Virginia Historical Magazine*, "Northumberland Post Office," Vol. XLVIII, The Northern Neck of Virginia Historical Society; Montross, Westmoreland County, VA, December 1998.

69 *Publication 100–The United States Postal Service: An American History 1775-2006*, November 2012, www.about.usps.com,

70 Ibid.

residents until the opening of Remo in 1913. Found among my parents' receipts is a copy of a money order (#3720) for $1.50, purchased in 1910 at this post office. (See photo on right.) Once serving as a combination of a post office and general store, it currently operates as a post office in the building that was the department store for Wicomico Church. Unlike during my years growing up in the area, Wicomico post office has an African American employee who is a female.

Remo post office. The Remo post office, located two miles east of Wicomico Church on Route 609, opened in 1913 with Joseph Delano as the first postmaster, followed by Albert E. Hanks in 1918. A. G. W. Christopher was appointed postmaster in 1928 and operated the general store in the same building. Residents of Bogey Neck followed what was often referred to as the "Post Office Trail" to pick up mail, packages, and even baby chickens that were shipped in crates. The post office closed in 1964, and the mail was delivered by a carrier from Heathsville Post Office. I was fortunate to get a photo of the century-old building before it was demolished. (Photo taken by Warren Jones, October 2012.)

Browns Store. Located three miles from Wicomico Church, Browns Store opened in 1870 with John Robertson serving as the first postmaster, and later Ira Hinton, Sr., filled the role. Like other post offices in the area, there was also a general store operated in the same building. In the 1870 federal census, Browns Store was listed as the post office for the following Bogey Neck families: Stafford Jones (ca. 1826), Betsy Ball (ca. 1826), Robert Wallace (ca. 1840), Frederick Warner (ca. 1847), and Steptoe Fallin (ca. 1863). Land records were not found between 1865 and 1911 for these individuals. Thus, one might assume that they lived in the Wicomico district.

CHAPTER VII—GENEALOGY OF THE FIRST FAMILIES

"In every conceivable manner, the family is link to our past, bridge to our future." —Alex Haley

This chapter begins with an introduction to the first-generation heads of households of the first Bogey Neck families who were born in slavery as reported in census records 1850–1870, followed by a brief introduction of subsequent generations. A historical sketch of the families will include the residence, race of neighbors, genealogy, and biographical sketches of some descendants. The genealogy of the families identifies over eight hundred descendants from this rural two-mile road in an area called Snowden Park.

In addition to listing names, I made an attempt to include dates of birth and death, place of birth, current residences, parents, siblings, spouses, children, and occupations. Eight of the ten heads of households of the first generation were born in the Wicomico Church district. There is no record of the actual community in Wicomico where the first generation lived before African Americans moved to Bogey Neck in early 1900. The family names have been traced to Wicomico, Northumberland County, VA, through the census. It is my belief that with the exception of two families, the first-generation families of Jones, Walters, and Warner lived somewhere in Snowden Park until it was divided into the small communities in the Wicomico Church district—namely, Remo, Mila Neck, Harvest Neck, Bogey Neck, and Harcum Wharf.

> The source of information in the "Biographical Sketch" section in this chapter will be noted at the end of each bio.
>
> Abbreviations used in this chapter are: b. *(born)*, d. *(died)*, B (*Black*), W (*White*), M (*Mulatto*), m. *(married)*, and AA (*African American*).

GENEALOGY OF BETSEY BALL (b. ca. 1826)

Generation 1: Betsey Ball—Introduction[71]

In 1870, Betsey Ball was about forty-four years old, widowed, and living in the Wicomico district, with an address of Browns Store Post Office. Living with her were her three children: Sallie Ball (age 16), Alice Ball (age 13), and John Ball (age 1). No record of the name of a husband or father of the children was found. The older daughter, Sallie, worked on a farm at the time of this census. Betsey's neighbors were Thomas Wheeler (W), Columbus Flynt (W), John Boyd (W), Stafford Jones (B), James Taylor (M), Henry Chesin (B), and Joseph Smith (B). Stafford B. Jones is an ancestor of three of the families who settled in Bogey Neck and will be discussed in Chapter VII.

---

71 Federal Census 1850, 1870, 1880.

In 1880, Betsey and her two sons, John Ball (about age ten) and William Ball (about age nine), lived in the home of Charles Snow, a merchant and farmer, and his wife Elizabeth Snow. Sally, who was about age twenty-six, was no longer listed in the census as living with the family. Betsey was a cook for the Snow family. (Note: the birth dates shown in 1870, 1880, and 1900 census reports vary; however, based on the ages and names of sons John and William, it appears that Betsey's birth date was about 1826.) Betsey's neighbors in 1880 were: John Lawson (B), Robert Wallace (B), Cyrus Crosby (B), William Simmons (W), Aaron Gordon (B), Octavius Bea (B), Hiriam Blackwell (W), Frederick Warner (B), and Betty Harding (W). Stafford B. Jones (B) was a neighbor in 1870 and 1880. Robert Wallace and Frederick Warner each had sons who lived in Bogey Neck, and they will be discussed in Chapter VII.

In 1900, Betsey was about seventy-five years old and living with her son John Ball in Bogey Neck. Her son William H. Ball lived on the adjacent property. By this time, land records indicate that African Americans had purchased land and were living in Bogey Neck. The African American and white neighborhoods were separated by two hills: north hill, leading to Barrett's Creek, and south, by a hill going toward Route 609. The neighbors were all African American: Columbus (Lombard) Jones, Joseph Jones, Raleigh Jones, Charles Johnson, Frederick Johnson, and William H. Ball. The white neighbors were below the north hill in the vicinity of Barrett's Creek and on the west side of Snowden Park above the south hill. There is no mention of Betsey Ball in the 1910 census. Thus, it could be assumed that she died between 1900 and 1910.

Generation 2—Children of Betsey Ball, born in Wicomico Church, VA[72]

1. **Sallie Ball** (b. ca. 1853), widowed by 1900; washwoman; lived in Wicomico Church district; children: Frank Ball (b. ca. 1877), Jeremiah Ball, Jr. (b. ca. 1882), Sarah Ball (b. ca. 1888), and Lela Ball (b. ca. 1891).

2. **Alice Ball** (b. ca. 1857), no record after 1880 census.

3. **John Ball, Sr.** (ca. 1869–1928), in 1885, m. Addie Ball (ca. 1870–1921); purchased a tract of land in Bogey Neck from brother William H. Ball in 1912 and lived there with his family;[73] farmer; children: Ellen A. Ball (b. ca. 1895), Moses Ball (b. ca. 1896), Betsy Ball (b. ca. 1898), and John Ball, Jr. (b. ca. 1900).

4. **William H. Ball** (b. ca. 1871), m. Addie L. King; purchased property and resided in Bogey Neck;[74] farmer and laborer; children: Helen Ball (b. 1900), William W. Ball, (b. 1903), Essie L. Ball (b. 1905), Edmund Ball (b. 1906), Etta Ball (b. 1908), Bernice Ball (b. 1909), Connie Ball (b. 1910), and Addie Ball (b. 1918); stepchildren: Levi King (b. ca. 1897), Howard King (b. ca. 1899), and Rosie King (b. ca. 1896).

Generation 3—Grandchildren of Betsey Ball[75]

Children of Sallie Ball, born in Wicomico and lived in Wicomico with mother:

1. **Frank Ball** (b. ca. 1877), about age 23; single; factory laborer.

---

72 Federal Census 1870, 1880, 1900.
73 Land Tax Books 1900, Northumberland County, VA.
74 Ibid.
75 Federal Census 1920, 1930, 1940.

2. **Jeremiah Ball** (b. ca. 1882), about age 18; single; factory hand.
3. **Sarah Ball** (b. ca. 1888), about age 12; single; house servant.
4. **Lela Ball** (b. ca. 1891), about age 9.

Children of John and Addie Ball, born in Wicomico and resided in Bogey Neck:

1. **Ellen A. Ball** (b. ca. 1895).
2. **Moses Ball** (b. ca. 1896), lived in Remo (1920); waterman; m. with one child.[76]
3. **Betsy Ball** (b. ca. 1898), about 12.
4. **John Ball, Jr**. (b. ca. 1900).
5. **Helen Ball** (b. ca. 1902), lived with parents; cooked for a private white family.

Children of William H. and Addie L. Ball:

1. **William W. Ball** (1903); m. Mazie Green, resided in Westmoreland County, VA, with Aunt Kate before moving to Bogey Neck community, Wicomico Church, VA, about 1933;[77] worked as a laborer and fisherman; children: William Gilbert "Cool Breeze" Ball (1930–1984), Essolene Ball Eskridge (b. 1932), James Linwood Ball (b. 1935), and Stanley Burnell Ball (1940–2009).
2. **Escelana Ball** (b. 1905), cook for private family.
3. **Edmund Ball** (b. 1906), son of William H. and Addie Ball; m. Bessie Ball; resided in Philadelphia (1925); worked as waiter

---

76 www.ancestry.com, draft registration.
77 Oral history, Deed Book XX, p. 126–127, Northumberland County, VA.

in a cafeteria; moved to Baltimore, MD (1940) on Woodyear Street; worked as a porter; children: Edmund Ball, Jr. (b. 1925), Helena Ball (b. 1931), Christine Ball (b. 1933), and Walter Ball (b. 1934).

4. **Etta Ball** (b. 1908), daughter of William H. and Addie Ball; moved to Philadelphia, PA, after finishing seventh grade at Mila Neck School.

5. **Bernice Ball** (b. 1909), son of William H. and Addie Ball; m. Marian Hudnall of Hacks Neck in 1955 at Howland Chapel, Northumberland County, VA; later m. to Mary Adeline Norris Caster of Wicomico Church in 1935.[78]

6. **Connie Ball** (b. 1910).

Generation 4—Great-Grandchildren of Betsey Ball; Grandchildren of William H. and Addie Ball[79]

Children of William W. and Mazie Ball, reared in Bogey Neck and attended school in the Wicomico Church district:

1. **William Gilbert Ball** (1930–1994), born in Westmoreland County, VA; reared in Bogey Neck; nickname: "Cool Breeze"; m. Lois V. Ross; fisherman; children: Carolyn Ball (1951), Constance Ball, Gilbert Ball Jr., Joyce Ball, Wayne Ball.

2. **Essolene Ball Eskridge** (1932), born in Westmoreland County, VA; m. Robert Eskridge of Lottsburg, VA, and lived there for a number of years; currently living with brother James Ball in Bogey Neck.

3. **James Linwood Ball** (b. 1935), born in Bogey Neck; m. Rose Conley; resides in Bogey Neck; worked as a fisherman, logger,

---

78 Marriage Records Colored 1917–1957, Northumberland County, VA.
79 Federal Census 1920, 1930, 1940.

well digger, landscaper; antique collector; caretaker for sister Essolene; child: J. Ball. [*See biographical sketch.*]

4. **Stanley Burnell Ball** (1940–2009), born in Bogey Neck community; first m. Evelyn Cox; second m. Christine B. Ball; buried in Mt. Olive Baptist Church cemetery, Wicomico Church, VA; children: Stanley Ball, Rose Ball, Dean Ball, Sharon Ball, (Burnell and Christine Ball).

Children of Edmund and Bessie Ball, born in Baltimore, MD:

5. **Edmund Ball Jr**. (b. 1925).
6. **Helena Ball** (b. 1931).
7. **Christine Ball** (b. 1933), resides in Philadelphia, PA.
8. **Walter Ball** (b. 1934), resides in Philadelphia, PA.

Generation 5—Great-Great-Grandchildren of Betsey Ball; Great-Grandchildren of William H. and Addie Ball; Grandchildren of William W. and Mazie Ball[80]

Children of Gilbert and Lois Ball, born in Bogey Neck (Oral history-2012):

1. **Carolyn Ball** (b. 1951), resides in Bogey Neck.
2. **Constance Ball,** resides in Clinton, MD.
3. **Gilbert Ball Jr.**, resides in LA.
4. **Joyce Ball**, resides in Bogey Neck, Wicomico Church, VA.
5. **Wayne Ball**, resides in Bogey Neck, Wicomico Church, VA.

---

80 Oral history 2012, 2013.

Son of James and Rose Ball:

6. J. Ball.

Children of Stanley Burnell and Evelyn Cox Ball:

7. Stanley Ball, resides in Lottsburg, VA.
8. Rose Ball, resides in Waldorf, VA.
9. Dean Ball, resides in Tappahannock, VA.
10. Sharon Ball, daughter of Stanley Burnell and Christine Ball.

BIOGRAPHICAL SKETCH — DESCENDANT OF BETSEY BALL

James Linwood Ball (1935) in Bogey Neck; son of William Ball, Jr. (1903–1974) and Mazie Green (1909– 1996); attended Mila and Anna T. Jeanes Elementary Schools; married Rose Conley (Lottsburg, VA); built home in Bogey Neck (1959) on land purchased from Louis Jones,  son of Lombard Jones; worked as fisherman, logger, landscaper, well digger; enjoys helping others. Some of his greatest deeds are: returned the body of a one-and-a-half-year-old boy from a sixty-five-foot well on the property of Louis Jones in Mila Neck; removed a black snake from Ellis Jones's house; helped Deacon Allen Yerby paint the steeple on Mt. Olive Church; father of one son and four grandchildren; antique collector, and among collection of antiques in living room are an eighty-year-old organ, a record player from the steamboat that once docked at Mila wharf, and a one-hundred-year-old Fisher woodstove that heats his three-bedroom home. James's favorite saying: "If God had not blessed me with a gift, I would be messed up." (*Source: James Ball, interview.*)

GENEALOGY OF MARY DAVENPORT (b. ca. 1880)

Generation 1: Mary Davenport—Introduction[81]

Mary Davenport (b. ca.1880); in 1910 census: widowed at age 30; resided in Bogey Neck, Wicomico Church, VA, district with six children (between ages 1 and 12 years old); worked as a washwoman for private white family; children: Addison Davenport (b. 1898); Ethel B. Davenport (b. 1901), William Davenport (b. 1903), Leroy J. Davenport (b. 1904), Estelle Davenport (b. 1907), Florence Davenport (b. 1909); neighbors: William H. Ball (B), Steptoe Fallin (B), Lombard Jones (B), and Joseph Jones (B). (No federal census found after 1910; possibly left the area; no land records found. It is believed that Mary Davenport was not a homeowner when she lived in Bogey Neck.)

Generation 2—Children of Mary Davenport

1. **Addison Davenport** (b. ca. 1898).
2. **Ethel Davenport** (b. ca.1901).
3. **William Davenport** (b. ca. 1903).
4. **Leroy Davenport** (b. ca. 1904).
5. **Estelle Davenport** (b. ca.1907).
6. **Florence Davenport** (b. ca. 1909).

Generations 3–7—Descendants of Mary Davenport

No records found in federal census. It is likely that Mary Davenport and children moved out of Bogey Neck between 1910 and 1920.

---

81 Federal Census 1910.

GENEALOGY OF JAMES FALLIN (b. ca. 1833)

Generation 1: James Fallin—Introduction[82]

James Fallin (b. ca. 1833), in Virginia; his wife Betsy (b. ca. 1850) was born in Virginia. They had three sons: Lewis (b. ca. 1854), John (b. ca. 1869), and Steptoe (b. ca. 1862), all residing in Wicomico at the time of the census. Also living with the Fallins was Robert Ball (age 17)—no relation. By the 1880 census, James was sixty-six years old and living in his home with son Steptoe Fallin, now eighteen years of age. Both worked as laborers. There is no record of James's and Betsy's death.[83]

Generation 2—Children of James and Betsy Fallin[84]

1. **Lewis Fallin** (b. ca. 1854), no other records found.
2. **John Fallin** (b. ca. 1869), no other records found.
3. **Steptoe Fallin** (b. ca. 1862), born in Wicomico Church, VA; in 1888 m. Bettie Taylor (b. ca. 1874); children: Nancy (b. ca. 1888); Eugene Fallin (b. ca. 1889); also living in the household was Steptoe's sixty-three-year-old mother-in-law, Esther Taylor; in 1908, Steptoe (about age forty-five) purchased four acres of land from Joseph W. Jones in Bogey Neck and was living there with his family; was a general farmer and worked for himself; according to the census reports, Steptoe could not read and write, but his wife and children could; daughter Nancy, at twenty-two years old, became a public school teacher; son, Eugene, at twenty-one years old, was working in the fishing industry;

---

82 Federal Census 1850, 1870.
83 Federal Census 1880, 1890, 1900, 1910.
84 Federal Census 1870, 1880, 1900, 1910, 1920.

a nephew, Levi Fallin (age 17), lived with Steptoe and worked in the fishing industry; by the 1920 census, Steptoe and Bettie's children were no longer living with them in Bogey Neck; Steptoe continued to farm on his land until his house was destroyed by fire, and he left the Bogey Neck community; daughter, Nancy Fallin Johns was the sole heir of Steptoe's property;[85] property sold to Elaine Jones Williams, the daughter of Joseph Jones and her husband, Leon Williams; Bogey Neck neighbors were: William H. Ball, Lombard Jones, Mary Davenport, Washington Walters, and Joseph Jones.

4. **Robert Fallin** (b. ca. 1861) born in Wicomico; no other records found.

Generation 3—Grandchildren of James and Betsy Fallin, Children of Steptoe and Bettie Fallin[86]

1. **Nancy Fallin Johns** (b. ca. 1888), public school teacher; no other records found.

2. **Eugene Fallin** (b. ca. 1889), laborer; no other records found.

Generation 4, 5, 6, 7—no records found.

---

85 Will Book, p. 672, Northumberland County, VA.
86 Federal Census 1900.

GENEALOGY OF STAFFORD B. JONES (b. ca. 1826)

Generation 1: Stafford B. Jones—Introduction[87]

Stafford B. Jones served in the Civil War with the Union Army in the District of Columbia Cavalry (1863– 1864) at the age of about thirty-seven. Stafford was discharged as an injured soldier. He applied for a pension and received a rejection notice on July 15, 1864. According to my father, Daniel Olin Jones (Stafford's grandson), Stafford lived in a log cabin between

Cross Hills Road and Remo Road in Wicomico Church.[88] My father and I took a walk to the site where it was believed Stafford's log cabin once stood. The house spot was clear and surrounded by beautiful oak trees. My dad pointed to the plantation where it was said that Stafford's wife, Susan Warner (b. ca. 1840), grew up as a slave girl.

In 1870, Stafford B. and Susan lived in Wicomico, and their post office was Browns Store. Stafford was a woodcutter, and Susan was a housekeeper. At the time, they had four children: Mary Jones (age 10), Ann Eliza Jones (age 7), Raleigh Doleman Jones (age 4), Joseph Warren Jones (age 2); Mary Carpenter and her son, Robert Carpenter (no relation), also lived in the home of Stafford. In the 1880 census, Stafford was farming, and Susan was caring for the house. The children

---

87 Federal Census 1850, 1870, 1880, 1900.
88 Sketch by William T. Jones, native of Bogey Neck; great-grandson of Stafford B. Jones, resides in Jacksonville, FL., 2012.

living with them were: Mary (age 17), Ann Eliza (16), Raleigh (13), Joseph (11), Lombard (7), and Susan (age 3). (Note: from one decade to the next, ages will vary in the census.) Also living in the house but no relation were: Sarah Turner (age 50), a laborer and single, and James Turner (age 7), Sarah's son. By the 1910 census, Susan Warner (age 75) was living in Bogey Neck with her son, Raleigh Jones, and his wife, Hannah. There are no census records beyond 1910 for Susan.

There were no records of land ownership found for Stafford B. Jones, having lived in Bogey Neck. However, three of his sons owned property and lived in Bogey Neck all their lives: Joseph Warren Jones, Lombard Coleman Jones, and Raleigh Doleman Jones. Stafford's grandsons—Daniel Olin Jones, Ellis Dubois Jones, Onard Jackson Jackson, Walter Kennard Kennard—and granddaughter, Elaine Jones Williams, lived in Bogey Neck. Kennard lived with his parents and remained on the family property until his death; Stafford's grandson, Joseph Russell Jones, purchased property in Bogey Neck (1930) and lived there with his wife, Sarah; Joseph's property was auctioned in 1939. The Jones properties are currently owned by fourth- and fifth-generation descendants—Stafford and Susan's great-grandchildren and great-great-grandchildren. One of the original homes built about 1918 and one of the last two homes left was owned by Stafford Jones's grandsons: first by Clarence "Bert" Jones who lost the house, and it was purchased by his brother, Daniel Olin, from Stuart and Imogene Blackwell in 1933. Records show that the deed was issued to Daniel Olin and Vera Sebree Jones in 1943. It took ten years for Daniel and Vera to pay off the note of $550 for the house and five acres.[89]

---

89   Land Records, Northumberland County, 1943-44.

Generation 2—Children of Stafford B. and Susan Warner Jones, born in Wicomico, Northumberland County, VA[90]

1. **Mary Jones** (ca.1863–1937) lived in a one-room log cabin on the property of brother, Joseph Jones; blind; unmarried; buried in Bogey Neck on property of niece, Elaine Jones Williams.

2. **Ann Eliza Jones** (b. ca. 1864); buried in cemetery on property of brother, Joseph Jones.

3. **Raleigh Doleman Jones** (ca.1867–1944); m. Hannah Johnson (b. ca. 1872); resided in Bogey Neck community all of his life; his two-story house sat on 6 4/5 acres in Snowden Park, purchased in 1913 from C. H. Walker; moved to son, Arthur Reid's house next door when his house became unlivable; according to 1930 federal census, Raleigh was sixty-seven years old, a widower, and lived alone; buried in family cemetery on his property; children: Arthur Reid Jones (b. ca. 1892), Julia Ann Jones Jackson (b. ca. 1893), William Scott Jones (b. ca. 1896), Raleigh Dolman Jones, Jr. (b. ca. 1901), and Martin Luther Jones (b. ca. 1903); neighbors: Julia Washington (B), John Brown (B), J. Conley (W), Sylvester

Warner (B), Washington Walters (B), Ernest Walters (B), Adolphus Wallace (B), and Willie Wilson (B).

4. **Joseph Warren Jonas** (ca. 1869–1940); in 1893, m. Mary L. Jackson (ca. 1875–1958); resided in Bogey Neck; farmer and also worked as carpenter; lived in two-story house on about twelve acres, where he and

---

90 Federal Census 1870, 1880; oral history; Marriage Records–Northumberland County, VA.

Mary raised thirteen of their
fourteen children;[91] son
Arthur Reid died at birth in
1908 and buried in family
cemetery behind the house;
known as "Papa Joe," Joseph
was a man of medium build;

wife Mary took care of the house and the children and worked
for the Hardings as a maid; raised turkeys to sell and hogs for
food; maintained a fruit orchard on the farm; owned horses that
served him well on his farm and as a mode of transportation to
church. On Sunday morning, Joseph hitched the horses to the
wagon and with his wife and half of his children, he headed off
to Mt. Olive Church, where he directed the choir for many years.
There were too many children to put in the buggy at one time,
so the children took turns riding and walking behind the buggy.
Joseph and his wife are buried in the old Mt. Olive Baptist
Church cemetery. Children: (recorded in Family Bible) Paul
Jones (1894–1928), Clarence D. Jones (1895–1947), Eula Jones
(1897–1988), Walter Kennard Jones (1891–1981), Glesner
Jones (1901–1968), Gladys Theresa Jones (1903–1979), Joseph
Russell Jones, Jr. (1905–1967), Daniel "Flossie" Olin Jones
(1907–1986), Onard "Sanny" Jackson Jones (1909–1993),
Logan Aster Jones (1912–1967), Miriam Tabitha Jones (1914–
1971), Ellis "Cap" Dubois Jones (1918–2004), and Mertice
Elaine Jones (1920–2007). Neighbors (1910): William H. Ball

---

91   Sketch by William T. Jones, 2010.

(B), Lombard Jones (B), Steptoe Fallin (B), Mary Davenport (B), and Washington Walters (B).

5. **Lombard Coleman Jones** (b. ca. 1873); first marriage to Annie Thompson (b. ca. 1871) in 1895; lived in Bogey Neck in a small two-story house next door to his brother Joseph and sister Mary; had two children: Robert Jones, Louis (Lewis) Thomas Jones (1905–1987) who was adopted. The house had two rooms downstairs (small kitchen big enough for a stove and icebox, a sitting/dining room in front used also for eating, one bedroom, and a hallway upstairs (the hallway was where the boys slept); fisherman and helped farm brother Joe's land, which extended several acres in the back of Joe's house; often heard praying in his outhouse by neighbors' children on their way to school; widowed by age fifty-two; second marriage to Lavinia Dameron (b. ca. 1886) in 1930 at Howland Chapel; willed his property to adopted son, Louis Thomas, in 1955;[92] widowed for the second time and resided in Bogey Neck in his home until death; buried in Old Mt. Olive cemetery.

6. **Susan Jones** (b. ca. 1877) no other records.

7. **Hannah Jones** (died at birth).

8. **Margaret Jones** (died at birth).

---

92   Will Book E, Northumberland County, VA, pp. 505-506.

Generation 3—Grandchildren of Stafford B. and Susan Jones[93]
<u>Children of Joseph and Mary L. Jackson Jones:</u>

1. **Paul Jones** (1894–1928); preacher; m. Susan Carter (b. 1898) in Ditchely, VA; resided in Wicomico Church, VA; moved to Baltimore, MD, in 1920s; buried in family cemetery at the homeplace in Bogey Neck along with wife, Susan. Children: Ernest H. Jones (b. 1915) and Clarence Jones (1918–2000).

2. **Clarence D. "Bert" Jones** (1895–1947), WWI (age 22); m. Mary King (b. 1898); purchased land in Bogey Neck and resided there until he lost his home; moved to New York in early 1900; steamboat cook while living in VA; employed by sanitation department in New York.

3. **Eula B. "Sis" Jones Ross Ingram** (1897–1988); m. Oscar Ross (b. ca. 1894), a WWI veteran from Regina, VA; was residing in Wicomico in 1930 when Oscar was killed by fallen tree; after Oscar's death, Eula moved to Trenton, NJ; m. William Ingram; child: Darrel Ross (b. 1922).

4. **Walter Kennard Jones** (1898–ca. 1981); resided in Bogey Neck all of his life, living most of his years with his parents and in a trailer on his parents' property; m. Cora Braxton Wallace (1931), widow of Adolphus Wallace of Bogey Neck Road; buried in Mt. Olive Church old cemetery.

5. **Glesner Jones** (1901–1968), m. Allie Kate Hankins (b. 1902) of North Carolina; resided at 29 Sumpter StreetKings, NY; chauffeur (trucking company); buried in Brooklyn, NY. Children: Glesner

---

93 Federal Census 1880, 1900, 1910; oral history; obituaries; marriage records.

Jones, Jr. (b. 1924), Eugene Jones (b. 1928), and Inez Jones (b. 1932).

6. **Gladys Theresa "Gakkie" Jones Taylor Thompson** (1903–1979); first m. (1930) to Moses Taylor of Northumberland County, VA; resided in Philadelphia, PA; second m. to Moses Thompson; employed by state hospital in Norris Town, PA; buried in Philadelphia, PA. Stepdaughters: Vernice Taylor Byrd Jones and Betty Taylor Anderson.

7. **Joseph "Joe Buck" Russell Jones** (1905–1967); first marriage to Sarah A. Walters; resided and worked in Newport News, VA, as a salesman in fishing industry in 1930s; moved to Philadelphia, PA; second marriage to Lucille (*maiden name unknown*); third marriage to Vernice Taylor Byrd (1915–2007), daughter of Moses Taylor and stepdaughter of Gladys Jones Taylor, Joseph's sister; buried in Philadelphia, PA; children: Coolidge Jones (Joseph and Sarah Jones), and Joyce Jones Roche (Joseph and Vernice Taylor Jones); stepchildren: Lorraine Byrd Sylva, Mingo Byrd, and Jerome Byrd (Vernice Taylor Byrd Jones).

8. **Daniel "Flossie" Olin Jones** (1907–1986); left school after seventh grade and went to work on Christopher's farm; m. Vera Sebree (1909–2003) in 1933; both buried in new Mt. Olive cemetery. Children: William Thomas Jones (b. 1928), David Samuel Jones (1935–2009), Daniel Rudolph Jones (1935–1975), Mary Mahalia Jones Day (b. 1940), and John I. Jones (b. 1946). [*See biographical sketch.*]

9. **Arthur Reid Jones** (1908–1908).

10. **Onard "Sandy" Jackson Jones** (1909–1993); resided in Bogey Neck; first m. to Mildred Pope in 1916 of Browns Store; second

m. to Alice Carter Smith in 1965; resided in Bogey Neck until death; auto mechanic and first repair shop in parents' backyard, oysterman. Children: Paul Jones (Onard and Mildred Pope Jones); Sheila Jones Lewis and William "Billy" Jones (Onard and Grace Rousby).

11. **Logan "Casey" Aster Jones** (1912–1967); in 1936, m. Beatrice Hazel Wallace (1918–1967); lived in house with Beatrice's mother (Cora Braxton Wallace) in Bogey Neck; moved to Philadelphia, PA, and remarried. Child: Pauline Jones of Philadelphia, PA.

12. **Miriam Telitha "Toe" Jones Palmer Jackson** (1914–1971); first m. to Travis Palmer of Regina, VA, in 1933; moved to Baltimore, MD, in 1939; second m. to Robert Jackson in 1955; clerk in jewelry store in Edmonson Village in Baltimore, MD; resided in Baltimore until her death; buried in old Mt. Olive Church cemetery.

13. **Ellis Dubois "Cap" Jones** (1918–2004); m. Hortense Walters (1922–2013) of Bogey Neck in 1941; resided in Bogey Neck; auto mechanic; buried in new Mt. Olive Church cemetery. Children: Barbara Mastine Jones (b. 1941), Elwood Lavern Jones, Sr. (b. 1945), and Warren Jones (b. 1968). [*See biographical sketch.*]

14. **Mertice Elaine Jones Williams** (1920–2007); m. Leon Williams (1910–1967) of Wicomico, VA; resided in Bogey Neck; buried in old Mt. Olive Church cemetery next to husband, Leon Williams. Children: Milfret Williams (b. 1940), Deloris Williams Gordon (b. 1941), Maurice Williams (b. 1947), Duval Williams (b. 1948), and Christopher Jones (b. 1958).

Generation 4—Great-Grandchildren of Stafford B. and Susan Warner Jones[94]

Grandchildren of Joseph and Mary L. Jackson Jones:

1. **Ernest H. Jones, Sr.** (1915–1994), son of Paul D. and Susan Carter Jones; born in Northumberland County, VA; m. Dorothy Campbell in 1940; moved to Baltimore, MD, in 1943; buried in Arbutus Memorial Park, Arbutus, MD. Children: Ernest Jones, Jr., and Edna Brown Smith.

2. **Clarence Carter Jones** (1918–2000); son of Paul D. and Susan Carter Jones; born in Baltimore, MD; m. childhood sweetheart, Henrietta Henly of Baltimore, MD; resided in Cherry Hill, MD; buried in Baltimore, MD. [*See biographical sketch.*]

3. **Darrel Ross** (b. 1922) son of Eula Jones and Oscar Ross; born in Wicomico, VA.

4. **Glesner Jones, Jr.** (b. 1924), son of Glesner, Sr., and Allie Kate Hankins Jones; born in Brooklyn, NY.

5. **Eugene Jones** (b. 1928**)**, son of Glesner, Sr., and Allie Kate Hankins Jones; born in Brooklyn, NY.

6. **Inez Jones** (b. 1932), daughter of Glesner, Sr., and Allie Kate Hankins Jones; born in Brooklyn, NY.

7. **Coolidge Jones** (b. 1929), son of Joseph Russell and Sarah Walters Jones; born in Bogey Neck; resided in Virginia with his grandparents until he left for college (Hampton Institute, Hampton, VA); mathematics teacher; resided in Maryland after graduating from Hampton; relocated to Philadelphia, PA, where he taught school and retired; buried in Philadelphia, PA.

---

94 Federal Census 1920, 1930; oral history; Marriage Records–Northumberland County, VA.

8. **Joyce Jones Roche**, daughter of Joseph Russell and Vernice Jones; born and resides in Philadelphia, PA; retired teacher. Child: Antoine Small..

9. **William Thomas Jones** (b. 1928), son of Daniel Olin and Vera Sebree Jones; born in Mila Neck; m. Mary Kathryn McGlone (1932–2007) of Ahoskie, NC; retired architect; resides in Jacksonville, FL; children: James Daniel Jones (b. 1964), adopted, and Vera Jones Soleyn (b. 1966). [*See biographical sketch.*]

10. **Daniel Rudolph Jones** (1935–1975), son of Daniel Olin and Vera Sebree Jones; born in Bogey Neck Community, Wicomico Church, Northumberland County, VA; m. Marian Hall; resided in Baltimore, MD; medical technician; buried in Mt. Olive Baptist Church cemetery. [*See biographical sketch.*]

11. **David Samuel Jones** (1935–2009), son of Daniel Olin and Vera Sebree Jones; born in Bogey Neck; m. Esther Smith of Baltimore, MD, in 1935; resided in Baltimore, MD; retired teacher; buried in Baltimore County, MD; children: Mark S. Jones (b. 1962), Stephanie M. Jones Wilkins (b. 1964), D. Michael Jones (b. 1969), and Michelle M. Jones (b. 1971), adopted. [*See biographical sketch.*]

12. **Mary Mahalia Jones Day** (b. 1940), daughter of Daniel Olin and Vera Sebree Jones; born in Bogey Neck; in 1963, m. Robert Eugene Day, Sr. (b. 1941) of Heathsville, VA; resides in Columbia, MD; retired educator (teacher, counselor, high school principal); author, *My Father's Journey;* children: Robert Eugene Day, Jr. (b. 1965) and Timothy Alan Day (b. 1973).

13. **John Irvin Jones** (b. 1946), son of Daniel Olin and Vera Sebree Jones; born in Bogey Neck; first m. to Sharon Robinson (1946–

2000); second m. to Gloria Conway; third m. to Vashti Savage of Baltimore, MD; retired accountant; currently a real estate agent; resides in Northumberland County, VA; child: Jonathan E. Jones (b. 1969), son of John and Sharon Robinson Jones. [*See biographical sketch.*]

14. **Barbara Mastine Jones** (b. 1941), daughter of Ellis Dubois and Hortense Walters Jones; born in Bogey Neck; resides in Bogey Neck. [*See biographical sketch.*]

15. **Elwood Lavern Jones, Sr.** (b. 1945), son of Ellis Dubois and Hortense Walters Jones; born in Bogey Neck; first marriage to the late Bonner Curry of Northumberland County, VA; second marriage to Erna Savoy (b. 1946) of Ditchley, VA; resides in Alexander, VA; retired auto mechanic. Children: Dawn M. Jones (b. 1967) and Elwood Jones Jr. (b. 1970), (Elwood, Sr., and Bonner Curry Jones); Andrea Jones Mosley, (Elwood, Sr., and Erna Savoy Jones). [*See biographical sketch.*]

16. **Warren Dubois Jones** (b. 1968), son of Ellis Dubois and Hortense Walters Jones; born in Bogey Neck; formerly married to Rochelle Taylor Jones; resides in Alexandria, VA; children: Ariel Jones (b. 1995) and Ashley Jones (b. 1999). [See biographical sketch.]

17. **Milfret Williams** (1940–1977), son of Elaine Jones and Leon Mason Williams; born in Bogey Neck; m. Cora Williams; resided and buried in Westmoreland County VA; children: Joy Williams Veney and Sherwin Williams.

18. **Miriam Deloris Williams Gordon** (b. 1941), daughter of Elaine Jones and Leon Mason Williams; born in Bogey Neck; m. John

Gordon of SC; resided in Philadelphia, PA, prior to retiring in North Carolina.

19. **Maurice Williams, Sr.** (b. 1947), son of Elaine Jones and Leon Williams; born in Bogey Neck; formerly m. to Vernadine Cartwright; resides in Fort Washington, MD; children: Maurice Williams, Jr., and Kendra Williams Morris.

20. **Duval Williams** (b. 1948), born in Bogey Neck, Wicomico Church, VA; son of Elaine Jones and Leon Mason Williams of Wicomico, VA; former first wife, Beverly Williams; child: Nicole Williams; former second wife, Verna Freeman Williams; Duval resides in Maryland.

21. **Christopher Jones** (b. 1958), born in Bogey Neck; son of Elaine Jones; m. the late Rena Carter of Northumberland County, VA; children: Christopher Williams, Jr., and Anthony Williams.

22. **Pauline Jones**, daughter of Logan Aster Jones, born in Philadelphia, PA.

23. **Paul Onard Jones**, son of Onard Jackson Jones and Mildred Pope Jones; reared by John Henry and aunt Edith Pope Parker of Horse Head, VA; resides in Philadelphia, PA; children: Timothy E. Jones and Vincent A. Jones.

24. **Sheila Jones Lewis** (b. 1943), daughter of Onard Jackson Jones and Grace Rousby; born in Remo, VA; resides in NJ; m. Willie Lewis; children: Sheila Lewis Fisher (b. 1960), Marshall D. Lewis (b. 1962), William A. Lewis (b. 1963), and Mary E. Lewis (b. 1964).

25. **William "Billy" Jones** (1942–1990), son of Onard Jackson Jones and Grace Rousby ; born in Remo, VA.

Generation 5—Great-Great-Grandchildren of Stafford B. and Susan Jones[95]

Great-Grandchildren of Joseph and Mary Jackson Jones:

1. **Ernest Jones, Jr**. (b. 1940), son of Ernest Jones, Sr., and Dorothy Campbell Jones; grandson of Paul and Susan Carter Jones; child: Kevin Jones.
2. **Edna Brown Smith,** daughter of Ernest Jones, Sr., and Margaret Brown; granddaughter of Paul and Susan Carter Jones; resides in Baltimore, MD; children: Danise Smith and Valarie Smith.
3. **Antoine Small, Jr.**, son of Joyce Jones Roche; grandson of Josesph and Vernice Taylor Byrd Jones; children: Shanice Small (b. 1988) and Nasir Small (b. 2003).
4. **Dawn Jones** (b. 1967), daughter of Elwood, Sr., and Bonner Curry Jones; granddaughter of Ellis Dubois and Hortense Walters Jones; born in Alexandria, VA; resides in Atlanta, GA; lawyer and nurse.
5. **Elwood Jones, Jr**. (b. 1970), son of Elwood, Sr., and Bonner Curry Jones; born in Alexandria, VA; grandson of Ellis Dubois and Hortense Walters Jones; children: Jerrell Jones, Jerrick Jones, Jasmine Jones, and Shawn Jones.
6. **Andrea Jones Mosley** (b. 1980), daughter of Elwood, Sr., and Erna Savoy Jones; granddaughter of Ellis Dubois and Hortense Walters Jones; born in Alexandria, VA; m. Marcell Mosley; resides in Woodbridge, MD. Children: Venessa Mosley and Elijah Mosley.

---

95 Oral history.

7. **Ariel Jones** (b. 1995), daughter of Warren and Michelle Taylor Jones; granddaughter of Ellis Dubois and Hortense Walters Jones; resides in Arlington, VA.

8. **Ashley Jones** (b. 1999), daughter of Warren and Michelle Taylor Jones; granddaughter of Ellis Dubois and Hortense Walters Jones; resides in Arlington, VA.

9. **James Daniel Jones** (b. 1964), adopted son of William Thomas and Mary Kathryn McGlone Jones; grandson of Daniel Olin and Vera Sebree Jones; resides in Florida; formerly m. to Deidre Jones. Child: Anthony Jones (b. 1990).

10. **Vera Jones Soleyn** (b. 1966), daughter of William Thomas and Mary Kathryn McGlone Jones; born in San Bernardino, CA; resides in FL; granddaughter of Daniel Olin and Vera Sebree Jones; formerly m. to Stephen Soleyn; basketball coach, motivational speaker, writer, award-winning television and radio broadcaster. Child: Andrew Soleyn (b. 1998). [*See biographical sketch.*]

11. **Mark S. Jones** (b. 1962), son of David Samuel and Esther Smith Jones; grandson of Daniel Olin and Vera Sebree Jones; born in Baltimore, MD; first m. to Cheryl Totten of Baltimore, MD; second m. Tina Gross of Baltimore, MD; accountant; children: Kelli Jones Mayfield (b. 1988) and Brandi Jones (b. 1996). [*See biographical sketch.*]

12. **Stephanie Jones Wilkins** (b. 1964); daughter of David Samuel and Esther Smith Jones; born in Baltimore, MD; granddaughter of Daniel Olin and Vera Sebree Jones; m. Col. Audie Wilkins (b. 1964) of Baltimore, MD; resides in Fredericksburg, VA; organizational industrial psychologist; child: Audie M. Wilkins, Jr. (b. 2001). [*See biographical sketch.*]

13. **David Michel Jones** (b. 1969); son of David Samuel and Esther Smith Jones; born in Baltimore, MD; grandson of Daniel Olin and Vera Sebree Jones; m. Tracey Bryant; resides in Leesburg, VA; electrical engineer. [*See biographical sketch.*]

14. **Michelle M. Jones** (b. 1971); youngest of four children raised by David Samuel and Esther Smith Jones; granddaughter of Daniel Olin and Vera Sebree Jones; resides in Baltimore County, MD; children: Jeffrey Keyser (b. 1990) and Guy Jones (b. 1993). [*See biographical sketch.*]

15. **Robert Eugene Day, Jr.** (b. 1965); son of Mary Jones and Robert E. Day, Sr.; born in Baltimore, MD; grandson of Daniel Olin and Vera Sebree Jones; formerly m. to Michelle Sterrett (b. 1963); resides in Columbia, MD; global business executive; children: Ryan A. Day (b. 1992), Rachel M. Day (b. 1996), and Andrew S. Day (b. 1998). [*See biographical sketch.*]

16. **Timothy Alan Day** (b. 1973); son of Mary Jones and Robert E. Day, Sr.; born in Baltimore, MD; grandson of Daniel Olin and Vera Sebree Jones; formerly m. to Charlene Pittman (b. 1971) of Greensboro, NC; resides in Howard County, MD; marketing and sales representative; child: Emmanuel Timothy Day (b. 2006); stepdaughter: Chasity Pittman. [*See biographical sketch.*]

17. **Jonathan E. Jones** (b. 1969), son of John and Sharon Robinson Jones; born in Washington, DC; grandson of Daniel Olin and Vera Sebree Jones; m. Maria Gregoria of New York; resides in Severn, MD; child: Harley Jones (b. 2007). [*See biographical sketch.*]

18. **Sheila Lewis Fisher,** daughter of Sheila Jones and Willie Lewis; granddaughter of Onard Jackson Jones; resides in Chesapeake, VA; children: Alexis Fisher (b. 1962) and Nicholas Fisher (b. 1998).

19. **Marshall D. Lewis** (b. 1962), son of Sheila Jones and Willie Lewis; grandson of Onard Jackson Jones; resides in East Hampton, CT; children: Shamora Lewis and Brandon Lewis.

20. **William A. Lewis** (b. 1963), son of Sheila Jones and Willie Lewis; grandson of Onard Jackson Jones; resides in Pomona, CA; children: William Lewis, Jr. (b. 1982), Latasha Lewis (b. 1979), William Lewis (b. 1985), and Zsaté Lewis (b. 1991).

21. **Mary E. Lewis** (b. 1964), daughter of Sheila Jones and Willie Lewis; granddaughter of Onard Jackson Jones; resides in White Plains, NY.

22. **Vincent A. Jones** (b. 1967), son of Paul Onard. Jones; grandson of Onard Jackson Jones; m. Tanya Jones; children: Vincent Jones, Anthony Jones, Chanelle Jones, Andrea Jones;

23. **Timothy E. Jones**, son of Paul Onard Jones; grandson of Onard Jackson Jones m. April Thompson; children: Jaela Jones, Timothy Jones, Olivia Jones

24. **Christopher Jones, Jr.,** son of Christopher and Rena Carter Jones; resides in Richmond, VA; grandson of Elaine Jones and Leon Williams.

25. **Anthony Jones,** son of Christopher and Rena Carter Jones; grandson of Elaine Jones and Leon Mason Williams; resides in Richmond, VA.

26. **Kendra Williams,** daughter of Maurice Williams, Sr.; granddaughter of Elaine Jones and Leon Mason Williams.

27. **Maurice Williams, Jr.,** son of Maurice Williams, Sr.; grandson of Elaine Jones and Leon Mason Williams.

28. **Joy Williams Veney,** daughter of Milfret Williams and Cora Williams-Roy; granddaughter of Elaine Jones and Leon Mason Williams; first m. Rodney Brannum; second m. Howard Veney; children: Tia Brannum, Leon Williams, Kaisha Williams, and Rayshawn Williams.

29. **Sherwin Williams, Sr.,** son of Milfret Williams and Cora Williams-Roy; m. Sharion Williams; grandson of Elaine and Leon Mason Williams; children: Sherwin Williams, Jr., Demetrice Williams, Harold Williams, and Jarroda Williams.

Generation 6—Great-Great-Great-Grandchildren of Stafford B. and Susan Warner Jones[96]

Great-Great-Grandchildren of Joseph and Mary Jackson Jones; Great-Grandchildren:

1. **Kevin Jones**, son of Ernest Jones, Jr.; grandson of Ernest, Sr., and Dorothy Campbell Jones; great-grandson of Paul and Susan King Jones.

2. **Valarie Smith** (b. 1955); daughter of Edna Brown Smith, granddaughter of Ernest, Sr., and Dorothy Campbell Jones, great-granddaughter of Paul and Susan King Jones; child: Elliott Tast.

3. **Danise Smith** (b. 1956); daughter of Edna Brown Smith, granddaughter of Ernest, Sr., and Dorothy Campbell Jones, great-granddaughter of Paul and Susan King Jones; child: Elliott Tast.

---

96 Oral history.

4. **Venessa Mosley** (b. 2001), daughter of Andrea Jones and Marcell Mosley; granddaughter of Elwood and Erna Jones; great-granddaughter of Ellis Dubois and Hortense Walters Jones.

5. **Elijah Mosley** (b. 2007), son of Andrea Jones and Marcell Mosley; grandson of Elwood and Erna Jones; great-grandson of Ellis Dubois and Hortense Walters Jones; resides with parents in Arlington, VA.

6. **Jerel Jones** (b. 1991), son of Elwood Jones, Jr., and Ursula Bell; grandson of Elwood, Sr., and Erna Savoy Jones; great-grandson of Ellis Dubois and Hortense Walters Jones.

7. **Jerick Jones** (b. 1993), son of Elwood Jones, Jr., and Ursula Bell; grandson of Elwood, Sr., and Erna Savoy Jones; great-grandson of Ellis Dubois and Hortense Walters Jones.

8. **Jasmine Jones** (b. 1989), daughter of Elwood Jones, Jr., and Ursula Bell; granddaughter of Elwood and Erna Savoy Jones; granddaughter of Elwood, Sr., and Erna Savoy Jones; great-granddaughter of Ellis Dubois and Hortense Walters Jones; children: Anaya (b. 2008), Sana (b. 2010), and Josiah (b. 2012).

9. **Shawn Jones** (b. 2000), son of Elwood Jones, Jr., and Ursula Bell; grandson of Elwood, Sr., and Erna Savoy Jones; great-grandson of Ellis Dubois and Hortense Walters Jones.

10. **Harley Jones** (b. 2007), daughter of Jonathan and Maria Gregoria Jones; granddaughter of John and Sharon Jones; great-granddaughter of Daniel Olin and Vera Sebree Jones; born and resides in Severn, MD.

11. **Anthony Jones** (b. 1990), son of James Daniel and Deidre Jones; grandson of William and Kathryn Jones; great-grandson of Daniel Olin and Vera Sebree Jones.

12. **Andrew Soleyn** (b. 1998), son of Vera Jones and Steven Soleyn, born in FL; grandson of William and Kathryn Jones; great-grandson of Daniel Olin and Vera Sebree Jones; honor student at Florida School for Deaf and Blind.

13. **Ryan Alexander Day** (b. 1992), son of Robert E., Jr., and Michelle Sterrett, born in Los Angeles, CA.; grandson of Mary Jones and Robert E. Day, Sr., great grandson of Daniel Olin and Vera Sebree Jones; resides in New York; attended St. John's University, NY; currently enrolled at York College, NY.

14. **Rachel Michelle Day** (b. 1996), daughter of Robert E., Jr., and Michelle Sterrett; born in Baltimore, MD; granddaughter of Mary Jones and Robert E. Day, Sr.; great-granddaughter of Daniel Olin and Vera Sebree Jones; resides in Columbia, MD; honor student at Atholton High School, Howard County, MD.

15. **Andrew Sterrett Day** (b. 1998); son of Robert E. Day, Jr., and Michelle Sterrett; born in Baltimore, MD; grandson of Mary Jones and Robert E. Day, Sr.; great-grandson of Daniel Olin and Vera Sebree Jones; resides in Columbia, MD; honor student, St. Paul's School, Baltimore, County, MD.

16. **Emmanuel Timothy Day** (b. 2006); son of Timothy Day and Charlene Pittman; born in High Point, NC; grandson of Mary Jones and Robert E. Day, Sr., great-grandson of Daniel Olin and Vera Sebree Jones; resides in Maryland.

17. **Kelli Jones Mayfield** (b. 1988); daughter of Mark Jones and Cheryl Totten; born in Baltimore, MD; granddaughter of Esther and David S. Jones; great-granddaughter of Daniel Olin and Vera Sebree Jones; resides in Baltimore, County, MD; nurse; child: Aryana Mayfield (b. 2011).

18. **Brandi Jones** (b. 1996); daughter of Mark Jones and Cheryl Totten; granddaughter of Esther and David S. Jones; great-granddaughter of Daniel Olin and Vera Sebree Jones; born in and resides in Maryland.

19. **Audie M. Wilkins, Jr.** (b. 2001); son of Stephanie Jones and Audie Wilkins, Sr.; grandson of Esther and David S. Jones; great-grandson of Daniel Olin and Vera Sebree Jones; resides in Fredericksburg, VA.

20. **Jeffrey Keyser** (b. 1990); son of Michelle Jones and Jeffrey Keyser; born in Baltimore, MD; grandson of Esther and David S. Jones; great-granddaughter of Daniel Olin and Vera Sebree Jones; attended Morgan State University; resides in Baltimore County, MD.

21. **Lorenzo Guy Jones** (b. 1993); son of Michelle Jones; born in Baltimore, MD; grandson of Esther and David S. Jones; great-granddaughter of Daniel Olin and Vera Sebree Jones; resides in Baltimore County, MD; honor student at Frostburg University, MD.

22. **Tia Veney Brannum**, daughter of Joy Brannum Veney and Rodney Brannum; granddaughter of Milfret Williams and Cora Williams-Roy; great-granddaughter of Elaine Jones and Leon Mason Williams; children: Renika, Keith, and Tiaja.

23. **Leon Veney**, son of Joy Williams and Howard Veney; grandson of Milfret Williams and Cora Williams-Roy; great-grandson of Elaine Jones and Leon Mason Williams.

24. **Kaisha Veney**, daughter of Joy Williams and Howard Veney; granddaughter of Milfret and Cora Williams-Roy; great-granddaughter of Elaine Jones and Leon Mason Williams.

25. **Rayshawn Veney,** son of Joy Williams and Howard Veney; grandson of Milfret Williams and Cora Williams-Roy; great-grandson of Elaine Jones and Leon Mason Williams.

26. **Sherwin Williams, Jr.,** son of Sherwin, Sr., and Sharion Williams, Sr; grandson of Milfret Williams and Cora Williams-Roy; great-grandson of Elaine Jones and Leon Mason Williams.

27. **Demetrice Williams,** daughter of Sherwin, Sr., and Sharon Williams, Sr.; granddaughter of Milfret Williams and Cora Williams-Roy; great-granddaughter of Elaine Jones and Leon Mason Williams.

28. **Harold Williams,** son of Sherwin, Sr., and Sharon Williams, Sr.; grandson of Milfret Williams and Cora Williams-Roy; great-grandson of Elaine Jones and Leon Mason Williams.

29. **Jarroda Williams,** daughter of Sherwin and Sharon Williams, Sr.; granddaughter of Milfret Williams and Cora Williams-Roy; great-granddaughter of Elaine Jones and Leon Mason Williams.

30. **Alexis Fisher** (b.1993), daughter of Sheila Lewis Fisher; granddaughter of Sheila Jones and Willie Lewis; great granddaughter of Onard Jackson Jones and Grace Rousby.

31. **Nicholas Fisher** (b. 1998); son of Sheila Lewis Fisher; granddaughter of Sheila Jones and Willie Lewis; great grandson of Onard Jackson Jones and Grace Rousby.

32. **Shamora Lewis**, daughter of Marshall D. Lewis; granddaughter of Sheila Jones and Willie Lewis; great grandson of Onard Jackson Jones and Grace Rousby.

33. **Brandon Lewis**, son of Marshall D. Lewis; grandson of Sheila Jones and Willie Lewis; great grandson of Onard Jackson Jones and Grace Rousby.

34. **William Lewis, Jr**. (b.1982), son of William A. Lewis, Sr and Deanne Richardson Lewis; grandson of Sheila Jones and Willie Lewis; great grandson of Onard Jackson Jones and Grace Rousby; resides in Lindenwold, N.J.

35. **Latasha Lewis** (b. 1979), daughter of William A. Lewis, Sr. and Deanne Richardso; granddaughter of Sheila Jones and Willie Lewis; great granddaughter of Onard Jackson Jones and Grace Rousby. resides in Atlantic City, NJ.

36. **William Lewis** (b. 1985), son of William A. Lewis Sr. and Marcella McClean); grandson of Sheila Jones and Willie Lewis; great grandson of Onard Jackson Jones and Grace Rousby. resides in Atlantic City.

37. **Zsaté Lewis** (b. 1991), daughter of William A. Lewis Sr. and Marcella McClean; granddaughter of Sheila Jones and Willie Lewis; great granddaughter of Onard Jackson Jones and Grace Rousby; resides in Virginia Beach, VA.

38. **Vincent Jones**, son of Vincent A. Jones; grandson of Paul Onard Jones; great grandson of Onard Jackson and Mildred Pope Jones.

39. **Anthony Jones**, son of Vincent A. Jones; grandson of Paul Onard Jones; great grandson of Onard Jackson and Mildred Pope Jones.

40. **Chanelle Jones**, daughter of Vincent A. Jones; granddaughter of Paul Onard Jones; great granddaughter of Onard Jackson and Mildred Pope Jones

41. **Andrea Jones**, daughter of Vincent A. Jones; granddaughter of Paul Onard Jones; great granddaughter of Onard Jackson and Mildred Pope Jones

42. **Jaela Jones**, daughter of Timothy E. Jones; granddaughter of Paul Onard Jones; great granddaughter of Onard Jackson and Mildred Pope Jones

43. **Timothy Jones**, son Timothy E. Jones; grandson of Paul Onard Jones; great grandson of Onard Jackson and Mildred Pope Jones.

44. **Olivia Jones,** daughter of Timothy E. Jones; granddaughter of Paul Onard Jones; great granddaughter of Onard Jackson and Mildred Pope Jones Jackson and Mildred Pope Jones

45. **Shanice Small** (b. 1988), daughter of Antione Small, Jr.; granddaughter of Joyce Jones Roche; great granddaughter of Joseph and Vernice Taylor Byrd Jones; resides in Philadelphia, PA.

46. **Nasir Small** (2003), son of Antione Small, Jr.; grandson of Joyce Jones Roche; great grandson of Joseph and Vernice Taylor Byrd Jones; resides in Philadelphia, PA.

Generation 7—Great-Great-Great-Great-Grandchildren of Stafford B. and Susan Jones[97]

Great-Great-Great-Grandchildren of Joseph and Mary Jackson Jones:

1. **Anaya** (b. 2008), daughter of Jasmine Jones; granddaughter of Elwood Jones, Jr.; great-granddaughter of Elwood Jones, Sr.; great-great-granddaughter of Ellis Dubois and Hortense Walters Jones.

2. **Sana** (b. 2010), daughter of Jasmine Jones; granddaughter of Elwood Jones, Jr.; great-granddaughter of Elwood Jones, Sr.; great-great-granddaughter of Ellis Dubois and Hortense Walters Jones.

97　Oral history and family records.

3. **Josiah** (b. 2012), son of Jasmine Jones; grandson of Elwood Jones, Jr.; great-grandson of Elwood Jones, Sr., great-great grandson of Ellis Dubois and Hortense Walters Jones.

4. **Aryana Mayfield** (b. 2011); born in Baltimore, MD; daughter of Kelli Jones Mayfield; granddaughter of Mark S. and Sherri Jones; great-granddaughter of David and Esther Smith Jones; great-great-granddaughter of Daniel Olin and Vera Sebree Jones; resides in Baltimore County, MD.

5. **Elliott Tast**, son of Valarie Smith; grandson of Edna Brown Smith; great-grandson of Ernest, Sr., and Dorothy Campbell Jones; great-great-grandson of Paul and Susan King Jones; attends Carnegie Mellon University, Pittsburgh, PA, on a full scholarship, majoring in engineering.

6. **Renika Barnnum**, daughter of Tia Barnnum; granddaughter of Joy Williams Veney; great-granddaughter of Milfret Williams and Cora Williams-Roy; great-great-granddaughter of Elaine Jones and Leon Mason Williams.

7. **Keith Barnnum,** son of Tia Barnnum, grandson of Joy Williams Veney; great-grandson of Milfret Williams and Cora Williams-Roy; great-great-grandson of Elaine Jones and Leon Mason Williams.

8. **Tiaja Barnnum,** daughter of Tia Barnnum; granddaughter of Joy Williams Veney; great-granddaughter of Milfret Williams and Cora Williams-Roy; great-great-granddaughter of Elaine Jones and Leon Mason Williams.

Generation 8—Great-Great-Great-Great-Great Grandchild of Stafford B. and Susan Jones[98]

Great-Great-Great-Great-Grandchild of Joseph and Mary L. Jones:

1. **Lyric Brannum**, daughter of Renika Brannum; granddaughter of Tia Brannum; great-granddaughter of Joy Williams Veney; great-great-granddaughter of Milfret Williams and Cora Williams-Roy; great-great-great granddaughter of Elaine Jones and Leon Mason Williams.

BIOGRAPHICAL SKETCH—DESCENDANTS OF STAFFORD B. AND SUSAN WARNER JONES (Joseph and Mary L. Jones)

Daniel Olin Jones (1907–1986), son of Joseph Warren. and Mary L. Jones; born and resided in Bogey Neck, Wicomico Church, Northumberland County, VA; began public schooling at Mila School (1914), leaving at end of seventh grade to work on Gus Christopher farm (1921) in Remo, VA, as a "farm boy"; married fifty-two years to Vera Sebree Jones of Mila Neck, Wicomico Church district; moved to Bogey Neck home in 1933; five children: William Thomas, David Samuel, Daniel Rudolph, John Irvin, and Mary Mahalia; employed at Newport News shipyard (1928); returned to Bogey Neck and worked as a Menhaden fisherman and oysterman; upon retiring, employed at Robert Northern seafood plant and caretaker for the Bowman family's property in

---

98 Oral history and family records.

Bogey Neck; joined Mt. Olive Baptist Church (1922), service covering a broad spectrum of active involvement in many organizations and church projects: trustee board, superintendent of Sunday school, elected and ordained deacon (1932); during tenure on Mt. Olive deacon board, unselfishly contributed energy, time, and talent to the growth and development of the church and the church community; superintendent of New Chapel Sunday School (1942); appointed chairman of deacon board (1949); organized the Northern Neck Deacons' Union (1952) and remained active in the organization until death; as a community activist, member of Mila and Anna T. Jeanes elementary school's Parent Teacher Associations (PTA); president of Julius Rosenwald High School PTA; member of Hospital Building Fund committee, Boy Scouts of America, Bogey Neck Community Annual Picnic; described by Evon Ervin as the "proverbial servant leader, father, mentor, and reluctant hero"; died in Baltimore County General Hospital, Randallstown, MD, after annual family Christmas dinner; buried in new Mt. Olive Church cemetery beside his wife and son, Daniel R. Jones. (*Source*: My Father's Journey, *by Mary J. Day, 2009.*)

Ellis Dubois Jones (1918–2004), one of fourteen children of Joseph Warren. and Mary L. Jackson Jones of Bogey Neck; m. Hortense Walters in 1941; attended Mila Neck School and furthered education through participation in many religious, civic, and community organizations; dedicated member of Mt. Olive Baptist Church, serving chair of trustee board for twenty-five years; member of usher board; member of men's chorus for fifty years; children look forward to "Mr. Ellis" picking them up on church bus for Sunday school and morning worship; proud of affiliation with Boy Scouts of America and traveled throughout Virginia with Robert E. Lee Council–Troop 224; as a skilled mechanic, worked for Crowther Car Dealership in Kilmarnock, VA, and Norris Service Station in Kilmarnock, VA. (*Source:Family*)

William Thomas Jones (b. 1928), great-grandson of Stafford B. Jones (b. ca. 1826), who fought in the Civil War, and Susan Warner (b. ca. 1840), both born in slavery in Northumberland County, VA; grandson of Joseph Warren Jones (ca. 1867–1940) and Mary L. Jackson Jones (ca. 1875–1958) of Bogey Neck, once a one lane dirt road in Snowden Park, Wicomico Church; the oldest of five children of Daniel Olin Jones (1907–1986) of Bogey Neck and Vera Sebree Jones (1909–2003) of Mila Neck, a small community in the Wicomico Church district; attended Mila and Anna T. Jeanes elementary schools and graduate of Julius Rosenwald High School (1946); received a BS degree in architectural engineering (1950) from Hampton Institute, Hampton, VA; employed by the US Army Corps of Engineers as a civil engineer for twenty-two years; first assignment in the territory of Alaska followed by Tehran, Iran, for two years; employed ten years with the District of Columbia government as director of design engineering, Department of General Services. After retiring from the federal government, was administrator with the Metropolitan Area Transit Authority for ten years; formerly a member of Mt. Olive Baptist Church, Wicomico, VA; currently a member and steward of A. M. E. Church, Palm Coast, FL;

formerly a two-term councilman in Palm Coast, FL; member of Omega Psi Phi Fraternity; resides in Jacksonville, FL; father of a son and daughter: James Daniel Jones, attended Bowie State College, MD, and Vera Jones Soleyn, a graduate of Syracuse University, NY; two grandsons: Anthony Jones (22) and Andrew Soleyn (14). (*Source: William T. Jones.*)

Clarence Carter Jones (1918–2000), born in Baltimore, MD, and resided there until death; son of the late Paul and Susan Carter of Northumberland County, VA; one brother, Ernest Jones, and a half-sister, Elnor Saulsbury; graduate of Douglas High School, Baltimore, MD (1950); married fifty-nine years to childhood sweetheart, Henrietta Henly; attained the rank of sergeant while serving in WWII, presented a certificate for exemplary military service by former Maryland governor, Herbert R. O'Connor; received a certificate of achievement in a career advanced program from Baltimore Urban League; employed by Edward Peck in Baltimore, MD, as a painter (1937–1939); pursued post-secondary studies at Morgan State University; retired from United States Postal Service (1980); received several commendations while employed with post office: "Outstanding Service" (1960), "Kind and courteous service" from group of local businesses on postal route (1965), "Outstanding contributions to the advance of the branch from the National Alliance of Postal Employees" (1965); community involvement: chairman and president of the LaRue Square Improvement Association, advocate for community improvements (such as pedestrian patrol, zoning changes, push-button pedestrian signal control); member of Morning Star Baptist Church and later Douglas Memorial Community Church, serving on trustee board, Steward Board, Usher Board, Sunday school teacher; member of Mt. Olive Baptist Church (Wicomico Church, VA) Helping Hand Club; member of local Libertarians, a social organization for men; known as an ardent biblical scholar, great dancer, proud and strong willed, caring, and generous with time and money. (*Source: Obituary.*)

David Samuel Jones (1935–2009) of Bogey Neck; one of five children born to the late Daniel Olin and Vera Sebree Jones; member of Mt. Olive Baptist Church, Wicomico, VA; sang in the junior choir and participated in all of the youth activities; m. to Esther Smith Jones of Baltimore for forty-eight years; followed a career path in education after earning a Bachelor of Arts degree from Virginia Union University and a Master of Education degree from Coppin State College, Baltimore, MD, and advanced studies at Loyola College, Baltimore, MD; committed to helping young children; served as a recreational leader in Baltimore County's summer program, Youth Counselor and Job Recruiter (summer programs) for the Maryland State Department of Economic Development, teacher of the Head Start program at Coppin State College; taught public school in Westmoreland County VA, Middleburg, VA, and retired from Baltimore County Public Schools (1990); involved with Boy Scouts of America of Baltimore County, MD; driver for Meals on Wheels at Douglas Memorial Community Church and visited the sick regularly in hospitals and nursing homes; member of Douglas Memorial Community Church for forty-six years and held positions as Superintendent of Church School, member of usher board, Samaritans and Gospel Choir; president of the Mt. Olive Baptist Church Helping Hand Club for thirty-one years; vice president and treasurer of the Miles W. Conner Alumni Chapter of Virginia Union University (membership, fifty-one years); treasurer of Phi Beta Sigma Fraternity Inc.; member Zeta Alpha Sigma Chapter of Columbia, MD, for twenty-one years; achieved numerous awards and honors: Alumnus of the Year, Miles W. Connor Alumni Chapter of VA Union University, Humanitarian Award, Mt. Olive Helping Hand Club, "Tribute in Appreciation for Faithful Service"; twenty-seven years Baltimore County Board of Education, Certificate of Training–Job Corp Program, "Keeping The Virginia Union Spirit Alive" Award, Certificate of Appreciation–Friends of Woodlawn Middle School, Charles J. Brown Award "recognition for outstanding effort and unselfish contribution to the advancement of the chapter fraternal goals," and Sigma Man of the Year (2007), Phi Beta Sigma Fraternity Inc., Alpha Sigma Chapter; friends and family describe David as "a quiet, humble, faithful, and Christian man. Children: Mark S. Jones, Stephanie Wilkins, D. Michael Jones, and Michelle Jones. (*Source: family.*)

Daniel Rudolph Jones (1935–1975) of Bogey Neck; one of five children born to the late Daniel Olin and Vera Sebree Jones; m. Marian Hall; member of Mt. Olive Baptist Church, Wicomico, VA; sang in the junior choir and participated in many of the youth activities; pursued postsecondary education by taking night classes in the medical field; worked as a technician in pathology for a number of years; enjoyed singing and was affiliated with many singing groups; joined Shiloh Baptist Church in Baltimore, MD, where he was active until his early death at age forty-one; friends and family remember Daniel as a kind and friendly person, one who loved singing and entertaining; favorite song was "Will The Circle Be Unbroken"; died in Johns Hopkins due to complications while recovering from surgery; buried in the Mt. Olive Baptist Church cemetery. (*Source: family.*)

John Irvin Jones (b. 1946), son of Daniel Olin and Vera Sebree Jones of Bogey Neck; graduate of Central High School, Northumberland County, VA; Bachelor of Science degree in accounting, Norfolk State College, Norfolk, VA; advanced studies at South Eastern College, Washington, DC; first m. Gloria Conway; second m. Sharon Robinson of Washington, DC; third m. Vashti Savage of Baltimore, MD, in 2001; employment: Martin Marietta, Quality Inn, Commercial Credit; retired and moved back to birthplace in VA; currently self-employed as real estate agent with REMAX Realty; reunited with Mt. Olive Baptist Church and assumes many leadership roles, including church treasurer, member of trustee ministry, food pantry, member of various committees, including homecoming, church aid, and constitution; maintains affiliation with Baltimore, MD, Helping Hand ministry; identified and placed markers on graves in church cemeteries; child: Jonathan E. Jones of Severn, MD (Sharon and John); granddaughter:

Halley Jones; stepsons and stepchildren. Active in community and enjoys people. (*Source: John Jones, interview.*)

Elwood Lavern Jones (b. 1945), son of Ellis Dubois and Hortense Walters Jones; graduate of Central High School, Northumberland County, VA; attended Virginia State College in Petersburg, VA; majoring in automotive mechanics, thanks to Dr. Morgan E. Norris who collected donations to buy the automotive tools needed to take to college; drafted in the United States Army and tour of duty included Ft. Jackson, SC, Fort Raleigh, KS, and Vietnam; upon returning to the United States from Vietnam, taught at Ft. Belvoir until discharged; worked in several dealerships as an auto mechanic before starting a company, E & E Automotive Repair (1975–2011); former member of Mt. Olive Baptist Church, Wicomico, VA; joined Alfred Street Baptist Church in Alexander, VA (1975); m. the former Erna Savoy of Ditchley, VA; three children: Dawn and Elwood Jones (Elwood Jones, Sr., and Bonner Curry) and Andrea Jones Mosley (Elwood Jones, Sr., and Erna Savoy Jones); four grandchildren: Jerel, Jerick, Jasmine, and Shawn Jones; great-grandchildren: Anaya, Santaa, and Josiah Jones; currently resides in Alexandria, VA; enjoys riding a motorcycle; frequently visits Bogey Neck to help care for mother who passed November 2013; maintains family home and entertains friends in trailer located next to the family home; owner of several acres of property in Bogey Neck, including grandparents' home site. (*Source: Elwood Jones.*)

Barbara M. Jones (b. 1941), great-granddaughter of two of the first families—Stafford B. and Susan Warner Jones and William W. and Addie Walters; granddaughter of Lena Walters Johnson and Joseph Warren and Mary L. Jones; daughter of Ellis Dubois and Hortense Walters Jones; grew up on Bogey Neck Road; attended Mila and Anna T. Jeanes Elementary Schools; attended Julius Rosenwald High School and graduated from Central High School, 1960; postsecondary training in nursing; employed as a nurse at Albert Einstein Medical Center in Philadelphia, PA, for forty-two years; member of Second Macedonia Baptist Church in Philadelphia; returned to Bogey Neck in 2004 after father's death to care for her mother; currently an active member of Mt. Olive Baptist Church, Wicomico, VA, serving in Sunday school, Church Aide, and various committees; has two brothers: Elwood Jones, Sr., and Warren Jones. (*Source: Barbara M. Jones.*)

Warren Dubois Jones, youngest of three children of Ellis Dubois Jones (1918–2004) of Bogey Neck and Hortense Walters Jones (1922–2013); attended Rehoboth Elementary (originally Anna T. Jeanes Elementary School), Fairfields Elementary, and Northumberland Middle and High Schools; attended Northern Neck Regional Vocational School for the residential electrical wiring program; graduated from Northumberland High School (1986); entered the military (1986); basic training at Ft. McClellan, AL; received skill training as an audio/TV production specialist (84F now 25V) at Lowry Air Force Base in Denver, CO; stationed in Korea

(Armed Forces Korea Network), Ft. Knox, KY (US Armor School), Korea again during first Gulf War (TSAK, Training Support Activity Korea); last duty station was Ft. Leavenworth, KS (BCTP, Battle Command Training Program); a reservist in the 1085th Map Distribution in Annapolis and IRR; a member of Cub Scouts and Boy Scouts (pack and troop 224); member of Mt. Olive Baptist Church, and served as junior usher; held employment at Mobil Oil Corporation (public affairs, Columbia, MD), Missile Defense Agency, National Military Command Center, and Office of Secretary of Defense (information systems directorate, present); a member of Arlington Lodge #58 (past master) and Shadrack Jackson Consistory #156; two daughters: Ariel Renee Jones and Ashley Dawn Jones. (*Source: Warren D. Jones.*)

Mark S. Jones (b. 1962), oldest of four children of David Samuel Jones (1935–2009) of Bogey Neck and Esther Smith Jones of Baltimore, MD; attended Thomas Jefferson Elementary School, Baltimore, MD; graduated from Woodlawn Senior High School (1980); received a BS in accounting from Virginia State University, Petersburg, VA (1985); currently working for Laureate Education, Inc., managing the accounting for the Santa Fe University Art and Design; resides with wife, Tina Gross Jones, in Reisterstown, MD; two daughters: Kelli D. Jones-Mayfield, a graduate of Anne Arundel Community College, and Brandi N. Jones (16), currently a junior at Arundel High School; one stepdaughter: Jennifer Gross; BS degree from Kent State University and MS degree from McDaniel College; granddaughter: Aryana Trinity Mayfield (3). (*Source: Mark D. Jones.*)

Vera Jones (b. 1966), motivational speaker, writer, award-winning television and radio broadcaster, and Syracuse University hall-of-fame athlete; most widely known for extensive background in broadcasting, serving as a women's basketball analyst and reporter for various networks over the past two decades, including ESPN, Fox Sports, Madison Square Garden Network, NBA-TV, and most recently, the Big Ten Network; enjoyed a professional career as a women's basketball coach, having been an Assistant Coach at the University of Dayton and Indiana University; resides in Delray Beach, FL, with fifteen-year-old son, Andrew (1998); former Assistant Coach for Florida Atlantic University; continues to make speaking appearances and lead motivational workshops as president of Vera's Voiceworks (www. verasvoiceworks.com); author of *Play through the Foul: Basketball Lessons for the Game of Life, New Best Friend: A Little Book of Faith,* and *The True Champion's 30-Day Challenge, a Christian Devotional,* coauthored with A. J. Ali; did not take a speaking, broadcasting, or coaching career for the name "Vera Jones" to become well-known, at least not in Northumberland County, VA; Vera Jones is named after a prominent relative of the same name of Bogey Neck Road—the late elder Vera Jones and husband Deacon Daniel Olin Jones were the parents of father, William Thomas Jones and, thus, grandparents to the younger Vera Jones. (*Source: Vera Jones.*)

David Michael Jones (b. 1969), one of four children of David Jones (1935-2009) of Bogey Neck and Esther Jones of Baltimore, MD; earned a BS in electrical engineering in 1992 from Hampton University, Hampton, VA; earned a master's in computer engineering in 1996 from Villanova University, Villanova, PA; currently enjoying a career as a software engineer; member of Mt. Pleasant Baptist Church in Herndon, VA; resides in Leesburg, VA, with wife (Traci); enjoys traveling, travel blogging, learning French, performing on piano and synthesizers, and spending time with family and friends. (*Source: D. Michael Jones.*)

Timothy Alan Day (b. 1973), born in Baltimore, MD; son of Robert E., Sr., and Mary J. Day, Sr., of Columbia, MD; 1991 graduate of Howard High School, Howard County, MD; earned a BS in marketing from North Carolina A & T University, Greensboro, NC, in 1996; attended Southeastern Baptist Theological Seminary, Wake Forest, NC, Master of Divinity candidate; served as youth minister of Columbia Baptist Fellowship (1999–

2009), Howard County, MD; employment history includes: Walmart, assistant manager; Applied Digital Solutions, sales representative; Verizon Wireless, business account executive; T Mobile, business development manager; resides in Howard County, MD; one son: Emmanuel Timothy Day and a stepdaughter, Chasity Pittman. (*Source: Timothy Alan Day.*)

Robert Eugene Day, Jr. (b. 1965) born in Baltimore, MD; grandson of the late Daniel and Vera Sebree Jones of Bogey Neck; son of Robert E., Sr., and Mary Jones Day of Columbia, MD; graduate of Wilde Lake High School, Columbia, MD (1983); earned MBA from California State University and Bachelor of Science degree in engineering from the United States Air Force Academy (1987); a seasoned global business executive with decades of experience; worked for large public companies such as IBM as well as small start-up, venture-capital-backed companies; leveraged experiences from a diverse background that includes being a successful international sales manager, stockbroker, aerospace engineer, pilot, and Desert Storm war veteran; has written, negotiated, and managed over one hundred international business transactions including global partnerships, sales contracts, and resell agreements; has negotiated business deals on nearly every continent and has deep experience all over the world, including China, Italy, Germany, Slovenia, and Great Britain, to name a few; author, *Street Smarts for Global Business: A*

Practical Guidebook for Global Business Executives; won 2009 Allbooks Review International Editors' Choice Award for business; resides in Columbia, MD, with three children: Ryan Alexander Day, attended St. Johns University and currently a student at York College in Queens, NY; Rachel Michelle Day, an honor student at Atholton High School in Columbia, MD; and Andrew Sterrett Day, an honor student at St. Paul's High School in Baltimore, MD. (*Source: Robert. E. Day, Jr.*)

Stephanie Jones Wilkins (b. 1964), granddaughter of Daniel Jones (1907–1986) of Bogey Neck and Vera Sebree (1909–2003) of Mila Neck, VA; one of four children to David S. Jones (1935–2009) of Bogey Neck and Esther Smith of Baltimore, MD; attended Thomas Jefferson and Johnnycake Elementary Schools in Baltimore, MD; graduated from Woodlawn Senior High School (1982); received a BA in psychology (1986) from Virginia Union University, Richmond, VA; earned a Master's degree in industrial organizational psychology (1988) from Radford University, Radford, VA; currently chief training officer for the US Department of Agriculture's Food Safety Inspection Service in Washington, DC; member of St. Bernadine's Roman Catholic Church, Baltimore, MD; member of Alpha Kappa Alpha Sorority, Inc.; resides with husband, Colonel Audie M. Wilkins and son, Audie M. Wilkins, Jr. (12) in Fredericksburg, VA. (*Source: Stephanie Jones Wilkins.*)

Michelle M. Jones (b. 1970), youngest of four children raised by David Samuel and Esther Smith Jones; administrator of Day Break LLC, a full-service human resource and business consulting firm in Baltimore, MD; over nineteen years of experience in human resource management; served as chief operating officer, administrator, and manager for nonprofit organizations, including University of Maryland Medical System and Johns Hopkins Institutions; earned an MBA from Johns Hopkins University; taught business and human resource management at Baltimore International College (1998–2004); a member of the Society for Human Resource Management and the National Black MBA Association; currently serves as a member of the board of directors for Tooney Town Early Learning Center and for Chosen Media; two sons: Jay Keyser and Lorenzo Guy Jones; resides in Baltimore County, MD (*Source: Michelle M. Jones.*)

Jonathan E. Jones (b. 1969) born in Washington, DC; son of John Jones and Sharon Robinson; graduate of Kensington High School in Kensington, MD; BS in recreation at Frostburg State University (1994) and MS in education (2001); married Maria Gregorio of New York City, also a graduate of Frostburg State University;

employed with Maryland National Capitol Park and Planning as a facility director; spent summers in Bogey Neck with grandparents, Daniel and Vera Jones, from about age five until completion of high school; helped grandparents in the garden and rode around with grandmother, who sold her quilts and vegetables; often fished with grandfather; favorite memory was kids chasing a neighbor's pig up Bogey Neck Road; going to church with his granddaddy three days a week and on Sunday was not the favorite pastime; floated his granddaddy's hand-carved boats made from scrap wood in the mud puddles or creek; raised chickens bought by his grandpa, and the fox came at night and stole the chickens; when checking on chickens in the morning, all that was left were the feathers; tried to catch rabbits in a shoe box; joined Boy Scouts of America at Mt. Olive Church; enjoys hunting, fishing, and cooking. (*Source: Jonathan Jones, interview.*)

Generation 1—Stafford B. Jones

Generation 2—Children of Stafford B. and Susan Jones

Generation 3—Grandson of Stafford B. and Susan Jones, Son of Lombard Coleman and Annie Thompson Jones[99]

1. **Louis Thomas Jones, Sr.** (b. ca. 1905) in Baltimore, MD; adopted by Lombard and Annie Thompson Jones; biological mother was Agnes Cook (ca. 1889–1912) who resided in Baltimore, MD (It was believed Agnes Cook was a maid for one of the passengers on the Titanic and drowned when the ship sank.); lived in Bogey Neck community until first marriage in 1925 to Fragia Sebree (1907–1954) of Mila Neck community; purchased land and built house on Mila Neck Road; after Fragia's death, second marriage to Emily Walters Smith, and after Emily's death, third marriage to Ethel Roane in 1966; worked entire adult life as a waterman; resided on Mila Road until death; buried in Mt. Olive Church cemetery, Wicomico Church, VA. Children: James Edward Jones (1925–1992), Louis Thomas Jones, Jr. (b. 1926), Grafton Jones (1927—2012), Alice Jones (1930–1930), Beatrice Jones Moody (b. 1931), Olethia Jones (1933–1933), Harry Jones (1934–1934), Leonard Jones (b. 1935), Lombard Jones (1936–1938), and Ulysees Jones (b. 1938).

2. **Robert Jones** (b. 1901), age nine at time of 1910 census. No record in subsequent censuses.

---

99 Federal Census 1910, 1920, 1930, 1940, oral history.

Generation 4—Great-Grandchildren of Stafford B. and Susan Warner Jones, Grandchildren of Lombard Coleman and Annie Johnson Jones, Children of Louis Thomas and Fragia Sebree Jones[100]

1. **James Edward Jones** (1925–1992); born in Baltimore, MD; drafted in US Army (1942); m. Ceddra Kistel Yerby of Mila Neck in 1946; resided in Mila Neck community with his parents prior to purchasing two acres of land and building a house in Bogey Neck (1951); worked as a waterman (fisherman, crab potter, oysterman); purchased an additional one tract of land adjacent to his property; buried in Mt. Olive Baptist Church cemetery; children: William Alfred Jones (1942–1999), Katherine Jones Milton Singleterry (b. 1947), Carolyn Jones Matthews (b. 1950), James Jones (b. 1957), Michael Jones (b. 1958), and Mark Jones (b. 1960).

2. **Louis Thomas Jones, Jr**. (1926–2010); left home at an early age, resided in New York most of his adult life; inspector in post office; buried in New York.

3. **Grafton Jones** (1927–2012); m. Lenora D. Copeland (1927-2003); resided in Baltimore, MD; buried in Baltimore, MD; children: Lenora Jones Cheatham, Linda Jones Johnson, and Ruby Jones.

4. **Beatrice Jones Moody** (b. 1931); m. Edward Moody (1929–1988); resides in Kilmarnock, Lancaster County, VA; crab picker; children: Brenda Moody Winstead (1954), Edward Moody, Jr. (1955), and Gregory Moody (b. 1958).

---

100 Federal Census 1930, 1940; oral history 2012.

5. **Leonard Jones** (b. 1934), born in Mila Neck; m. Carrie Edwards; drafted in US Army (1956); retired Maryland state employee; resides in Baltimore, MD; children: Alicia Colleen, Audrey Denise, Ansel Reginald, and Anita Lynn. [*See biographical sketch.*]

6. **Ulysees Jones** (b. 1938) in Mila Neck; m. Annie Kersey; resides in Baltimore, MD; children: Gwendolyn Jones (b. 1959), Myron Jones (b. 1961), and Demasceo Jones (b. 1965).

Generation 5—Great-Great-Grandchildren of Stafford B. and Susan Warner Jones; Great-Grandchildren of Lombard Coleman and Annie Johnson Jones; Grandchildren of Louis Thomas and Fragia Sebree Jones[101]

Children of Edward and Ceddra Kistel Yerby Jones of Bogey Neck:

1. **William Alfred Jones, Sr.** (1942–1999); born in Mila Neck and raised in Bogey Neck; m. Christine Chambers (b. 1963); resided in Baltimore, MD; children: William A. Jones, Jr., Brita Jones Dorsey, and Marvin Jones.

2. **Katherine Virginia Jones Milton-Singleterry** (b. 1947); first m. to John Milton; second m. to Melvin Singleteery; resides in Baltimore, MD; family support worker; retired; children: Wanda Milton-Watts and Kevin Milton, Sr. (1968–1991). Stepchildren: Prentiss Singleterry, Sharon Singleterry-Brown, Angela Singleterry-Gosby, Sylvester Singleterry, Robert Singleterry, and Floretta Boone.

---

101   Oral history 2012.

3. **Carolyn Deloris Jones Matthews** (b. 1950), m. Frederick Matthews; resides in Baltimore County, MD; administrative assistant; retired; children: Keith Jones and Tevis Jones-Henry.

4. **James E. Jones, Jr.** (b. 1957), m. Dixie Rich; twenty years of military service—Iraqi Desert Storm War/Iraqi Freedom; currently a dining facility manager in Afghanistan; wife resides in Oklahoma. Children: Jermaine Jones and Marcus Jones.

5. **Michael Jones, Sr.** (b. 1958), spouse: Sandra Jones; served in US Army; children: Senquoia Jones Chester, Michael Jones, Jr., Mikeisha Jonre Harrison, Jessica Wade, and Kaylene Taylor.

6. **Mark Jones** (b. 1960), m. Tamara Yvette Walden (b. 1983); twenty-four years in US Army; resides in Richmond, VA; children: Daniel Jones and Courtney Shavonne Jones.

Children of Grafton and Lenora D. Copeland Jones, born in Baltimore, MD:

7. **Lenora Jones Cheatham**, m. Wally Cheatham; children: Tony Cheatham and Maurice Cheatham.

8. **Linda Jones Johnson;** child: Waldia Johnson.

9. **Ruby Jones**.

Children of Beatrice Jones and Edward Moody, Sr., born in Kilmarnock, Lancaster County, VA:

10. **Brenda Moody Winstead** (b. 1954), m. William Winstead, Sr.; children: Tiffany Winstead Hutchings, William Winstead, Jr., and Ebony Beale.

11. **Edward Moody, Jr.** (b. 1955), m. Linda White; child: Rashida Moody Waters.

12. **Gregory Moody** (b. 1958), m. Alisha; children: T. J. Moody and Derrick Moody.

Children of Leonard and Carrie Jones, born in Baltimore, MD:

13. **Alicia Colleen Jones Hudson** (divorced); resides in Baltimore County, MD; technical engineer for Verizon; children: Dominick "Nick" Hudson Bryan, Candace Hudson, and Bryan Henderson. [*See biographical sketch.*]

14. **Audrey Denise Jones Jordan (Walter)**, retired; resides in Goldsboro, NC; children: Tyra, Warren Jason, Lea, and Ciara. [*See biographical sketch.*]

15. **Ansel Reginald Jones, Sr.;** resides in Baltimore, MD; owner of Kirby Vacuum Cleaner sales, service, and repair store in Woodlawn, MD; children: Marcus Jones and Ansel Jones, Jr. [*See biographical sketch.*]

16. **Anita Lynn Jones** (divorced); resides in Owings Mills, MD; employed with Department of Defense in Baltimore; children: Dorian Brown and Erin Erin Brown. [*See biographical sketch.*]

Children of Ulysees and Annie Kersey Jones:

17. **Gwendolyn Jones** (b. 1959), born and resides in Baltimore. MD. [*See biographical sketch.*]

18. **Myron Jones** (b. 1961); born and resides in Baltimore, MD.

19. **Demasceo Jones** (b. 1965); born and resides in Baltimore, MD; children: Demasceo C. Jones, Jr., and Courtney C, Jones.

Generation 6 — Great-Great-Great-Grandchildren of Stafford B. and Susan Warner Jones, Great-Great-Grandchildren of Lombard Coleman and Annie Johnson Jones, Great-Grandchildren of Louis Thomas and Fragia Sebree Jones[102]

Grandchildren of James Edward and Ceddra Kistel Yerby Jones:

1. **William Alfred Jones, Jr.,** son of the late William Alfred, Sr., and Christine Chambers Jones of Baltimore; born in Baltimore, MD; resides in Baltimore, MD; child: LaQuesha Jones.

2. **Brita Jones Dorsey,** daughter of the late William Alfred and Christine Jones of Baltimore, MD; m. Victor Dorsey; children: Taneisha Sampson (Brita and Samuel Sampson), Nicole Dorsey and Dominic Dorsey (Brita & Victor Dorsey); Stepchild: Ranika Ivy.

3. **Marvin Jones**, son of the late William Alfred and Christine Jones; m. Denise Jones; child: Christina Jones; stepchildren: (Marvin Jones and Angela Raymond) Marvin Raymond, Angelica Raymond, Anthony Raymond; (Marvin Jones and Denise) Aasem Deiab, Candace Tate, Ciera Tate, and Marc Sherrod.

4. **Wanda Milton Watts**, daughter of Katherine Milton Singleterry and John Carey Milton; m. Joseph Watts; resides in Baltimore, MD; child: Joseph Watts II.

---

102   Oral history, 2012.

5. **Kevin Milton, Sr.,** son of Katherine Milton Singleterry and John Carey Milton; children: Kevin Milton, Jr. (Kevin Milton, Sr., and Cylvonia), Felicia Milton (Kevin, Sr., and Felicia), and Tayshera Wilson (Kevin, Sr., and Stalicia).

6. **Keith Jones,** son of Carolyn Jones and Frederick Matthews, stepfather.

7. **Tevis Jones-Henry,** daughter of Carolyn Jones and Frederick Matthews.

8. **Jermaine Jones,** son of James and Dixie Jones.

9. **Marcus Jones,** son of James and Dixie Jones.

10. **Senquoia Jones-Chester,** daughter of Michael and Sandra Jones.

11. **Michael Jones, Jr.,** son of Michael and Sandra Jones.

12. **Mikeisha Jones Harrison,** daughter of Michael and Sandra Jones.

13. **Jessica Wade,** daughter of Michael Jones (Bertha).

14. **Kaylene Taylor,** daughter of Michael and Sandra Jones, stepmother.

15. **Daniel Jones,** son of Mark and Tamara Jones.

16. **Courtney Jones,** daughter of Mark and Tamara Jones.

17. **Demaceo C. Jones, Jr.** (b. 1990), son of Demaceo C. and Charlotte Jones; grandson of Ulysees and Annie Kersey Jones.

18. **Zalea Gaskins,** daughter of Kaylene Taylor; granddaughter of Michael and Sandra Jones.

19. **Courtney C. Jones** (b. 1992), daughter of Demaceo C. and Charlotte Jones; grandson of Ulysees and Annie Kersey Jones.

Grandchildren of Grafton and Lenora D. Copeland Jones:

20. **Tony Cheatham**, son of Lenora and Wally Cheatham.
21. **Maurice Cheatham**, son of Lenora and Wally Cheatham.
22. **Waldia Johnson**, daughter of Linda Jones Johnson.

Grandchildren of Beatrice Jones and the late Edward Moody:

23. **Tiffany Hutchins** (b. 1971), daughter of Brenda and William Winstead, Sr.; m. Toby Hutchings.
24. **William Winstead, Jr**. (b. 1974), son of Brenda and William Winstead, Sr.
25. **Ebony Beale** (b. 1985), daughter of Brenda and William Winstead, Sr.; m. Marcus Beale.
26. **Rashida Moody Waters** (b. 1983), m. Gerrick Waters, daughter of Edward Moody, Jr.
27. **Marcus "T. J." Moody** (b. 1982), son of Gregory and Alisha Moody.
28. **Derrick Moody** (b. 1983), son of Gregory and Alisha Moody.

Grandchildren of Leonard and Carrie Jones:

29. **Dominick "Nick" Hudson,** son of Alicia Colleen Hudson; honor student in senior year at Old Dominion University, Norfolk, VA.
30. **Candace Hudson,** daughter of Alicia Colleen Hudson; pursuing a career in nursing.
31. **Bryan Henderson,** son of Alicia Colleen Hudson; attends Montgomery County, MD, community college; married; children: Briyan, Brieyani, Brizae, and Bryndon.

32. **Tyra Jones Dickerson** (b. 1984), daughter of Audrey Denise Jones Jordan; attends Liberty University; resides with husband, Gerald, in North Carolina; child: Elijah Coleman Dickerson.

33. **Warren Jason Bronson** (b. 1982), son of Audrey Denise Jones Jordan; attended West Virginia State College; resides with wife, Vanessa, in North Carolina.

34. **Lea Jordan,** daughter of Audrey Denise Jones Jordan; resides in North Carolina; children: Nicole Jordan (b. 2008), Angelo Monroe III (b. 2010), and Auria Jordan (b. 2012).

35. **Ciara Jordan,** daughter of Audrey Denise Jones Jordan; resides in North Carolina; children: Caleb Jordan (b. 2007), Ava Jordan (b. 2008), and Joshua Jordan (b. 2009).

36. **Marcus Jones,** son of Ansel Reginald Jones; resides in Baltimore, MD.

37. **Ansel Jones,** Jr., son of Ansel Reginald Jones, Sr.; served in US Air Force in Iraq; resides in Baltimore, MD.

38. **Dorian Brown,** son of Anita Lynn Jones; electrician in US Air Force in Germany; pursuing a degree in electrical engineering while in the air force; was a defensive back for Northwestern High School, Baltimore, MD.

39. **Erin Jones,** daughter of Anita Lynn Jones and Anthony Patrick; resides in Owings Mills, MD.

Grandchildren of Ulysees and Annie Kersey Jones:

40. **Demasceo C. Jones, Jr.** (b.1990), son of Demaseo C., Sr., and Charlotte Jones.

41. **Courtney C. Jones** (b.1992), daughter of Demaseo C. Sr., and Charlotte Jones.

Generation 7—Great-Great-Great-Great-Grandchildren of Stafford B. and Susan Warner Jones; Great-Great-Great Grandchildren of Lombard Coleman and Annie Johnson Jones, Great-Great-Grandchildren of Louis and Fragia Sebree Jones[103]

Great grandchildren of James Edward and Ceddra Kistel Yerby Jones of Bogey Neck:

1. **LaQuesha Jones,** daughter of William Alfred Jones, Jr. (Elizabeth); granddaughter of William Alfred, Sr., and Christine Chambers Jones.
2. **Taneisha Sampso**n, daughter of Brita Jones-Dorsey and Samuel Sampson; granddaughter of William Alfred, Sr., and Christine Jones of Baltimore, MD; child: Kahlel Welch.
3. **Nicole Dorsey**, daughter of Brita and Victor Dorsey; granddaughter of William Alfred, Sr., and Christine Jones of Baltimore; child: Kiyanna Enoch.
4. **Dominic Dorsey**, son of Brita and Victor Dorsey; grandson of William Alfred, Sr., and Christine Jones of Baltimore, MD; children: Leilani Dorsey and Javian Dorsey.
5. **Ranika Ivy,** stepdaughter of Brita Jones-Dorsey and daughter of Victor Dorsey; stepgranddaughter of William Alfred, Sr., and Christine Jones of Baltimore, MD; child: Leilani Branagh.

---

103 Oral history, 2012.

6. **Marvin Raymond**, son of Marvin Jones (Angela); grandson of William Alfred, Sr., and Christine Jones of Baltimore, MD.

7. **Angelica Raymond,** daughter of Marvin Jones (Angela); granddaughter of William Alfred, Sr., and Christine Jones of Baltimore, MD; child: Daeson Sparks.

8. **Anthony Jones, Sr.,** son of Marvin Jones (Angela); grandson of William Alfred, Sr., and Christine Jones of Baltimore, MD; Child: Anthony Jones, Jr.

9. **Christina Jones**, daughter of Marvin and Denise Jones of Baltimore, MD; granddaughter of William Alfred, Sr., and Christine Jones of Baltimore, MD.

10. **Kevin Milton, Jr.,** son of the late Kevin, Sr., and Cylvonia of Baltimore, MD; grandson of Katherine Virginia Jones Milton Singleterry and the late John Carey Milton of Baltimore, MD; resides in North Carolina.

11. **Felicia Milton**, daughter of the late Kevin, Sr., and Felicia of Baltimore, MD; granddaughter of Katherine Virginia Jones Milton Singleterry and the late John Carey Milton of Baltimore, MD.

12. **Joseph Watts**, son of Wanda and Joseph Watts; grandson of Katherine Virginia Jones Milton Singleterry and the late John Carey Milton of Baltimore, MD.

13. **Tayshera Wilson**, daughter of Kevin Milton, Sr. (Stalicia); granddaughter of Katherine Virginia Jones Milton Singleterry and the late John Carey Milton of Baltimore, MD.

14. **Kaedin Jones**, son of Senquoia Jones-Chester and Roman Chester (stepfather); grandson of Michel and Sandra Jones.

15. **Nicholas Harrison II,** son of Mikeshia Jones-Harrison and Nicholas Harrison; grandson of Michael and Sandra Jones; great-grandson of James Edward and Ceddra Kistel Yerby Jones of Bogey Neck, Wicomico Church, Northumberland County, VA.

16. **Dorian Wade**, son of Jessica Wade; grandson of Michael and Sandra Jones.

17. **Morgan Wade**, daughter of Jessica Wade; granddaughter of Michael and Sandra Jones.

18. **Zaire Jackson,** daughter of Kaylene Taylor; granddaughter of Michael and Sandra Jones.

19. **Keith Jones, Jr.,** son of Keith Jones, Sr. (spouse, Dometria); grandson of Carolyn Jones-Matthews and Frederick Matthews.

20. **Deonta Jones**, son of Keith Jones, Sr. (spouse, Shewanda); grandson of Carolyn Jones-Matthews and Frederick Matthews.

21. **Keyshawna Jones**, daughter of Keith Jones, Sr. (spouse, Shewanda); granddaughter of Carolyn Jones-Matthews and Frederick Matthews.

22. **Shaniah Jones,** daughter of Keith Jones, Sr. (spouse, Shawntae); granddaughter of Carolyn Jones-Matthews and Frederick Matthews.

23. **Jasmine Dugger,** daughter of Tevis Jones (spouse, Damani Dugger); granddaughter of Carolyn Jones-Matthews and Frederick Matthews.

24. **Chyna Henry,** daughter of Tevis Jones-Henry and Lawrence Henry; granddaughter of Carolyn Jones-Matthews and Frederick Matthews.

25. **Brandon Henry,** son of Lawrence Henry and Tevis Jones-Henry (stepmother); step-grandson of Carolyn Jones-Matthews and Frederick Matthews.

26. **Janeal Henry**, daughter of Lawrence Henry and Tevis Jones-Henry (stepmother); step-granddaughter of Carolyn Jones-Matthews and Frederick Matthews.

27. **Aasem Deiab**, stepson of Marvin (Denise); step-grandson of William Alfred and Christine Chambers Jones.

28. **Candace Tate**, stepdaughter of Marvin (Denise); step-granddaughter of William Alfred and Christine Chambers Jones.

29. **Ciera Tate,** stepdaughter of Marvin (Denise); step-granddaughter of William Alfred and Christine Chambers Jones.

30. **Marc Sherrod,** stepson of Marvin (Denise); step-grandson of William Alfred and Christine Chambers Jones.

Great-grandchildren of Beatrice Jones and the late Edward Moody:

31. **Dorian Crawley** (b. 1991), son of Tiffany and Toby Hutchins.

32. **Jaylen Hutchins** (b. 1993), son of Tiffany and Toby Hutchins.

33. **Tyson Hutchins** (b. 1998), son of Tiffany and Toby Hutchins.

34. **Jayla Beale** (b. 2007), daughter of Ebony and Marcus Beale.

35. **Brandon Beale** (b. 2008), son of Ebony and Marcus Beale.

36. **Kyra Waters** (b. 2004), daughter of Rashida and Gerrick Waters.

37. **Kennedy Waters** (b. 2010), daughter of Rashida and Gerrick Waters.

38. **Tyrese Kennedy** (b. ca. 2002), son of William Winstead, Jr., and Sherinda Kennedy.

Great-grandchildren of Leonard and Carrie Jones:

39. **Elijah Coleman Dickerson,** son of Tyra Jones and Gerald Dickerson; grandchild of Audrey and Walter Jordan.

40. **Caleb Jordan** (b. 2007), son of Ciara Jordan; grandchild of Audrey and Walter Jordan.

41. **Ava Jordan** (b. 2008), daughter of Ciara Jordan; grandchild of Audrey and Walter Jordan.

42. **Joshua Jordan** (b. 2009), son of Ciara Jordan; grandchild of Audrey and Walter Jordan.

43. **Nicole Jordan** (b. 2008), daughter of Lea Jordan; grandchild of Audrey and Walter Jordan.

44. **Angelo Monroe III** (b. 2010), son of Lea Jordan; grandchild of Audrey and Walter Jordan.

45. **Auria Jordan** (b. 2012), child of Lea Jordan; grandchild of Audrey and Walter Jordan.

46. **Brian Henderson,** child of Brian Henderson; grandchild of Alicia Colleen Hudson.

47. **Brieyani Henderson,** child of Brian Henderson; grandchild of Alicia Colleen Hudson.

48. **Brizae Henderson,** child of Brian Henderson; grandchild of Alicia Colleen Hudson.

49. **Bryndon Henderson,** child of Brian Henderson; grandchild of Alicia Collen Hudson.

Generation 8—Great-Great-Great-Great-Great-Grandchildren of Stafford B. and Susan Warren Jones; Great-Great-Great-Great-Grandchildren of Lombard Coleman and Annie Johnson Jones; Great-Great-Great-Grandchildren of Louis Thomas and Fragia Sebree Jones.[104]

Great-great-grandchildren of James Edward and Ceddra Kistel Yerby Jones of Bogey Neck:

1. **Kahlel Welch**, son of Taneisha Sampson; grandson of Brita Jones-Dorsey and Victor Dorsey; great-grandson of William Alfred and Christine Chambers Jones.

2. **Kiyanna Enoch**, daughter of Nicole Dorsey; granddaughter of Brita Jones-Dorsey and Victor Dorsey; great-granddaughter of William Alfred and Christine Chambers Jones.

3. **Leilani Dorsey,** daughter of Dominic Dorsey; granddaughter of Brita Jones-Dorsey and Victor Dorsey; great-granddaughter of William Alfred and Christine Chambers Jones.

4. **Javian Dorsey**, son of Dominic Dorsey; grandson of Brita Jones-Dorsey and Victor Dorsey; great-grandson of William Alfred and Christine Chambers Jones.

5. **Lelani Branagh**, daughter of Ranika Ivy; step-granddaughter of Brita Jones-Dorsey and Victor Dorsey; great-granddaughter of William Alfred and Christine Chambers Jones.

6. **Daeson Sparks,** son of Angelica Raymond; grandson of Marvin Jones (Angela); step-great-grandson of William Alfred and Christine Chambers Jones.

---

104 Oral history.

7. **Anthony Raymond, Jr.,** son of Anthony Raymond, Sr.; grandson of Marvin Jones (Angela); step-great-grandson of William Alfred and Christine Chambers Jones.

8. **Adrienna Wheeler,** daughter of Ciera Tate; step-granddaughter of Marvin Jones (Denise); step-great-granddaughter of William Alfred and Christine Chambers Jones.

9. **Marques Coleman**, son of Ciera Tate; step-grandson of Marvin Jones (Denise); step-great-grandson of William Alfred and Christine Chambers Jones.

10. **Jeanine Tate**, daughter of Candace Tate; step-granddaughter of Marvin Jones (Denise); step great-granddaughter of William Alfred and Christine Chambers Jones.

11. **Cassidy Coleman**, daughter of Ciera Tate; granddaughter of Marvin Jones (Denise); great-granddaughter of William Alfred and Christine Chambers Jones.

BIOGRAPHICAL SKETCH—DESCENDANTS OF STAFFORD B. AND SUSAN WARNER JONES AND LOMBARD COLEMAN AND ANNIE JONES

Louis Thomas Jones (1905–1987); born in Baltimore, MD; son of Agnes Cook; adopted by Lombard Coleman and Annie Johnson Jones of Bogey Neck (1907), father believed to have been Frank Cook, who worked on the Panama Canal; resided in Bogey Neck with adopted parents until his marriage to Fragia Sebree Jones; second marriage, to Emily Smith Jones, and third marriage, to Ethel Roane; resided in Mila Neck, Remo, VA; according to an aunt, Agnes Cook was a maid for a passenger on the Titanic and drowned when the ship sank. (*Obituary and oral history.*)

Beatrice Jones Moody (b. 1931), born and reared in Remo, VA; adopted granddaughter of Lombard and Annie Jones; daughter of Lewis and Fragia Jones; two brothers living and five deceased brothers and one sister; married Edward Moody, Sr. (1929–1988); resides in Kilmarnock, VA; two sons: Edward, Jr., and Gregory Moody; one daughter, Brenda Winstead; six grandchildren; seven great-grandchildren; graduated from Julius Rosenwald High School; joined Mt. Olive Baptist Church at an early age; worked as a crab picker for over twenty years; enjoys children and grandchildren in retirement. (*Source: Interview.*)

Ansel Reginald Jones, Sr., born and resides in Baltimore, MD; great grandson of Lombard and Annie Jones; grandson of Louis and Fragia Jones of Mila Neck community, Wicomico, Northumberland County, VA; son of Leonard and Carrie Jones of Baltimore, MD; worked for the IRS after high school; currently owner of Kirby Vacuum Cleaner sales, service, and repair store located in Woodlawn, MD; two sons: Marcus and Ansel, Jr.; younger son served in the US Air Force in Iraq. Both sons live in Baltimore, MD. (*Source: Leonard Jones.*)

Anita Lynn Jones Payne (divorced), great-granddaughter of Lombard and Annie Jones; granddaughter of Louis and Fragia Jones of Northumberland County, VA; youngest daughter of Leonard and Carrie Jones; graduate of University of Maryland (UMBC), with degrees in psychology and information systems and Master's program in procurement, purchasing, and inventory management. Currently employed with the Department of Defense in Baltimore City; son Dorian is an electrician in the US Air Force in Germany, and upon discharge from air force, he expects to get a degree in electrical engineering;

was a defensive lineman for Northwestern High School football team in Baltimore, MD; daughter Erin in middle school; resides in Owings Mills, MD. (*Source: Leonard Jones.*)

Alicia Colleen Jones Hudson (divorced), resides in Baltimore County, MD; oldest daughter of Leonard and Carrie Jones of Baltimore, MD; granddaughter of Louis Thomas and Fragia Sebree Jones of Northumberland County, VA; great-granddaughter of Lombard C. and Annie Johnson Jones; worked as a technical engineer III for Verizon for more than twenty years; currently pursuing a degree in business administration and marketing at University of Maryland (UMBC), expecting to complete in 2013; has three children: youngest son, Dominick ("Nick"), is an honor student in his senior year at Old Dominion University, Norfolk, VA, pursuing a degree in mechanical engineering with aerospace design minor; daughter, Candace, is studying for RN degree; older son, Bryan, attended Montgomery County Community College and is married with four children. (*Source: Leonard Jones.*)

Leonard C. Jones (1935*)*, son of Louis Thomas and Fragia Sebree Jones of Mila Neck community, Wicomico, Northumberland County, VA; graduate of Julius Rosenwald High School of Northumberland County, VA (1952); earned a BS in industrial education from St. Paul's College, Lawrenceville, VA (1956); certificates from University of Tennessee, Knoxville (1969), Unemployment Insurance Claims Adjudicators Institute, Unemployment Insurance Law Program and an advanced certificate from University of Colorado, Boulder (1971), Unemployment Insurance Claims Adjudicators Institute, and a certificate in management and supervision from Hood College, Frederick, MD (1975); inactive member of Alpha Phi Alpha Fraternity, Inc.; received numerous awards—Bronze Metal (MD Senior Olympics) bowling (2012), National Alliance of Businessmen Outstanding Service to Veterans, Youth, Ex-Offenders, and Disabled Americans Award (1976), Department of Economic and Employment Development Outstanding Service to Citizens of MD Award (1990), Governor Schaeffer's Governors' Recognition of Distinguished Service Award (1992), US Department of Labor Older Workers Program Certificate of Excellence Award (1999); three times retired from state service; drafted into the US Army in December 1956; trained at Fort Belvoir Engineer Center in cartography; assigned to 2nd Army Missile Command Headquarters Co., General Staff Plans and Operations Division; four children: Alicia Colleen, Audrey Denise, Warren Jason, and Ansel, Sr.; six grandchildren: Dominick, Candace, Tara, Marcus, Ansel, Jr., and Dorian; five great-grandchildren: Bryan, Warren, Lea, Ciara, and Erin; resides in Baltimore, MD. (*Source: Leonard Jones.*)

Katherine Jones Milton-Singleteery, daughter of James Edward, Sr., and Ceddra K. Yerby Jones; raised in Bogey Neck community, Wicomico Church, Northumberland County, VA; attended Northumberland County Public Schools; in elementary school, enjoyed recess time—playing on the seesaw, sliding board, swings, dodge ball, hide-and-seek, Ring Around the Rosie, etc.; best day of the school year was May Day, where there was lots of food and games and wrapping the maypole; one of the first eighth graders to attend Central High School; highlights of attending a beautiful new school were taking graduation pictures, prom in twelfth grade, wearing class ring, and graduation (1965); moved to Baltimore after graduation from high school; held several positions prior to employment with the Department of Social Services (1972–1992) in the Family Preservation Reunification Unit; obtained work-related training at Wheelock College in (Boston, MA), St. Joseph College (Hartford, CT), Community College of Baltimore County, MD, School of Social Work, Coppin State College, Baltimore, MD, and conferences in Delaware, Washington, DC, and New Orleans; retired from Department of Social Services after thirty-seven years (2009); part-time employment (1999–2007) at Daisey Field Foundation working with children with physical, emotional, and social needs. (*Source: Katherine Jones Milton-Singleteery.*)

Gwendolyn Y. Jones (b. 1959), great-granddaughter of Lombard Coleman Jones of Bogey Neck, Wicomico, Northumberland County, VA; granddaughter of Louis Thomas and Fragia Sebree Jones of Mila Neck, Wicomico; daughter of Ulysses and Annie Jones, Baltimore, MD; one of three children: two brothers (Myron Jones and Demasceo Jones); attended Lynnhurst Elementary School and Woodlawn Junior High School; graduate of Milford Mill High School (1977); further education at Coppin State College (1981) with emphasis in medical sciences; currently employed as a certified medical coder; former member of The New Pleasant Grove Missionary Baptist Church for twenty-plus years; currently a member of New Rehoboth Baptist Church—both churches are located in Baltimore, MD; member of the music ministry and former church Biblical Evangelism Team, certificate through Mt. Pleasant Ministries. (*Source: Gwendolyn Y. Jones.*)

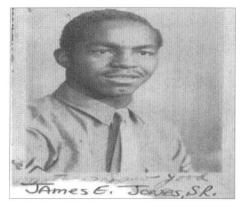

James Edward (Ed) Jones, Sr. (1924–1992), son of Louis Thomas and Fragia Sebree-Jones of Mila Neck community, Wicomico Church, Northumberland County, VA; attended the Mila Neck School; member of Mt. Olive Baptist Church; served in the US Army (1942–1945) as a cook earning the rank of corporal; married Ceddra Kistel Yerby (b. 1946); resided in Bogey Neck community, Wicomico Church, Northumberland County, VA; six children: William Alfred, Katherine Virginia (Snooks), Carolyn, James, Jr. (Jimmy), Michael, and Mark; worked as a fisherman, oyster shucker, and crab potter; retired from Stanley Products Corporation after thirty years; known for his holiday fruitcake; people person, loving and spoiling his children and grandchildren. (*Source: Family.*)

Michael Lorenzo Jones (b. 1958); son of the late James Edward (Ed) and Ceddra K. Jones and the late James (Ed) Jones, Sr.; married twenty-nine years to Sandra; five children: Jessica, Kaylene, Senquoia, Mikeshia, and Michael II; six grandchildren: Zaire, Dorien, Kaedin, Morgan, Zylela, and Nicholas; joined Mt. Olive Baptist Church at age ten; graduated from Northumberland High School (1977); served nine years in the US Army and earned the rank of staff sergeant; served as an army recruiter for two years; worked in civil service for six years, Juvenile Corrections Officer for twelve years; owned and operated a lawn service for fifteen years; opened a personal care home,

Pearson-Jones Residential Services (2007), under contract with the Augusta Veterans Administration, which cares for spinal-injured veterans from the WWII era to the Iraqi and Afghan wars; he says, "Thank God for the people who helped mold me: parents and family, Daniel and Vera Jones, Emerson Norris, Gilbert "Cool Breeze" Ball, employers of Smith Seafood, Sisson & Russell Oyster Houses, and my teachers at Northumberland High School, especially, Mrs. Margaret Campbell (business teacher)"; resides in Augusta, GA. (*Source: Michael Lorenzo Jones.*)

Carolyn D. Jones Matthews, third child of James Edward (Ed) and Ceddra K. Yerby-Jones; raised in Bogey Neck; attended Anna T. Jeanes Elementary School and a graduate of Central High School (1969), Northumberland County, VA; member of Mt. Olive Baptist Church of Wicomico Church, VA; moved to Baltimore, MD, after graduation from high school; first employment at Stewart Department Store in accounting department; other places of employment were: C&P Telephone Company as an information operator (*411), Department of Social Services in adoption department as an administrative assistant processing all adoption forms and reports, Citi Financial Commercial Credit (twenty-seven years) as a loan officer for mail-in out-of-state loans in the United States, senior customer service in various capacities; resides with husband, Frederick Matthews; two children: Keith Jones and Tevis Jones-Henry; six grandchildren: Keith, Jr., Jasmine, Deonta, Keyshawna, Chyna, and Shaniah; loves to cook, bake, paint, garden (flowers and vegetables), work in yard, talk on phone with family members, and plan dinners for family and special functions. (*Source: Carolyn D. Matthews.*)

Audrey Denise Jones Jordan, great-granddaughter of Lombard and Annie Jones; granddaughter of Louis and Fragia Jones of Mila Neck community, Wicomico, Northumberland County, VA; oldest daughter of Leonard and Carrie Jones of Baltimore, MD; began college studies at University of Maryland (UMBC) in biology; following some medical issues, changed to accounting; taught in Goldsboro, NC; retired due to medical issues; oldest daughter, Tyra, attended Liberty University and lives with husband, Gerald, in NC; son, Warren Jason, attended West Virginia State College and is currently married and living with his wife, Vanessa, in North Carolina; has two young daughters, Lea and Ciara, who live in North Carolina. *(Source: Leonard Jones.)*

William Alfred Jones, Sr. (1942–1999), oldest son of James Edward (Ed) and Ceddra Kistel Yerby Jones; known by some as "crow" and could sleep standing up; grew up in Bogey Neck, Wicomico Church, Northumberland County, VA; educated in Northumberland County Public Schools; member of Mt. Olive Baptist Church, Wicomico, VA; first job was crabbing (taught by grandmother, Fragia Jones); moved to Baltimore, MD, met and married Christine Chambers (b. 1963); three children: William Alfred, Jr., Brita, and Marvin; employed at Cloverland Dairy, Pepsi Cola Company, and Schmidt Blue Ribbon until his death; buried in Baltimore, MD. (*Source: Carolyn Matthews.*)

Mark Alonzo Jones (b. 1960), the youngest son of James Edward Jones, Sr., and Ceddra Kistel (Yerby) Jones; graduate of Northumberland County schools (1979); joined the US Army (1980) and retired at Fort Lee, VA (2004); attended basic training and advanced individual training at Ft. Bliss, TX during twenty-four years of service; duty locations included Ft. Lewis, WA; Berlin, Germany; Hampton, VA; Charlottesville, VA; Beckley, WV; and Richmond, VA; married Tamara Yvette Walden (b. 1983); two children: Daniel Allen Walden-Jones and Courtney Shavonne Jones; four grandchildren (two sets of twins): Coka Dahni and Ronin Dahvi (three years old) and Sofi Dai and Cannon Knight (ten months) by Daniel Jones and Kameren Harris; resides in Richmond, VA. (*Source: Michael A. Jones.*)

James E. Jones, Jr. (1957) was the fourth child born to James Edward (Ed) Jones and Ceddra Yerby Jones; grew up in Bogey Neck community, Wicomico Church, Northumberland County, VA; known by family and neighborhood friends as Jimmy; attended and graduated from the Northumberland County School System; upon graduation joined the US Army (1977); following basic training and Advanced Individual Training (AIT), assigned to Schofield Barracks in Oahu, HI (1979); united in marriage to Dixie Rich, daughter of Mary Rich and the late Odell Rich, Sr., of Northumberland County, VA; two sons: Jermaine and Marcus Jones., daughter-in-law, Danielle, wife of Jermaine; two granddaughters: Kaleah (b. 1997) and Aiyana (b. 1999); retired after twenty years of military service; during tenure in the military, traveled with family to Oahu, HI Ft. Riley, KS, Ft. Ritchie, MD (three years), Kirchgoens, Germany (six years), Fort Lee, Petersburg,

VA (seven months), and finally retired in Fort Sill, OK; served in Iraqi Desert Storm War/Iraqi Freedom; after retirement and a brief break, went to work at Treasure Lake Job Corp, Indiahoma, OK, as culinary arts training instructor, later promoted to dining facility manager; has many accomplishments; has touched many people in a positive manner; mentored disabled children in Hawaii and Oklahoma; consistently counseled and mentored troubled young adults; taught a trade at Treasure Lake; worked for Kellogg Brown and Root International for three years; currently employed with Dyna Corp International in Afghanistan as a dining facility manager. (*Source: James E. Jones, Jr.*)

Generation No. 3—Grandchildren of Stafford B. and Susan Jones, Children of Raleigh Doleman, Sr., and Hannah Johson

1. **Arthur Reid Jones** (b. ca. 1892).
2. **Julia Ann Jones Jackson** (b. ca. 1893–1987).
3. **William Scott Jones** (b. ca. 1896).
4. **Raleigh Doleman Jones, Jr.** (1901–1959); born in Bogey Neck; died in Brooklyn, NY; son of Raleigh Doleman, Sr., and Hannah Johnson (b. 1872); m. Hannah Eliza Palmer (1914–2001) born in Lancaster County, VA; died in Baltimore, MD; daughter of Johnny and Mary Palmer; child: Lionel Augustine Jones (b. 1936).
5. **Martin Luther Jones** (b. 1903).

Generation 4—Great-Grandson of Stafford B and Susan Jones; Grandson of Raleigh Doleman Jones, Sr.[105]

---

105   Oral history.

Lionel Augustine Jones, Sr. (1936–2013), son of Raleigh, Jr., and Hannah Palmer Jones; born in Northumberland County, VA; in 1959, m. Mary Elizabeth Bunn (b. 1936) in Baltimore, MD; children: Melinee Jones (b. 1960), Lionel Augustine Jones, Jr. (b. 1961), Raleigh Daniel Jones (b. 1962); Mary Parker (b. 1967), Wiley William Jones (b. 1963), and Monique Elizabeth Jones (b. 1969).

Generation 5—Great-Great-Grandchildren of Stafford B. and Susan Jones; Great-Grandchildren of Raleigh Doleman and Hannah Johnson Jones; Children of Lionel Augustine, Sr., and Mary Elizabeth Bunn Jones[106]

1. **Melinee Deidra Jones** (b. 1960), born in Baltimore, MD; m. Emery Cody, son of Emery Cody and Lue Spruell. Children: Jasmine Cody (b. 1987), Matthew Cody (b. 1988), and Nathaniel Cody (b. 1993).

2. **Lionel Augustine Jones, Jr**. (b. 1961); born in Verdon, France; m. Lagaunda Saunders, daughter of Irving Saunders and Marvina Brown of Washington, DC. Child: Lionel Jones III (b. 1997).

3. **Raleigh Daniel Jones** (b. 1962), born in Verdon, France; married Mary Parker (b. 2005).

4. **Wiley William Jones** (b. 1963), born in Verdon, France; in 1986, m. Kimberly Jo Hunt, born in Warren, OH (b. 1964); in 1996, married Kimberly Holly (b. 1963) in Montezuma Creek, UT, born in Shiprock, NM; children: William Dana Jones (b. 1986), (Wiley William and Kim Hunt Jones) and Aaron Williams Jones (b. 1998) (Wiley William and Kimberly Holly).

---

106   Oral history.

5. **Monique Elizabeth Jones** (b. 1968), born in Baltimore, MD; married Gregory Cephas of Baltimore, MD; child: Chikiera Cephas (b. 1964).

Generation 6—Great-Great-Great-Grandchildren of Stafford B. and Susan Jones; Great-Great-Grandchildren of Raleigh Doleman and Hannah Johnson Jones; Great-Grandchildren of Raleigh, Jr., and Hannah Palmer Jones; Grandchildren of Lionel Augustine, Sr., and Mary Elizabeth Bunn Jones[107]

1. **Jasmine Cody** (b. 1987), born in Landsthul, Germany, daughter of Melinee Jones Cody; child: Jeremiah Leonard Cody (b. 2007).
2. **Matthew Cody** (b. 1988), born in Lansthul, Germany, son of Melinee Jones Cody.
3. **Nathaniel Cody** (b. 1992), born in Phoenix AZ, son of Melinee Jones Cody.
4. **Lionel Jones III** (b. 1997), born in Alabama, son of Lionel and Lagaunda Saunders Jones.
5. **William Dana Jones** (b. 1986), born in Baltimore, MD; son of Wiley and Kimberly Hunt Jones.
6. **Aaron William Jones** (b. 1998), born in Columbia, MD; son of Wiley and Kimberly Holly Jones.
7. **Chikiera Cephas** (b. 1994), born in Baltimore, MD; daughter of Monique Jones and Gregory Cephas.

Generation No. 7—Great-Great-Great-Great-Grandchild of Stafford B. and Susan Jones; Great-Great-Great-

---

107   Oral history.

Grandchild of Raleigh Doleman and Hannah Johnson Jones; Great-Great-Grandchild of Raleigh, Jr., and Hannah Palmer Jones; Great-Grandchild of Lionel Augustine, Sr., and Mary Elizabeth Bunn Jones[108]

1. **Jeremiah Leonard Cody** (b. 2007), born in Newport News, VA, son of Jasmine and Brandon Hill.

BIOGRAPHICAL SKETCH—Descendant of Raleigh D. Jones

Lionel Augustine Jones (1936–2013), born in Northumberland County, VA, to Raleigh Doleman Jones and Hannah Eliza Palmer; moved to Baltimore, MD, at an early age and raised by a cousin, Florence Smith; educated in the Baltimore City School system and graduated from Douglas High School (1955); matriculated at Morgan State College and later enlisted in the US Army; served in France, Germany, Korea, Vietnam, and US Army post Tobyhanna; Pacific, WA, Fort Huachuca, AZ; served at Schofield Barracks, HI, White Sands, NM, Fort Bragg, NC, Fort Belvoir, VA, Fort Lee, VA, and Suitland, MD; retired from Fort Richard, AL, in 1981 as a sergeant major; attended Mt. Olive Baptist Church, Wicomico, VA; baptized at Fulton Baptist Church in Baltimore; met wife, Mary Bunn, at Fulton Baptist; resided with wife Mary in Baltimore, MD; father of five: Melanie D., Lionel

---

108   Oral history.

A., Raleigh D., Wiley W., and Monique E; buried in Baltimore, MD. (*Source: Family.*)

GENEALOGY OF ROBERT WALLACE (b. ca. 1840)

Generation 1: Robert Wallace—Introduction[109]

Robert Wallace (b. ca. 1840), born in Virginia, was living in Wicomico, VA, in 1870 with his wife, Ellen Wallace (b. ca. 1845); post office: Browns Store; farmer; neighbors: Frederick Warner (B), James Hudson (W), John Cole (W), Lucinda White (B), Hiriam Cockrell (B), and Moredan Blackwell (W) (1870 census); the 1880 census reports Robert and his wife, Ellen, had two children: William (age 3) and Mary E (age 1), daughter in-law, Winey A. Winsey (age 15) lived in his household, and Robert's parents were born in Maryland. Neighborhood changed from a mixed neighborhood in 1870 to all black in 1880; neighbors: Fielding Brown, James Taylor, Robert Lee, Walter Rico, James Vino, Henry Fisher, and Martha Johnson.

In 1900, the census reports Robert and Ellen as having been married thirty years. Children living in the household were: Adolphus (age 21), Elizabeth (age 19), Margaret (age 18), George (age 17), Thomas (age 12), and a nephew, Alfred Coleman (age 8). The neighbors were: Isaiah Smith (B), Steptoe Fallin (B), Patty Coyewter (W), Julia Harding (W), William Waters (B), James Jessup (B), William Doggett (W), and Welford Day (B).

There were no records of land ownership for periods 1865–1922 in Northumberland County, VA.

---

109 Federal Census 1870, 1880.

Generation 2—Children of Robert and Ellen Wallace, born and reared in Bogey Neck[110]

1. **Adolphus Wallace** (ca. 1879–1930); m. Cora Lee Braxton (ca. 1882–1974); resided in Bogey Neck community; after Adolphus's death, Cora Wallace m. Walter K. Jones of Bogey Neck and lived in her family home in Bogey Neck with her son, George Otha, and his wife, Eula, until her death in 1974.
2. **Elizabeth Wallace** (b. ca. 1879).
3. **Margaret Wallace** (b. ca. 1882).
4. **George Otha Wallace** (b. ca. 1883)
5. **Thomas Wallace** (b. ca. 1889); resided in Wicomico Church; m. Blanche Beatrice Butler (ca. 1908–1993) of Browns Store.

Generation 3—Grandchildren of Robert and Ellen Wallace; Children of Adolphus and Cora Braxton Wallace[111]

1. **Elizabeth Wallace Washington** (1902–1966); m. John James Washington; resided in Philadelphia, PA; moved back to Bogey Neck and resided there until her death; buried in family cemetery in Bogey Neck. Child: Fannie Washington (b. 1928).
2. **Robert Wallace** (1903–1974); in 1929 m. his uncle Thomas Wallace's widow, Blanche Beatrice Butler Wallace (1903–1993); resided in Wicomico Church, VA, until his death; buried in family cemetery in Bogey Neck. Children: Sarah Beatrice Wallace (b. 1935) and deceased children (names unknown).

---

110 Federal Census 1870, 1880, 1900.
111 Federal Census 1900, 1910, 1920.

3. **George Otha Wallace** (1908–1970), m. Eula Smith (1913–1970) of Wicomico; resided in Bogey Neck; child: raised Synethia Taylor (five months to age fifteen) until his death in 1970.

4. **Hilda Modelle Wallace Norris** (1911–1986), m. Harvey Norris; resided in Brooklyn, NY.

5. **Alonzo Louis Wallace** (1914–1929).

6. **Beatrice Hazel Wallace Jones** (1916–1967), m. Logan Jones (1912–1967); resided with mother and brother in Bogey Neck before she and Logan moved to Philadelphia, PA; husband, Logan Jones, was the brother of stepfather, Walter K. Jones.

Generation 4—Great-Grandchildren of Robert and Ellen Wallace; Grandchildren of Adolphus and Cora Braxton Wallace[112]

1. **Fannie Washington Wood** (1921–1994), daughter of Elizabeth and John James Washington; m. Melvin Wood (1911–1970); resided in Philadelphia, PA. Children: Richard (b. 1938), Robert (b. 1940), Ronald (b. 1940), Delores (b. 1941), Antoinette (b. 1947), b. Anthony (b. 1950), Irene (b. 1952), and Anita (b. 1957).

2. **Sarah Beatrice Wallace Brassfield** (b. 1935), daughter of Robert and Beatrice Wallace; m. Arthur Brassfield; resides in Wicomico Church. [See biograqphical sketch.]

---

112 Federal Census 1920, 1930, 1940; oral history.

Generation 5—Great-Great-Grandchildren of Robert and Ellen Wallace; Great-Grandchildren of Adolphus and Cora Braxton Wallace; Grandchildren of Elizabeth and John James Washington; Children of Fannie and Melvin Wood.

1. **Richard Wood** (b. 1938); children: (Richard and Teresa Wood) Miko Wood (b. 1968), Richard Brian Wood (b. 1969), Malvin Curtis Wood (b. 1971); (Richard and Celestine Fleming) Richard Fleming, Martino Fleming, and Antoinette Fleming.

2. **Ronald Wood** (b. 1940), wife: Barbara. Child: Rhonda (Hill) Wood.

3. **Robert Wood, Sr.** (1940–2005), wife: Barbara; children: Robert Wood, Jr., and Duane Freeman.

4. **Delores Wood Hammond** (b. 1941), m. Leon Hammond. Children: Leon Hammond, Jr., Derrell Hammond, and Trina Hammond.

5. **Antoinette Wood Johnson** (b. 1947), m. Daniel Johnson; children: Eric Wood and Celeste Wood.

6. **Anthony Wood** (b. 1950); children: Tyrone Gaines Wood, Melba Wood, and Travis Wood.

7. **Irene Wood** (1952–1978).

8. **Anita Wood** (b. 1957).

Generation 6—Great-Great-Great-Grandchildren of Robert and Ellen Wallace; Great-Great-Grandchildren of Adolphus and Cora Braxton Wallace; Great-Grandchildren of Fannie and John James Washington[113]

1. **Miko Wood Sampson** (b. 1968), daughter of Richard and Teresa Wood; m. Austin Sampson; children: Samiya Sampson (b. 1993) and Justina Sampson (b. 1999).

2. **Richard Brian Wood** (b. 1969), son of Richard and Teresa Wood.

3. **Malvin Curtis Wood** (b. 1971), son of Richard and Teresa Wood.

4. **Richard Fleming**, son of Richard Wood, Sr., and Celestine Fleming.

5. **Martino Fleming**, son of Richard Wood, Sr., and Celestine Fleming.

6. **Rhonda (Hill) Wood**, daughter of Ronald and Sarah Wood.

7. **Robert Wood, Jr.**, son of the late Robert Wood, Sr., and Barbara Wood.

8. **Duane Freeman**, son of the late Robert Wood, Sr., and Barbara Wood.

9. **Leon Hammond, Jr**. (b. 1960), son of Delores Wood and Leon Hammond, Sr.; wife: Sherri; children: Gina Lyles (b. 1977), Leon Hammond III (b. 1985), Erica Hammond (b. 1990), Zaccai Millee Hammond (b. 1999), and Zalia Millee Hammond (b. 2001).

---

113 Oral history.

10. **Derrell Hammond, Sr.** (b. 1961), son of Delores Wood and Leon Hammond, Sr.; wife: Marcia Perry; children: Siahai Hammond (b. 2008), Sanai Hammond (b. 2010), Derrell Hammond, Jr. (b. 2012), Sumaugh Perry (b. 2006), and Leroy Burrell (b. 1997).

11. **Trina Hammond** (b. 1963), daughter of Delores and Leon Hammond, Sr.; children: Shakeya Hammond (b. 1981) and Tyreek Hammond (b. 1991).

12. **Eric Wood**, son of Antoinette Wood Johnson.

13. **Celeste Wood**, daughter of Antoinette Wood Johnson.

14. **Tyrone Gaines Wood**, son of Anthony and Rosetta Wood.

15. **Melba Wood**, daughter of Anthony and Rosetta Wood.

16. **Travis Wood**, son of Anthony and Rosetta Wood.

Generation 7—Great-Great-Great-Great-Grandchildren of Robert and Ellen Wallace; Great-Great-Great Grandchildren of Adolphus and Cora Braxton Wallace; Great-Great Grandchildren of Elizabeth Wallace and John James Washington; Great-Grandchildren of Fannie Washington and Melvin Wood.[114]

1. **Gina Lyles** (b. 1977), daughter of Leon, Jr., and Sherri Hammond.

2. **Shakeva Hammond** (b. 1981), daughter of Trina Hammond.

3. **Tyreek Hammond** (b. 1991), son of Trina Hammond.

4. **Leon Hammond III** (b. 1985), son of Leon, Jr., and Sherri Hammond.

5. **Erica Hammond** (b. 1990), daughter of Leon, Jr., and Sherri Hammond.

---

114 Oral history.

6. **Zaccai Millee Hammond** (b. 1999), son of Leon, Jr., and Sherri Hammond.

7. **Zalia Millee Hammond** (b. 1991), daughter of Leon, Jr., and Sherri Hammond.

8. **Siahai Hammond** (b. 2008), daughter of Derrell and Marcia Hammond.

9. **Derrell Hammond, Jr**. (b. 2012), son of Derrell and Marcia Hammond.

10. **Sumaugh Perry** (b. 2006), daughter of Derrell and Marcia Hammond.

11. **Leroy Burrell** (b. 1997), son of Darrell and Marcia Hammond.

12. **Samiya Sampson** (b. 1993), daughter of Miko and Austin Sampson.

13. **Justina Sampson** (b. 1999), daughter of Miko and Austin Sampson.

Biographical Sketch — Descendants of Adolphus Wallace

Sarah Beatrice Wallace Brassfield, second of two granddaughters of Adolphus Wallace (1877–1930) and Cora Lee Braxton (1882–1974) of Bogey Neck, Wicomico, Northumberland County, VA; one surviving daughter of several siblings born to Robert Wallace (1903–1974) and Blanche Beatrice Butler (1908–1993) of Browns Store, VA; attended Anna T. Jeanes Elementary School and Julius Rosenwald High School, graduating in 1953; graduate of Virginia Union University, receiving a BS in business administration (1957); employed as bank clerk and teller by the Industrial Bank of Washington, DC (1957–1959); elementary school teacher in Lancaster County, VA (1960–1967); Social Security Administration (1967–1995), Baltimore, MD; retired from Social Security and returned to her roots in Wicomico Church, VA, with husband of forty years, Arthur C. Brassfield, of Meridian, MS; reunited with Mt. Olive Baptist Church (Wicomico Church, VA); stepmother of three: Gloria D. Wilson, (Meridian, MS), Debra L. Crowell (Birmingham, AL), and Arthur C. Brassfield, Jr. (Meridian, MS); five grandchildren and five great grandchildren. (*Source: Sarah B. Wallace.*)

Anthony "Tony" Wood (1950), son of Fannie Washington and Melvin Wood; grandson of Elizabeth Wallace and James John Washington; great grandson of Adolphus and Cora Lee Braxton Wallace; founder and Executive Director of Carmen

Ministries, a nonprofit Christian organization that provides holistic services to juvenile offenders while they are in institutions and after they are released back into their home communities; passion for troubled teens started in the mideighties while volunteering in a juvenile home in Tennessee; over the past years, has worked in the NJ Warren County Youth Detention Center through the Gideon International Ministry; holds a chaplain certificate from the United Chaplain International Worldwide Outreach Inc. and participates annually in numerous workshops, lectures, and local mission trips involving teens at risk; as executive director, is dedicated to Carmen Ministries' development as a benevolent Christian force within the state of NJ; to this end, Carmen Ministries holds weekly Bible studies in seven state facilities and two county facilities and provides one-on-one mentoring for incarcerated and released teens; continues to personally help at-risk teens and is "dad" to many of the teens mentored; awarded the NAACP 2010 Community Service Award for Warren and Hunterdon, NJ, counties. A 1972 graduate of Delaware Valley College, DE; resides in northern New Jersey with wife, Rosetta; three children: Tyrone, Melba, and Travis; was an employee at USA Master Foods (formerly M&M Mars) for twenty-two years, serving as a quality assurance manager and corporate trainer; elected early retirement in 2001; helps teens full-time through work in Carmen Ministries; family attends the Washington Assembly of God church with Pastor Gerald Scott, Jr. (*Source: Tony Wood.*)

GENEALOGY OF WILLIAM W. WALTERS, Sr.
(ca. 1840–ca.1905)

Generation 1: William W. Walters, Sr.—Introduction[115]

William W. Walters, born in Maryland, m. first wife, Ann V. Walters, and resided in Wicomico, VA; farmed for a living; ten children: Sarah E. Walters (b. ca.1864), Abby Walters (b. ca. 1867), Milley J. Walters (b. ca. 1872), William S. Walters (b. ca. 1875), John Walters (b. ca. 1877), George Walters (b. ca. 1882), William W. Walters (b. ca. 1880), Frank Walters (b. ca. 1886), Annie Walters (b. ca. 1880), Luella Walters (b. ca. 1894); m. Addie Walters (b. ca. 1899); William W. Walters, Sr., purchased 8¾ acres of land near Harcum Wharf (1889) in Mila Neck, where he lived with his wife and family;[116] neighbors in 1900 federal census record were: Robert Jessup (B), Fred Warner (B), Charles Norris (B), Roy Jessup (B), John T. Davenport (W), William Rowe (W), Bear Barrett (W), and Lucious Barrett (W); two sons lived in Bogey Neck: John Walters and William Washington Walters, Jr., whose descendants will be presented in this chapter.

Generation 2—Children of William W. and Ann V. Walters[117]

1. **Sarah E. Walters** (b. ca. 1864).
2. **Abby Walters** (b. ca. 1867.
3. **Milley J. Walters** (b. ca. 1872).
4. **William Solomon Walters** (b. ca. 1875).

---

115 Federal Census 1850, 1900.
116 Northumberland County, VA, Land Records, 1900–1913.
117 Federal Census 1850.

5. **John Walters** (ca. 1877–1930); m. Emma Johnson (ca. 1883–1922); resided in Bogey Neck; fisherman; children: Edward Walters (b. 1900), Elvin Walters (b. 1903), Emily B. Smith (1904–1963), John C. Walters (b. 1906), George F. Walters (b. 1909), Grace C. Walters (1911–1986), Julia G. Walters (b. 1913), Stewart C. Walters (b. 1916), Harold Walters (b. 1918), and Annie Walters (b. 1920).

6. **George Walters** (b. ca. 1882), m. Lucy Corbin; resided in Mila Neck, Wicomico Church district; laborer in fishing industry; wife, Lucy, shucked oysters. Children: Prentice (b. 1904), Lewis (b. 1912), and Annie (b. 1919); others in household: nephew Homer Walters and sister-in-law Lola Walters.

7. **William Washington Walters** (b. ca. 1880); m. Maggie Carter (b. ca. 1884) of Mila; resided in Bogey Neck community in Wicomico Church district; worked as laborer in fishing industry; children: Ernest Walters (b. 1900), Lena Walters (b. 1903), Henry Walters (b. 1905), Washington Walters, Jr. (b. 1907), Sarah Walters (1908–1928), Solomon Walters (b. 1909), Unnamed (1910–1910), Luther Walters (b. 1912), and Gertrude Walters (b. 1917).

8. **Frank Walters** (b. ca. 1886), lived with brother George Walters in 1910 (age 23).

9. **Annie Walters** (b. ca. 1890), lived with brother George Walters in 1910 (age 20).

10. **Luella Walters** (b. ca. 1894), lived with brother George Walters in 1910 (age 15).

Generation 3—Grandchildren of William W. and Ann V. Walters.[118]

Children of John and Emma J. Walters, children born in Bogey Neck Community, Remo Post Office:

1. **Edward Walters** (b. 1900); single; lived with John Walters for a short period; believed to have drowned at an early age.
2. **Elvin Walters** (b. 1903); m. Rosie Walters; resided in Maryland; one adopted child.
3. **Emily B. Walters** (1904–1963); m. Travis Smith (1899–1948); resided in Harvest Neck community. Children: Anna M. Smith (1920–1975), Winder Smith (1921–1922), Travis W. Smith (b. 1923), Oneil Smith (b. 1924), Mildred C. Smith Bromley (1926–1998), Emma C. Smith Jones (b. 1927), Mervin C. Smith (b. 1930), Elvin Smith (b. 1931), Rose Smith Jones (b. 1933), Thelma Smith Austin (b. 1934), Jaunita Smith (1934–1934), Edward M. Smith (b. ca. 1930), Grace Smith (1935–1947), Jean Smith Noel (1937–1969), Carroll Smith (b. 1939), Emmaline Smith Johnson (b. 1940), Lewis Smith (1942–2005), and Fannie Mae Smith Kennedy (b. 1943). [*See biographical sketch*]
4. **John Cecil Walters** (b. 1906); resided in MD.
5. **George F. Walters** (b. 1909); resided in MD.
6. **Grace C. Walters** (1911–1986); m. Emerson Norris (1909–1992) of Wicomico Church district; resided in Bogey Neck community, Remo, VA, post office. Children: Gladys Norris Cottrell (b. 1930), Jennis P. Norris (1932–1954), Violet J. Norris

---

118 Census 1880, 1900.

(b. 1933), Emerson W. Norris, Jr. (b. 1934), Randolph Norris (b. 1936), Douglas Norris (b. 1938), Helen Norris Ball (b. 1939), Otis Norris (1940–2012); Joyce Norris Wilson (b. 1941), Stanley Norris (b. 1943), Kermit Norris (1943–1993), Patricia Norris Abraham (b. 1948), and Raymond Norris (1950–1969); stepchild of Grace Norris: Eva Taylor Brown (b. 1928), daughter of Emerson Norris and Beatrice Taylor.

7. **Julia Gladys Walters** (b. 1913); lived in Philadelphia, PA.
8. **Stewart C. Walters** (b. 1916); lived with sister Emily after father's death; died at an early age.
9. **Harold J. Walters** (b. 1918); lived with sister Grace after father's death.
10. **Annie Walters** (b. 1920); m. Thomas Morris (b. 1937); lived in Baltimore, MD, (Stricker Street) as a boarder with Clarence Barber; housekeeper for private family.

Generation 4—Great-Grandchildren of William W. and Ann V. Walters; Grandchildren of John W. and Emma J. Walters of Bogey Neck community

Children of Emily Walters and Travis Smith, resided in Harvest Neck Community, Remo Post Office, Wicomico Church district:

1. **Anna M. Smith Blair** (1920–1975); resided in Baltimore, MD; worked as housekeeper and caretaker for sick and elderly; children: Mary Taylor Middleton, Ricardo "Ricky" Day, and Cheryl Blair.
2. **Winder Smith**, died at age one.
3. **Travis W. Smith** (b. 1923); m. Inez Roane; children: William D. Smith, James E. Smith, Ethel N. Smith, and Frank O. Smith.

4. **Oneil Smith** (b. 1924–d.); m. Mary Helen Blackwell (1928-1963) of Fairfield, VA; served in US Navy; resided in Baltimore, MD; children: Debra Smith Johnson (b. 1955), Carolyn Smith, Gail Smith Rooks (b. 1960), Catherine Smith (b. 1962), and Joan Smith Askins (b. 1963).

5. **Mildred C. Smith Bromley** (1926–1998), m. Orsie Bromley; resided in Remo, Wicomico Church district; children: Louis Bromley, Jacqueline Bromley Short, James Bromley, Sr. (1953–2012), and Steven Bromley.

6. **Emma C. Smith Jones** (b. 1927), m. Joseph Jones (1927–2004); resides in Mila Neck, Wicomico, VA; children: Doris Jones Colclough (b. 1946), Joseph E. Jones, Edward V. Jones (b. 1947), Sherman M. Jones (1949–1976), Grace Jones Spencer (b. 1950), Morris Jones (1951–2005), Debra Jones (b. 1953), and Walter Jones (b. 1956-d.). [*See biographical sketch*]

7. **Elvin Smith** (b. 1931); first m. Hattie Hill (b. 1934); second m. Peggy Peterson (b. 1934); resides in Baltimore, MD.

8. **Rose Smith Jones** (1932–2013); m. Leonard "Sky Joe" Jones (1929–2006); resided in Heathsville, VA; child: Sheila Jones Waller.

9. **Thelma Smith Austin** (b. 1934–d.); m. Edwood Austin; children: Preston Smith, Darlene Harriday, Anwar Muhammad, Sr., Dannetta Austin, Vicki Austin Terry, and Yvonne Rená Austin Sweetwine.

10. **Jaunita Smith** (lived ten months).

11. **Edward M. Smith** (b. ca. 1930).

12. **Grace Smith** (1935–1947).

13. **Jean Smith Noel** (1936–1969); m. Robert Noel, Sr.; children: Phyllis Noel Brown Tomlin, Robert Noel, Jr., Carroll Noel, Carolyn Ball Crockett, Rose Noel Claiborne, and Ninitia Noel.

14. **Carroll Smith** (b. 1938); m. Walice Edwards; resides in Harvest Neck, Wicomico Church district; child: Jeraldine Smith Clayton (1955–2006). [*See biographical sketch.*]

15. **Emmaline Smith Johnson** (b. 1940); m. Joseph Johnson; child: Tanya Johnson.

16. **Lewis Smith, Sr.** (1942–2005); m. Bernice Holden; children: Gary Smith, Sr., Lewis Smith, Jr., and Mardiko Smith.

17. **Fannie Mae Smith Kennedy** (b. 1943), m. Ivory Kennedy; resides in New Jersey; children: Fannie McMillan (b. 1963), Murvin Lionel Smith (b. 1962), and Desiree McMiller (b. 1967).

Children of Grace Walters and Emerson Norris, Sr., resided in Bogey Neck Community, Remo Post Office, Wicomico Church district, Northumberland County, VA:

18. **Gladys L. Norris Cottrell** (1930); m. Samuel Cottrell (1926–1982); resides in Baltimore, MD; employed as health service worker; children: Angelo Cottrell (1954), Dale Cottrell (1959). [*See biographical sketch.*]

19. **Jennis P. Norris** (1931–1954); the musician of the family; taught himself to play his grandfather's organ; resided in Bogey Neck with parents until his death.

20. **Violet Norris Davenport** (b. 1933); m. John Davenport; resides in Washington, DC; children: Jacqueline Davenport (b. 1949)

and Shirley Davenport Farrow (b. 1954). [*See biographical sketch.*]

21. **Emerson W. Norris** (b. 1934); m. Grace Conley; resides in Heathsville, VA; children: Emerson Norris III (1954–1994) and Yvette Norris Jones Harding. [*See biographical sketch.*]

22. **Randolph Norris** (b. 1936); m. Elsie Coleman; resides in Bogey Neck; children of Randolph: JoAnne Norris Crocker (b. 1956) and Eric Duane Harcum (Ricky).

23. **Douglas Norris** (b. 1938); m. Margaret Keeve; resides in Baltimore, MD; children: Douglas Avery Norris (b. 1958), Yvonne Norris Walker (b. 1959), and Kirt Norris (b. 1961).

24. **Helen Norris Ball** (b. 1939); m. Donald Ball; resides in Silver Spring, MD; children: Lori Ball Fenner (b. 1958) and Kim M. Ball (b. 1962).[*See biographical sketch*]

25. **Otis Norris** (1940–2012); resided in Baltimore, MD; m. Mary Shipley; children: Kevin B. Norris (1960–1979), Keith Norris (b. 1961), Karen Norris (b. 1965), and Jeffrey R. Norris (b. 1969).

26. **Joyce Norris Thomas Wilson** (b. 1942); first marriage, James W. Thomas; second marriage, Ernest Wilson (1936–1996); resides in Washington, DC; children: Alan Thomas (b. 1967) and Shanelle Thomas Goss (1968). [*See biographical sketch.*]

27. **Stanley Norris** (b. 1943); m. Phyllis Keeve; resides in Reedsville, VA; children: Carlos L. Norris (b. 1959) and Brian O. Norris (b. 1973).

28. **Kermit Norris** (1946–1993); m. Norma Keeve (d. 1993); child: Anthony Norris (1983–1993).

29. **Patricia Norris Walton** (b. 1948); m. Abraham B. Walton, Jr. (1947–2006); resides in Bowie, MD. [*See biographical sketch.*]

30. **Raymond Norris** (1950–1969); died while on active duty, private in US Marine Corp.

31. **Eva Taylor Brown** (b. 1928); stepdaughter of Grace Norris; daughter of Emerson and Bernice Taylor; m. Benjamin Brown; resides in Baltimore, MD; children: Bernadette Brown Murphy, Ava Brown, Shelley Brown, James Brown, Venessa Brown, Darnel Brown, Carmilla Brown, and Raheem Hakim.

Generation 5—Great-Great Grandchildren of William W. and Ann V. Walters; Great-Grandchildren of John W. and Emma J. Walters of Bogey Neck community, Remo Post Office, Wicomico district, Northumberland County, VA[119]

Grandchildren of Emily Walters and Travis Smith, Sr., resided in Harvest Neck Community, Remo Post Office, Wicomico Church district:

1. **Mary Taylor Middleton**, daughter of Anna M. Smith Blair; children: Synethia Taylor, Minerva Current, Sharon Nails, Thomas Middleton, Jennifer Yearwood, Gerald Middleton, Emily Roberts, and Anna "Peaches" Middleton. [*See biographical sketch.*]

2. **Ricardo "Ricky" Day**, son of Anna M. Smith Blair; resides in Suffolk, VA; children: Anthony and Stacey.

3. **Cheryl Blair** (b. 1962), daughter of Anna M. Smith and Nathaniel Blair; child: Shannon Blair Washington (b. 1982).

4. **William D. Smith** (b. 1945); son of Travis, Jr., and Inez Roane Smith; first m. Elsie L. Walters, second m. Kathryn Walters, third m. Barbara Smith (d. 1998); resides in Detroit, MI; children:

---

119 Oral history.

William Tye Smith (b. 1968), Ranelle (b. 1970), Vaneta (b. 1972), and Demetrius Smith (1979—2007).

5. **James E. Smith** (b. 1947); son of Travis, Jr., and Inez Roane Smith; resides in Cambridge, MA; children: Darrell Smith, Bridgette Smith, Daria Smith, William E. Holloman, and Joshua Smith (b. 1993).

6. **Ethel M. Smith** (b. 1952), daughter of Travis, Jr., and Inez Roane Smith.; m. Branch Delano Coleman, Jr.; resides in St. Mary's County, MD; children: Branch Delano III (b. 1978) and Brandon Andrew Coleman (b. 1983).

7. **Frank O. Smith,** son of Travis, Jr., and Inez Roane Smith.; resides in MD.

8. **Debra Smith Johnson** (b. 1955); born in Baltimore, MD; daughter of Oneil and Mary Helen Blackwell Smith; raised by foster mother, Edith Bowie, following mother's death (1963); resides in Baltimore, MD; children: Charles Johnson, Jr. (b. 1978), Gabriel Johnson (b. 1987), Christina Jones (b. 1989), and Milan Jones (b. 1994).

9. **Carolyn Smith,** born in Baltimore, MD; daughter of Oneil and Mary Helen Blackwell Smith; raised by foster mother, Edith Bowie, following mother's death (1963); resides in Baltimore, MD; children: Jermaine Cox and Lyra Hopewell.

10. **Gail Smith Rooks** (b. 1960); daughter of Oneil and Mary Helen Blackwell Smith; raised by foster mother, Edith Bowie, following mother's death (1963); children: Monica Rooks and Glen Rooks.

11. **Catherine Smith** (b. 1962); born in Baltimore, MD; daughter of Oneil and Mary Helen Blackwell Smith; raised by foster mother, Mable Carmabatch, following mother's death (1963).

12. **Joan Smith Askins** (b. 1963); daughter of Oneil and Mary Helen Blackwell Smith; raised by foster mother, Mable Carmabatch, following mother's death (1963); resides in Baltimore, MD; children: Calvin Askins (b. 1984) and Clifton Oneil Askins (b. 1988).

13. **Louis Bromley**, son of Mildred Smith and Orsie Bromley; m. Bessie Nickens; resides in Baltimore, MD; served in US Army (1966–1968); children: Darryl Bromley (b. 1971) and Shayelle Bromley (b. 1981).

14. **Jacqueline Bromley Short**, daughter of Mildred Smith and Orsie Bromley; formerly m. William Short, Sr.; resides in Irvington, NJ; children: William Short, Jr. (b. 1970) and Jennora Short (b. 1978).

15. **James A. Bromley, Sr.** (1953–2012), son of Mildred Smith and Orsie Bromley; served in US Army; landscaper, waterman; resided in Remo, VA; child: James Bromley, Jr.

16. **Steven Bromley** (b. 1968); son of Mildred Smith and Orsie Bromley; m. Darlene Bromley.

17. **Doris Jones Colclough** (b. 1946), daughter of Emma and Joseph Jones; m. Herbert Colclough; children: Michael Colclough, Jr., and Monica Colclough. [*See biographical sketch*]

18. **Joseph E. Jones**, son of Emma and Joseph Jones; m. Darlene Tracey; children: Vincent Jones and Diannetta Jones.

19. **Edward V. Jones, Sr.** (b. 1947), son of Emma Smith and Joseph Jones; m. Jacqueline; children: Edward Jones, Jr. (deceased) and Tara Jones.

20. **Sherman M. Jones** (1949–1976), son of Emma Smith and Joseph Jones; served in US Army.

21. **Grace Jones Spencer** (b. 1950), daughter of Emma Smith and Joseph Jones; m. Andrew Tracey; resides in Washington, DC. children: Rene Jones Forney (b. 1967), Keyetta Stoner Mills, Mervin Spencer, Mershom Spencer, and Keraly Spencer.

22. **Morris Jones** (1951–2005), son of Emma Smith and Joseph Jones; m. Margaret Hudnall; SFC US Army; child: Derrick Jones.

23. **Debra Jones Sydnor** (b. 1953), daughter of Emma Smith and Joseph Jones; m. Ralph Sydnor; children: Brian Sydnor, Christopher Sydnor, and Danny Sydnor.

24. **Walter Jones** (b. 1956–d.), son of Emma Smith and Joseph Jones; served in US Army.

25. **Sheila Jones Waller**, daughter of Rose Smith and Leonard Jones; child: Thornton.

26. **Mubarak Mahmood (Preston Smith)** (b. 1951), son of Thelma Smith; children: Sabrina Smith Potter (b. 1970) and Angela Nicole Smith (b. 1984).

27. **Darlene Austin Harriday**, daughter of Thelma Smith and Edwood Austin; m. George Warren Harriday; children: Edwin Harriday and Marcus Harriday.

28. **Anwar Muhammad, Sr.**, son of Thelma Smith and Edwood Austin; children: Anwar Muhammad, Jr., Shahidah Austin, and Elijah Muhammad.

29. **Diannetta Austin**, daughter of Thelma Smith and Edwood Austin.

30. **Vicki Austin Terry**, daughter of Thelma Smith and Edwood Austin; child: Niles Terry.

31. **Yvonne Rená Austin Sweetwine**, daughter of Thelma Smith and Edwood Austin; child: Alburt Sweetwine.

32. **Phyllis Noel Tomlin**, daughter of Jean Smith and Robert Noel, Sr.; resides in Wicomico Church, VA; children: Corey Lamont Brown (b. 1975) and Derrick (1977–1998).

33. **Robert Noel, Jr.**, son of Jean Smith and Robert Noel, Sr.; resides in LA; children: Tramaine, Troy, and Taylor.

34. **Carroll Noel**, son of Jean Smith and Robert Noel, Sr.; resides in Browns Store, VA; children: Carroll, Jr., Sherrell, and Brittany Nunev.

35. **Carolyn Noel Crockett**, daughter of Jean Smith and Robert Noel, Sr.; m. Norman Crockett; resides in Village, VA; children: Dwayne Noel (b. 1977), Shantoria Noel (b. 1978), Tiana Noel (b. 1980), and William Lionell Ball (b. 1984).

36. **Rose Noel Claiborne**, daughter of Jean Smith and Robert Noel, Sr; m. Edwin Claiborne; resides in Richmond, VA; children: Erin Claiborne and Nicole Claiborne.

37. **Ninitia Noel** (b. 1963), daughter of Jean Smith and Robert Noel, Sr; resides in Kilmarnock, VA; children: Jean Noel (b. 1983) and Kareem Noel (b. 1988).

38. **Jarlene Smith Clayton** (1955–2006), daughter of Carroll and Walice Edwards Smith; m. Gary Clayton; child: Danielle Clayton.

39. **Tanya Johnson**, daughter of Emmaline and Joseph Johnson.

40. **Gary Smith, Sr.**, son of Lewis and Bernice Holden Smith; child: Gary Smith, Jr.

41. **Lewis Smith, Jr.**, son of Lewis and Bernice Holden Smith; child: Dwayne Smith.

42. **Mardiko Smith,** daughter of Lewis and Bernice Holden Smith.

43. **Fannie McMillan** (b. 1963), daughter of Fannie Mae Smith Kennedy; m. Danny McMillan; children: Quidir Smith Harris (b. 1982), Lakecia Smith Harris (b. 1985); Tiffany Smith (b. 1988), Bobbi Mabry (b. 1990), Bernard Smith (b. 1992), Danielle McMillan (b. 1994), Destiny McMillan (b. 1997), and Jeramiah McMillan (b. 2006).

44. **Murvin Lionel Smith** (b. 1962), son of Fannie Mae Smith Kennedy; m. Adriane Douglas (b. 1965); children: Davione Smith (b. 1987), Adriane Smith (b. 1988); Christopher Smith (b. 1991), Justin Smith (b. 1990), Anthony Smith (b. 1994); stepdaughter: Melissa Douglas (b. 1993).

45. **Desiree McMiller** (b. 1967), daughter of Fannie Mae Smith Kennedy.

Grandchildren of Grace Walters and Emerson Norris, Sr., resided in Bogey Neck Community, Remo Post Office, Wicomico Church district, Northumberland County, VA:

1. **Angelo Cottrell** (b. 1954), son of Gladys and Samuel Cottrell; m. Janice Cottrell; resides in Baltimore, MD; children: Adrienne Cottrell (b. 1979) and Angela Cottrell (b. 1981).

2. **Dale Cottrell** (b. 1959), son of Gladys and Samuel Cottrell; m. Rosalind; resides in Richmond, VA; children: Nathan Cottrell (1989–1999), Ryan Cottrell (b. 1992), and Arnissa Cottrell (b. 1993).

3. **Jacqueline "Jackie" Davenport** (b. 1949); daughter of Violet Norris and John Davenport; resides in Upper Marlboro, MD; child: Stephanie Jackson Pace (1969–2010). [See biographical sketch.]

4. **Shirley "Mootney" Davenport Farrow,** daughter of Violet Norris and John Davenport; m. Tyrone Gary Farrow; resides in Washington, DC; children: Rashad Farrow (b. 1986), Camille Farrow (b. 1986), and Chantal Farrow (1981–1993). [See biographical sketch.]

5. **Emerson Norris III** (1954–1994); son of Emerson, Jr., and Grace Conley Norris; children: Emerson Norris IV and Michael Norris.

6. **Yvette Norris Jones Harding** (b. 1959); daughter of Emerson, Jr., and Grace Conley; resides in Reedville, VA; children: Jason Lamont Jones (b. 1977) and Addrian Terrell Jones (b. 1980).

7. **Carlos L. Norris** (b. 1967); son of Stanley and Phyllis Keeve Norris; m. Jennifer Norris; resides in Dale City, VA; children: Ashley Mizell (b. 1989) and Paris Norris (b. 1999).

8. **Brian O. Norris** (b. 1973); son of Stanley and Phyllis Keeve Norris; m. Kenya Norris; resides in Washington, DC; child: Brian O. Norris, Jr.

9. **Lori Ball Fenner** (b. 1958); daughter of Helen Norris and Donald Ball; resides in Silver Spring, MD.

10. **Kim Ball** (b. 1962), daughter of Helen Norris and Donald Ball; resides in Silver Spring, MD; child: Alivia Grace Ball Thomas (b. 2004).

11. **Alan W. Thomas, Jr.** (b. 1967); son of Joyce Norris Thomas Wilson and James W. Thomas, m. Felicia Knight; resides in

Prince Georges County, MD; children: Anthony Thomas (b. 1986), Kevin Thomas and Keith Thomas (b. 1988), Alan Wesley Thomas III (b. 1991), and Allison Thomas (b. 1992).

12. **Shanelle Thomas Goss** (b. 1968), daughter of Joyce Norris Thomas Wilson and James W. Thomas.; resides in Greenbelt, MD; children: Corric Crawford (b. 1989), Clifton James Crawford (b. 1990), Kamerin Goss (b. 1999), and Justin Goss (b. 2000).

13. **JoAnne Norris Crocker,** daughter of Randolph Norris; resides in Washington, DC; children: Jarvis Crocker (b. 1981) and Javon Crocker (b. 1982).

14. **Anthony Norris** (1983–1993), son of Kermit and Norma Keeve Norris.

15. **Kevin B. Norris** (1960–1979), son of Otis B. and Mary Shipley Norris.

16. **Keith Norris** (b. 1961), son of Otis B. and Mary Shipley Norris; resides in Baltimore, MD.

17. **Karen Norris** (b. 1965), daughter of Otis B. and Mary Shipley Norris; resides in Baltimore, MD.

18. **Jeffrey R. Norris** (b. 1969), son of Otis B. and Mary Shipley Norris; spouse: Jenine; resides in Windsor Mill, MD; children: Jasmine Smith (b. 1989) and Terrance Smith (b. 1990).

19. **Yvonne Norris Walker** (b. 1959), daughter of Douglas and Margaret Keeve Norris; m. Johnny Walker; resides in Baltimore, MD; children: Tyler Walker (b. 1993) and Travis Walker (b. 1996).

20. **Douglas Avery Norris** (b. 1958), son of Douglas and Margaret Keeve Norris; resides in Baltimore, MD; children: Avery Norris, Jr. (b. 1989) and Ava Norris (b. 1991).

21. **Kirk Norris** (b. 1961), son of Douglas and Margaret Keeve Norris; resides in Acworth, GA. Children: Jordan Norris (b. 1988) and Jillian Norris (b. 1990).

22. **Bernadette Brown Murphy,** daughter of Eva Taylor Brown; m. Daniel Murphy; resides in Atlanta, GA; child: Lynn Murphy Mikos.

23. **Ava Brown,** daughter of Eva Taylor and Benjamin Brown; resides in Baltimore, MD.

24. **Me'Shelly Brown,** daughter of Eva Taylor and Benjamin Brown; resides in Baltimore, MD.

25. **James Brown,** son of Eva Taylor and Benjamin Brown; resides in Baltimore, MD.

26. **Vanessa Brown,** daughter of Eva Taylor and Benjamin Brown; resides in Baltimore, MD.

27. **Darnell Brown,** daughter of Eva Taylor and Benjamin Brown; resides in Virginia.

28. **Carmella Brown,** daughter of Eva Taylor and Benjamin Brown; resides in Texas.

29. **Raheem Hakim,** son of Eva Taylor and Benjamin Brown; resides in Baltimore, MD.

30. **Eric Duane "Ricky" Harcum** (b. 1959); son of Randolph Norris; resides in Richmond, VA; children: Teia Walters (b. 1979) and Dontá Davis (b. 1990).

Generation 6—Great-Great-Great-Grandchildren of William W. and Addie Walters; Great-Great-Grandchildren of John W. and Emma J. Walters of Bogey Neck, Remo Post Office, Wicomico district, Northumberland County, VA[120]

Great-Grandchildren of Emily Walters and Travis Smith, resided in Harvest Neck Community, Remo Post Office, Wicomico Church district:

1. **Synethia Taylor** (b. 1954), daughter of Mary Taylor Middleton; granddaughter of Anna M. Smith Blair; raised by Otha and Eula Wallace until their deaths (1970); resides in Baltimore, MD; children: Kevin Taylor, William Powell, and Tisha Powell. [*See biographical sketch*]

2. **Minerva M. Current**, daughter of Mary Taylor Middleton; granddaughter of Anna M. Smith Blair, resides in Seattle, WA; teacher; children: John, Jr., and Faith Current Anderson.

3. **Sharon M. Nails**, daughter of Mary Taylor Middleton; granddaughter of Anna M. Smith Blair; resides in Newport News, VA; children: Chiquita and Shadana.

4. **Thomas A. Middleton,** son of Mary Taylor Middleton; grandson of Anna M. Smith Blair; m. Cathy Middleton; resides in Richmond, VA.

5. **Jennifer M. Smith Yearwood,** daughter of Mary Taylor Middleton; granddaughter of Anna M. Smith Blair; resides in Brandywine, MD; children: Aaron Smith and Tillie-Danielle Edwards; m. Raoul Edwards.

120 Oral history.

6. **Gerald T. Middleton,** son of Mary Taylor Middleton, grandson of Anna M. Smith Blair; resides in Elizabeth, VA; children: Genella and (one name not available).

7. **Emily M. Roberts,** daughter of Mary Taylor Middleton; granddaughter of Anna M. Smith Blair; m. Robert Roberts; resides in Richmond, VA; child: Alicia.

8. **Anna ("Peaches") M. Middleton,** daughter of Mary Taylor Middleton, granddaughter of Anna M. Smith Blair; resides in Richmond, VA; children: Deja Middleton, Mikall Wiggins, and India Wiggins.

9. **Anthony Day,** son of Ricardo "Ricky" Day; grandson of Anna M. Smith Blair.

10. **Stacey Day,** daughter of Ricardo "Ricky" Day; granddaughter of Anna M. Smith Blair.

11. **Shannon Blair Washington** (b. 1982), daughter of Cheryl Blair; granddaughter of Anna M. Smith Blair; child: Ari Washington.

12. **William Tye Smith** (b. 1968), son of William D. Smith; grandson of Travis, Jr., and Inez Roane Smith.

13. **Ranelle Smith** (b. 1970), daughter of William D. Smith; granddaughter of Travis Smith, Jr.

14. **Vaneta Smith** (b. 1972), daughter of William D. Smith, granddaughter of Travis, Jr., and Inez Roane Smith; children: Christopher, Joshua, and Jada.

15. **Demetrius Smith** (1979–2007), son of William D. Smith; grandson of Travis, Jr., and Inez Roane Smith.

16. **Darrell Smith,** daughter of James E. Smith, granddaughter of Travis, Jr., and Inez Roane Smith; child: James Smith.

17. **Bridgette Smith,** daughter of James E. Smith; granddaughter of Travis, Jr., and Inez Roane Smith; children: Shantori Smith, Dasandra Smith, Kia Smith, Dexter Smith, and DJ Smith.

18. **Daria Smith,** daughter of James E. Smith; granddaughter of Travis, Jr., and Inez Roane Smith; child: Travis Smith.

19. **William E. Holloman,** son of James E. Smith; grandson of Travis, Jr., and Inez Roane Smith.

20. **Branch Delano Coleman III** (b. 1978), son of Ethel Smith and Branch Delano Coleman, Jr.; grandson of Travis, Jr., and Inez Roane Smith; daughter: Basil December Coleman (b. 1911); resides in Baltimore, MD.

21. **Brandon Andrew Coleman** (b. 1983), son of Ethel Smith and Branch Delano Coleman; grandson of Travis, Jr., and Inez Roane Smith; resides in Ellicott City, MD.

22. **Charles Johnson, Jr.** (b. 1978), son of Debra Smith; grandson of Oneil and Mary Helen Blackwell Smith.

23. **Gabrielle Jones** (b. 1987), daughter of Debra Smith; granddaughter of Oneil and Mary Helen Blackwell Smith.

24. **Christina Jones** (b. 1989), daughter of Debra Smith; granddaughter of Oneil and Mary Helen Blackwell Smith.

25. **Milan Jones** (b. 1994), daughter of Debra Smith; granddaughter of Oneil and Mary Helen Blackwell Smith.

26. **Jermaine Cox**, son of Carolyn Smith; grandson of Oneil and Mary Helen Blackwell Smith.

27. **Lyra Hopewell,** daughter of Carolyn Smith; granddaughter of Oneil and Mary Helen Blackwell Smith.

28. **Monica Smith**, daughter of Gail Smith; granddaughter of Oneil and Mary Helen Blackwell Smith.

29. **Glenn Rooks**, son of Gail Smith; grandson of Oneil and Mary Helen Blackwell Smith.

30. **Calvin Askins** (b. 1984), son of Joan Smith Askins; grandson of Oneil and Mary Helen Blackwell Smith.

31. **Clifton Oneil Askins** (b. 1988), son of Joan Smith Askins; grandson of Oneil and Mary Helen Blackwell Smith.

32. **Darryl Bromley,** son of Louis and Bessie Bromley; grandson of Mildred Smith and Orsie Bromley; m. Adrienne Bromley; children: Maecyn Bromley (b. 2006) and Taylor Bromley.

33. **Shayell Bromley** (b. 1981), daughter of Louis and Bessie Bromley; granddaughter of Mildred Smith and Orsie Bromley.

34. **William Short, Jr.** (b. 1970), son of Jacqueline Short and William Short, Sr.; grandson of Mildred Smith and Orsie Bromley; resides in Woodbridge, NJ; children: William Anthony Short (b. 1991), Chantel Short (b. 1997), and Xavier Short (b. 2002).

35. **Jannora Short,** daughter of Jacqueline Bromley and William Short, Sr.; granddaughter of Mildred Smith and Orsie Bromley; resides in Irvington, NJ; children: Javonna Short (b. 1994), Javante Dorisme (b. 1999), Joeqel Dorisme (b. 2002), and Jahqie (b. 2004).

36. **Michael Colclough, Jr.,** son of Doris Jones and Herbert Colclolugh, Sr.; grandson of Emma Smith and Joseph Jones.

37. **Monica Colclough,** daughter of Doris Jones and Herbert Colclolugh, Sr.; granddaughter of Emma Smith and Joseph Jones.

38. **Vincent Jones,** son of Joseph E. and Darlene Tracey Jones; grandson of Emma Smith and Joseph Jones.

39. **Danetta Jones,** daughter of Joseph E. and Darlene Tracey Jones; granddaughter of Emma Smith and Joseph Jones.

40. **Edward V. Jones, Jr.,** son of Edward V. Jones, Sr., and Jacqueline Johnson; grandson of Emma Smith and Joseph Jones; children: Jasmine Jones (b. 1997), Amber Jones, Britney Jones (b. 2000), and Nyema Jones.

41. **Tara Jones,** daughter of Edward V. Jones; granddaughter of Emma Smith and Joseph Jones.

42. **Rene Jones Forney,** daughter of Grace and Andrew Spencer; m. Marshall Forney; granddaughter of Emma Smith and Joseph Jones; children: Marshall Forney, Jr., and Kierstin Forney.

43. **Kenyetta Stoner Mills,** daughter of Grace and Andrew Spencer; granddaughter of Emma Smith and Joseph Jones.

44. **Mervin Spencer,** son of Grace and Andrew Spencer; grandson of Emma Smith and Joseph Jones.

45. **Marshon Spencer,** son of Grace and Andrew Spencer; grandson of Emma Smith and Joseph Jones.

46. **Keraly Spencer,** daughter of Grace nd Andrew Spencer; granddaughter of Emma Smith and Joseph Jones.

47. **Derrick Jones,** son of Morris and Margaret Hudnall Jones; grandson of Emma Smith and Joseph Jones; children: Diaundra Jones and Jaden Jones.

48. **Brian Sydnor,** son of Debra Jones and Ralph Sydnor; grandson of Emma Smith and Joseph Jones.

49. **Christopher Sydnor,** son of Debra Jones and Ralph Sydnor; grandson of Emma Smith and Joseph Jones.

50. **Danny Sydnor,** son of Debra Jones and Ralph Sydnor; grandson of Emma Smith and Joseph Jones.

51. **Thornton Jones**, son of Sheila Jones Wilder; grandson of Rose Smith and Leonard Jones.

52. **Angela Nicole Smith** (b. 1984), daughter of Mubarak Mahmood (Preston Smith); granddaughter of Thelma Smith and Edwood Austin; resides in Baltimore, MD.

53. **Sebrina Smith Potter** (b. 1970)**,** daughter of Mubarak Mahmood (Preston Smith); granddaughter of Thelma Smith and Edwood Austin; resides in Baltimore, MD; children: Kenneth Stewart and Sean Potter.

54. **Edwin Amos Harriday** (b. 1992), son of Darlene Austin and George Warren Harriday; grandson of Thelma Smith and Edwood Austin.

55. **Marcus Harriday** (b. 1988), son of Darlene Austin and George Warren Harriday; grandson of Thelma Smith and Edwood Austin.

56. **Anwar Muhammad, Jr.,** son of Anwar Muhammad, Sr.; grandson of Thelma Smith and Edwood Austin.

57. **Shahidah Austin,** daughter of Anwar Muhammad, Sr.; granddaughter of Thelma Smith and Edwood Austin.

58. **Elijah Muhammad,** son of Anwar Muhammad, Sr.; grandson of Thelma Smith and Edwood Austin.

59. **Alburt Sweetwine,** son of Yvonne Rená Sweetwine; grandson of Thelma Smith and Edwood Austin.

60. **Corey Lamont Brown** (b. 1975)**,** son of Phyllis Noel Brown and Clifford Tomlin; grandson of Jean Smith and Robert Noel, Sr.; resides in Colorado; children: Nateisa Richardson

(b. 1995), Mercedes Brown (b. 1999), LaDerrick Brown (b. 2001), Tyrik Green (b. 1995), Armani Brown (b. 2002), Jada Brown (b. 2007), Destiny Brown (b. 2009), and Aubreana Brown (b. 2010).

61. **Derrick Brown** (1977–1998), son of Phyllis Noel Brown and Clifford Tomlin; grandson of Jean Smith and Robert Noel, Sr.; child: Malik Brown.

62. **Mario Brown** (b. 1982), m. Ashely Brown; resides in Colorado; children: Maria ("Raye") Brown (b. 2006) and Devonte Brown (b. 2007).

63. **Tramaine Noel,** son of Robert Noel, Jr.; grandson of Jean Smith and Robert Noel, Sr.

64. **Troy Noel,** son of Robert Noel, Jr.; grandson of Jean Smith and Robert Noel, Sr.

65. **Carroll Noel, Jr.,** son of Carroll Noel, Sr.; grandson of Jean Smith and Robert Noel, Sr.

66. **Sherrell Noel,** daughter of Carroll Noel, Sr.; granddaughter of Jean and Robert Noel, Sr.

67. **Brittany Nunev,** daughter of Carroll Noel, Sr.; granddaughter of Jean Smith and Robert Noel, Sr.

68. **Dwayne Noel** (b. 1977), son of Carolyn Noel Crockett; grandson of Jean Smith and Robert Noel, Sr.

69. **Shantoria Noel** (b. 1978), daughter of Carolyn Noel Crockett; granddaughter of Jean Smith and Robert Noel, Sr.

70. **Tiana Noel** (b. 1980), daughter of Carolyn Noel Crockett; granddaughter of Jean Smith and Robert Noel, Sr.

71. **William Lionell Ball** (b. 1984), son of Carolyn Noel Crockett; grandson of Jean Smith and Robert Noel, Sr.

72. **Erin Claiborne,** daughter of Rose Noel Claiborne; granddaughter of Jean Smith and Robert Noel, Sr.

73. **Nicole Claiborne,** daughter of Rose Noel Claiborne; granddaughter of Jean Smith and Robert Noel, Sr.

74. **Kareem Noel,** son of Ninitia Noel; grandson of Jean Smith and Robert Noel, Sr.

75. **Jean Noel,** daughter of Ninitia Noel; granddaughter of Jean Smith and Robert Noel, Sr.

76. **Danielle Clayton** (b. 1988), daughter of Jarlene Varleda and Gary Clayton; granddaughter of Carroll and Walice Edwards Smith; resides in Glen Allen, VA.

77. **Gary Smith, Jr.,** son of Gary Smith, Sr.; grandson of Lewis and Bernice Holden Smith.

78. **Dwayne Smith,** son of Lewis Smith, Jr.; grandson of Lewis and Bernice Holden Smith.

79. **Quidar Smith,** son of Fannie Smith McMillan; grandson of Fannie Mae Smith and Ivory Kennedy.

80. **Lakecia Smith Harris McMillan** (b. 1985), daughter of Fannie Smith McMillan; granddaughter of Fannie Mae Smith and Ivory Kennedy.

81. **Tiffany Smith** (b. 1988), daughter of Fannie Smith McMillan; granddaughter of Fannie Mae Smith and Ivory Kennedy; children: Tyvon Smith and Chris Smith.

82. **Bobbie Smith Mabry** (b. 1990), daughter of Fannie Smith McMillan; granddaughter of Fannie Mae Smith and Ivory Kennedy; child: Quincy Mabry.

83. **Bernard Smith Johnson** (b. 1992), son of Fannie Smith McMillan; grandson of Fannie Mae Smith and Ivory Kennedy.

84. **Danielle McMillan** (b. 1994), daughter of Fannie Smith McMillan; granddaughter of Fannie Mae Smith and Ivory Kennedy.

85. **Destiny McMillan** (b.1997), daughter of Fannie Smith McMillan; granddaughter of Fannie Mae Smith and Ivory Kennedy.

86. **Jeramiah McMillan** (b. 2006), son of Fannie Smith McMillan; grandson of Fannie Mae Smith and Ivory Kennedy.

87. **Davione Smith** (b. 1987), son of Murvin Lionel and Adriane Smith; grandson of Fannie Mae Smith and Ivory Kennedy.

88. **Anthony Smith** (b. 1994), son of Murvin Lionel and Adriane Smith; grandson of Fannie Mae Smith and Ivory Kennedy.

89. **Christopher Smith** (b. 1991), son of Murvin Lionel and Adriane Smith; grandson of Fannie Mae Smith and Ivory Kennedy.

90. **Justin Smith** (b. 1990), son of Murvin Lionel and Adriane Smith; grandson of Fannie Mae Smith and Ivory Kennedy.

91. **Adriane Smith** (b. 1988), daughter of Murvin Lionel and Adriane Smith; granddaughter of Fannie Mae Smith and Ivory Kennedy.

92. **Melissa Douglas** (b. 1993), stepdaughter of Lionel Smith; daughter of Adriane Douglas Smith.

Great-Grandchildren of Grace Walters and Emerson Norris, resided in Bogey Neck Community, Remo Post Office, Wicomico Church district, Northumberland County, VA:

1. **Alivia Grace Ball Thomas** (b. 2004), daughter of Kim M. Ball and Partner Lori A. Thomas; granddaughter of Helen Norris and Donald D. Ball; resides in Silver Spring, MD.

2. **Stephanie Jackson Pace, PhD** (1969–2010), daughter of Jacqueline Davenport; granddaughter of Violet Norris and John Davenport; child: Kendall Pace (b. 1996).

3. **Rashad Farrow** (b. 1986), son of Shirley Davenport Farrow; grandson of Violet Norris and John Davenport; resides in Washington, DC.

4. **Camille Farrow** (b. 1986), daughter of Shirley Davenport Farrow; granddaughter of Violet Norris and John Davenport; resides in Washington, DC.

5. **Chantal Farrow** (1981–1993), daughter of Shirley and Tyrone Gary Farrow; granddaughter of Violet Norris and John Davenport.

6. **Jasmine Smith** (b. 1989), daughter of Jeffrey Norris; granddaughter of Otis B. and Mary Shipley Norris; US Marine Corp.; resides in Beaufort, SC; child: Payton Smith (b. 2012).

7. **Terrace N. Smith** (b. 1990), son of Jeffrey Norris; grandson of Otis B. and Mary Shipley Norris; US Marine Corp.; resides in Baltimore, MD.

8. **Jordan Norris** (b. 1988), daughter of Kirk Norris; granddaughter of Douglas and Margaret Keeve Norris; resides in Atlanta, GA.

9. **Jillian Norris** (b. 1990), daughter of Kirk Norris; granddaughter of Douglas and Margaret Keeve Norris; resides in Atlanta, GA.

10. **Avery "AJ" Norris, Jr.** (b. 1989); son of Avery Norris, Sr.; grandson of Douglas and Margaret Keeve Norris; resides in Baltimore, MD.

11. **Ava Norris** (b. 1991); daughter of Avery Norris, Sr.; granddaughter of Douglas and Margaret Keeve Norris; resides in Baltimore, MD.

12. **Tyler Walker** (b. 1993); daughter of Yvonne Norris Walker; granddaughter of Douglas and Margaret Keeve Norris; resides in Baltimore, MD.

13. **Travis Walker** (b. 1996); son of Yvonne Norris Walker; grandson of Douglas and Margaret Keeve Norris; resides in Baltimore, MD.

14. **Paris Norris** (b. 1999), daughter of Carlos and Jennifer Norris; granddaughter of Stanley and Phyllis Keeve Norris; resides in Dale City, VA.

15. **Ashley Mizelle** (b. 1989), daughter of Carlos and Jennifer Norris; granddaughter of Stanley and Phyllis Keeve Norris; resides in Richmond, VA; child: Alex Harris (b. 2012).

16. **Brian O. Norris, Jr.** (b. 2011), son of Brian and Kenya Norris; grandson of Stanley and Phyllis Keeve Norris; resides in Washington, DC.

17. **Jason Lamont Jones** (b. 1977), son of Yvette Norris Jones Harding; grandson of Emerson, Jr., and Grace Conley Norris; child: Jamyra Jones (b. 2006).

18. **Addrain Terrell Jones** (b. 1980), son of Yvette Norris Jones Harding; grandson of Emerson, Jr., and Grace Conley Norris; children: Jamier Jones (b. 2006) and Jordan Jones (b. 2000).

19. **Emerson Norris IV** (b. 1974), son of Emerson Norris III; resides in Heathsville, VA; children: Terrick Norris (b. 2005), Isiah Norris (b. 2003), and Carlos Norris (b. 2001).

20. **Michael Norris** (b. 1976) son of Emerson Norris III; resides in Heathsville, VA; children: Taylor Norris (b. 1997) and Christopher Ball (b. 1995).

21. **Corric Crawford** (b. 1989), son of Shanelle Thomas Goss; grandson of Joyce Norris Wilson; resides in Detroit, MI; child: Kennidi Crawford (b. 2010).

22. **Clifton James Crawford** (b. 1990), son of Shanelle Thomas Goss; grandson of Joyce Norris Wilson; resides in Detroit, MI.

23. **Kamerin Goss** (b. 1999), son of Shanelle Thomas Goss; grandson of Joyce Norris Wilson.

24. **Justin Goss** (b. 2000), son of Shanelle Thomas Goss; grandson of Joyce Norris Wilson; resides in Greenbelt, MD.

25. **Anthony Thomas** (b. 1986), son of Alan W. and Felicia Knight Thomas; grandson of Joyce Norris Wilson; resides in Upper Marlboro, MD.

26. **Kevin Thomas** (b. 1988), son of Alan W. and Felicia Knight Thomas; grandson of Joyce Norris Wilson; resides in Upper Marlboro, MD; children: Kristian Thomas (b. 2009) and Kassidy Thomas (b. 2011).

27. **Keith Thomas** (b. 1988), son of Alan W. and Felicia Knight Thomas; grandson of Joyce Norris Wilson; resides in Upper Marlboro, MD.

28. **Alan Wesley Thomas** (b. 1991), son of Alan W. and Felicia Knight Thomas; grandson of Joyce Norris Wilson; resides in Upper Marlboro, MD.

29. **Allison Thomas** (b. 1992), daughter of Alan W. and Felicia Knight Thomas; granddaughter of Joyce Norris Wilson; resides in Upper Marlboro, MD; child: Jordan Thomas (b. 2012).

30. **Adrienne Cottrell Yongye** (b. 1979), daughter of Angelo and Janice Cottrell; granddaughter of Gladys Norris and the late Samuel Cottrell; child: Eliel Yongye (b. 2011).

31. **Angela Cottrell** (b. 1981), daughter of Angelo and Janice Cottrell; granddaughter of Gladys Norris and the late Samuel Cottrell; resides in Baltimore, MD.

32. **Nathan Cottrell** (1989–1999); son of Dale and Rosalind Cottrell; grandson of Gladys Norris and the late Samuel Cottrell; lived in Baltimore, MD.

33. **Ryan Cottrell** (b. 1992), son of Dale and Rosalind Cottrell; grandson of Gladys Norris and the late Samuel Cottrell; resides in Richmond, VA.

34. **Arnissa Cottrell** (b. 1993), daughter of Dale and Rosalind Cottrell; granddaughter of Gladys Norris and the late Samuel Cottrell; resides in Richmond, VA.

35. **Jarvis Crocker** (b. 1981), son of JoAnne Norris Crocker; grandson of Randolph Norris; resides in Washington, DC; child: Laila Sorinmade (b. 2007).

36. **Javon Crocker** (b. 1982), son of JoAnne Norris Crocker; grandson of Randolph Norris; resides in Washington, DC; child: Giavanni Crocker (b. 2002).

37. **Teresa Brown,** daughter of Carmilla Brown; granddaughter of Eva Taylor and Benjamin Brown; US Air Force; resides in Upper Marlboro, MD.

38. **Sean Brown,** son of Ava Brown; grandson of Eva Taylor and Benjamin Brown; resides in Atlanta, GA.

39. **Lynn Murphy Mikos,** daughter of Bernadette Brown Murphy; granddaughter of Eva Taylor and Benjamin Brown; resides in Silver Spring, MD.

40. **JaMichael Gaskins** (b. 1989), son of Eric Duane Harcum; grandson of Randolph Norris; resides in Richmond, VA; child: Markari Carter (b. 2011).

41. **Donta' Davis** (b. 1990), son of Eric Duane Harcum; grandson of Randolph Norris; resides in Raleigh, NC.
42. **Teia Walters** (b. 1979), daughter of Eric Duane Harcum; granddaughter of Randolph Norris; resides in Lancaster County, VA.

Generation 7 — Great-Great-Great-Great-Grandchildren of William W. and Addie Walters; Great-Great-Great-Grandchildren of John W. and Emma J. Walters of Bogey Neck, Wicomico, Northumberland County, VA[121]

Great-Great-Grandchildren of Emily Walters and Travis Smith, Sr., resided in Harvest Neck Community, Remo Post Office, Wicomico Church district:

1. **Christopher Rodgers,** son of Vaneta Smith and Wayne Rodgers; grandson of William D. Smith; great-grandson of Travis, Jr., and Inez Roane Smith.
2. **Joshua Rodgers,** son of Vaneta Smith and Wayne Rodgers; grandson of William D. Smith; great-grandson of Travis, Jr., and Inez Roane Smith.
3. **Jada Rodgers,** daughter of Vaneta Smith and Wayne Rodgers; granddaughter of William D. Smith; great-granddaughter of Travis, Jr., and Inez Roane Smith.
4. **Tyreek Jason Smith**, son of William Tye Smith; grandson of William D. Smith; great-grandson of Travis, Jr., and Inez Roane Smith.

---

121 Oral history.

5. **Nickelous Smith,** son of William Tye Smith; grandson of William D. Smith; great-grandson of Travis, Jr., and Inez Roane Smith.

6. **James Smith,** son of Darrell Smith; grandson of James E. Smith, Jr.; great-grandson of Travis and Inez Roane Smith.

7. **Dexter Smith,** son of Bridgette Smith; grandson of James E. Smith; great-grandson of Travis, Jr., and Inez Roane Smith.

8. **Shantori Smith,** daughter of Bridgette Smith; granddaughter of James E. Smith; great-granddaughter of Travis, Jr., and Inez Roane Smith.

9. **Dasandra Smith**, daughter of Bridgette Smith; granddaughter of James E. Smith; great-granddaughter of Travis, Jr., and Inez Roane Smith.

10. **Kia Smith**, daughter of Bridgette Smith; granddaughter of James E. Smith.

11. **Travis Smith,** son of Daria Smith; grandson of James E. Smith; great-grandson of Travis, Jr., and Inez Roane Smith.

12. **(Baby boy),** son of William E.Holloman; grandson of James E. Smith; great-grandson of Travis, Jr., and Inez Roane Smith.

13. **Joyena,** daughter of Genrva; great-granddaughter of Travis, Jr., and Inez Smith.

14. **Basil December Coleman** (b. 2011), daughter of Branch Delano Coleman III; granddaughter of Ethel Smith and Branch Delano Coleman Jr.; great-granddaughter of Travis, Jr., and Inez Roane Smith.

15. **William Anthony Short** (b. 1991), son of William Short, Jr.; grandson of Jacqueline Bromley and William Short, Sr; great-

grandson of Mildred Smith and James Orsie Bromley; resides in Irvington, NJ.

16. **Chantel Short** (b. 1997), daughter of William Short, Jr.; granddaughter of Jacqueline Bromley and William Short, Sr; great-granddaughter of Mildred Smith and James Orsie Bromley; resides in Irvington, NJ.

17. **Xavier Short** (b. 2002), son of William Short, Jr.; grandson of Jacqueline Bromley and William Short, Sr.; great-grandson of Mildred Smith and James Orsie Bromley; resides in Irvington, NJ.

18. **Javonna Short** (b. 1994), daughter of Jennora Short, granddaughter of Jacqueline Bromley and William Short, Sr.; great-granddaughter of Mildred Smith and James Orsie Bromley; resides in Irvington, NJ; child: Armani Cooper (b. 2013).

19. **Javante Short Dorisme** (b. 1999), son of Jennora Short, grandson of Jacqueline Bromley and William Short, Sr.; great-grandson of Mildred Smith and James Orsie Bromley; resides in Irvington, NJ.

20. **Joeqel Dorisme** (b. 2000), son of Jennora Short, grandson of Jacqueline Bromley and William Short, Sr.; great-grandson of Mildred Smith and James Orsie Bromley; resides in Irvington, NJ.

21. **Jahqie Dorisme** (b. 2004), son of Jennora Short, grandson of Jacqueline Bromley and William Short, Sr.; great-grandson of Mildred Smith and James Orsie Bromley; resides in Irvington, NJ.

22. **Michael Colclough, Jr.,** son of Michael and Sonya Colclough Sr.; grandson of Doris and Herbert Colclough; great-grandson of Emma Smith and Joseph Jones.

23. **Sasha Colclough,** daughter of Michael and Sonya Colclough Sr.; granddaughter of Doris and Herbert Colclough; great-granddaughter of Emma Smith and Joseph Jones.

24. **Diaundra Jones,** child of Derrick and Christy Jones; grandchild of Morris and Margaret Jones; great-grandchild of Emma Smith and Joseph Jones.

25. **Jaden Jones,** daughter of Derrick and Christy Jones; granddaughter of Morris and Margaret Jones; great-granddaughter of Emma Smith and Joseph Jones.

26. **Marshall Forney,** son of Marshall and Rene Forney; grandson of Rene and Herbert Forney; great-grandson of Emma Smith and Joseph Jones.

27. **Kierstin Forney,** daughter of Marshall and Rene Forney; granddaughter of Rene and Herbert Forney; great-granddaughter of Emma Smith and Joseph Jones.

28. **Jasmine Jones** (b. 1997), daughter of Edward V. Jones, Jr.; granddaughter of Edward V. Jones, Sr.; great-granddaughter of Emma Smith and Joseph Jones.

29. **Amber Jones,** daughter of Edward V. Jones, Jr.; granddaughter of Edward V. Jones, Sr.; great-granddaughter of Emma Smith and Joseph Jones.

30. **Britney Jones** (b. 2000), daughter of Edward V.. Jones, Jr.; granddaughter of Edward V. Jones, Sr.; great granddaughter of Emma Smith and Joseph Jones.

31. **Nyema Jones,** daughter of Edward V. Jones; granddaughter of Edward V. Jones, Sr.; great-granddaughter of Emma Smith and Joseph Jones.

32. **Savana Sydnor,** daughter of Danny Sydnor; granddaughter of Debra Jones Synder; great-granddaughter of Emma Smith and Joseph Jones.

33. **Pehro Spencer,** son of Mervin Spencer; grandson of Grace Jones and Andrew Spencer; great-grandson of Emma Smith and Joseph Jones.

34. **Toreh Jones,** child of Mershom Spencer; grandchild of Grace Jones and Andrew Spencer; great-grandchild of Emma Smith and Joseph Jones.

35. **Quincy Mabry,** son of Bobbie Smith and Quincy Mabry; grandson of Fannie McMillian; great-grandson of Fannie May Smith and Ivory Kennedy.

36. **Nasir Smith**, son of Davione Smith; grandson of Fannie McMillian; great-grandson of Fannie Mae Smith and Ivory Kennedy.

37. **Chyla Smith,** child of Davione Smith; grandchild of Fannie McMillian; great-grandchild of Fannie Mae Smith and Ivory Kennedy.

38. **Chayanne Smith,** child of Davionne Smith, grandchild of Fannie McMillian; great-grandchild of Fannie Mae Smith and Ivory Kennedy.

39. **Tyyon Smith**, son of Tiffany Smith, grandson of Fannie McMillian, great-grandson of Fannie Mae Smith and Ivory Kennedy.

40. **Christopher Smith,** son of Tiffany Smith, grandson of Fannie McMillian, great-grandson of Fannie Mae Smith and Ivory Kennedy.

41. **Jaysiyah Murphy,** child of Justin Smith; grandchild of Lionell Smith; great-grandchild of Fannie Mae Smith and Ivory Kennedy.

42. **Josiah Smith**, child of Justin Smith; grandchild of Lionell Smith; great grandchild of Fannie Mae Smith and Ivory Kennedy.

Great-Great-Grandchildren of Grace Walters and Emerson Norris, resided in Bogey Neck Community, Remo Post Office, Wicomico Church district, Northumberland County, VA:

1. **Kendall Pace** (b. 1996), son of the late Stephanie Jackson Pace, PhD; grandson of Jacqueline Davenport; great-grandson of Violet Norris and John Davenport; high school class of 2013; offered full scholarship to attend Columbia University (NY); resides in Suitland, MD.

2. **Payton Norris** (b. 2012), daughter of Jasmine Smith; granddaughter of Jeffrey Norris; great-granddaughter of Otis B. and Mary Shipley Norris.

3. **Taylor Norris** (b. 1997), daughter of Michael Norris; granddaughter of Emerson Norris III; great-granddaughter of Emerson, Jr., and Grace Conley Norris.

4. **Christopher Ball** (b. 1995), son of Michael Norris; grandson of Emerson Norris III; great-grandson of Emerson, Jr., and Grace Conley Norris.

5. **Giavonni Crocker** (b. 2002), daughter of Javon Crocker; granddaughter of JoAnne Crocker; great-granddaughter of Randolph Norris.

6. **Laila Sorinmade** (b. 2007), daughter of Jarvis Crocker; granddaughter of JoAnne Crocker; great-granddaughter of Randolph Norris.

7. **Kennidi Crawford** (b. 2010), daughter of Corric Crawford; granddaughter of Shanelle Thomas Goss; great granddaughter of Joyce Norris Wilson.

8. **Kristian Thomas** (b. 2009), son of Kevin Thomas; grandson of Alan W. Thomas, Jr,; great-grandson of Joyce Norris Wilson.

9. **Kassidy Thomas** (b. 2011), daughter of Kevin Thomas; granddaughter of Alan W. Thomas, Jr; great-granddaughter of Joyce Norris Wilson.

10. **Jordan Thomas** (b. 2012), son of Alison Thomas; grandson of Alan W. Thomas, Jr.; great-grandson of Joyce Norris Wilson.

11. **Alex Harris** (b. 2012), son of Ashley Mizell; grandson of Carlos Norris; great-grandson of Stanley and Phyllis Norris.

12. **Eliel Yongye** (b. 2011), son of Adrienne Cottrell Yongye; grandson of Angelo Cottrell; great-grandson of Gladys Norris and the late Samuel Cottrell.

13. **Markari Carter** (b. 2011), son of Michael Gaskins; grandson of Erick "Ricky" Duane Harcum; great-grandson of Randolph Norris.

14. **Jamyra Jones** (b. 2006), son of Jason Lamont Jones; grandson of Yvette Norris Jones Harding; great-grandson of Emerson, Jr., and Grace Conley Norris.

15. **Jamier Jones** (b. 2002), son of Addrain Jones; grandson of Yvette Norris Jones Harding; great-grandson of Emerson, Jr., and Grace Conley Norris.

16. **Jordan Jones** (b. 2003), daughter of Addrain Jones; granddaughter of Yvette Norris Jones Harding; great granddaughter of Emerson, Jr., and Grace Conley Norris.

17. **Terick Norris** (b. 2005), son of Emerson Norris IV; grandson of Emerson, III; great-grandson of Emerson Norris Jr., and Grace Conley Norris.

18. **Isiah Norris** (b. 2003), son of Emerson Norris IV; grandson of Emerson, III; great-grandson of Emerson Norris, Jr., and Grace Conley Norris.

19. **Carlos Norris** (b. 2001), son of Emerson Norris IV; grandson of Emerson, III; great-grandson of Emerson Norris, Jr., and Grace Conley Norris.

Generation 8 — Great - Great-Great-Great-Great-Grandchildren of William W. and Addie Walters; Great-Great-Great-Great-Grandchildren of John W. and Emma J. Walters of Bogey Neck, Wicomico, Northumberland County, VA[122]

Great-Great-Great-Grandchildren of Emily Walters and Travis Smith, Sr., resided in Harvest Neck Community, Remo Post Office, Wicomico Church district:

1. **Amani Nicole Cooper** (b. 2013), daughter of Javonna Short; granddaughter of Jannora Short; great-granddaughter of Jacqueline Bromley and William Short, Sr.; great-great-granddaughter of Mildred Smith and James Orsie Bromley; resides in Irvington, NJ.

BIOGRAPHICAL SKETCH — Descendants of William and Addie Walters

(John and Emma Johnson Walters)

Helen Roberta Norris Ball (b. 1939), the seventh child of Emerson and Grace Norris; named by cousin Raleigh Jones and became the favorite of his daughter, cousin Julia Ann Jones Jackson; received pennies in some type of a jar from each of cousin Julia's visits from Philadelphia; of course, pennies were lost while skipping down the path home; like most of the sisters and brothers, began education in the Mila School, a one-room school on Bogey Neck Road, under the tutelage of Mrs. Lillian P. Sebree; upon the closing of the school, all students were transferred to the Anna T. Jeanes School, which included grades one

---

122 Oral history.

through seven; upon graduation from the seventh grade, entered Julius Rosenwald High School (1952), the year Queen Elizabeth became the queen of England, and the family was able to see this historic event unfold on its first television set; the freshman class of 1952 was the first high school class to graduate from the twelfth grade; prior to that, high school classes ended at the eleventh grade; upon graduating in 1957 with no means of going to college, packed graduation gift luggage set and moved to Baltimore, MD, to live with her oldest sister, Gladys Norris Cottrell; married Donald D. Ball (1958), and relocated to Washington, DC, (1959) for better employment opportunities; enrolled and graduated from the Atlanta Business College; following in parents' footsteps, became an active member in the Saint Mary's Baptist Church; employed for thirty-five years in the United States Postal Service and the United States National Central Bureau-INTERPOL; both positions afforded the freedom to enjoy travel throughout the United States and abroad; two adult daughters: Lori Ball Fenner and Kim Ball; one lovely granddaughter, Alivia Grace. (*Source: Helen Norris Ball.*)

Doris Jones Colclough, daughter of Emma Smith and Joseph Jones; granddaughter of Emily Walters and Travis Smith; great-granddaughter of John and Emma Johnson Walters; great-great-granddaughter of William W. and Ann V. Walters; a blessed child of God from humble beginnings, coming from the Northern Neck of Virginia; along with late husband, Herbert Colclough, Jr., so blessed and grateful to have raised two wonderful children: Michael Colclough, Sr., and Monica Colclough Roebuck; both children are still working as productive citizens in the federal and state governments in investigations and education respectively; retired federal auditor; currently, family serving the Lord at The First Baptist Church of Glenarden, MD, along with daughter-in-law Sonya, and two grandchildren: seven-year-old Michael, Jr., and six-year-old Sasha. (*Source: Doris Jones Colclough.*)

Gladys Norris Cottrell (b.1930), granddaughter of John and Emma Walters; daughter of Grace Walters and Emerson Norris; wife of the late Samuel Cottrell (1926–1982); 1949 graduate of Julius Rosenwald High School; member of Perkins Square Baptist Church in Baltimore, MD, for fifty years, serving with nurses' ministry and seniors' ministry; retired from State of Maryland Department of Health Services; helped organize high school forty- and fifty-year class reunions; worked with community association for several years; enjoys traveling in United States and abroad; highlight of travel was a cruise on the Queen Mary 2; very proud of granddaughter Adrienne and her husband—both PhD graduates of University of Georgia in biology and chemistry, respectively; Adrienne is currently teaching on the college level in Florida. (*Source: Gladys Norris Cottrell.*)

Violet Norris Davenport (b. 1933), born in Bogey Neck, Wicomico Church, VA; the third child of Grace and Emerson Norris, Sr.; named by cousin Julia Jones Jackson, who also gave older sister Gladys the nickname of Buttercup; attended the old and new Mila schools, Anna T. Jeanes Elementary School and Julius Rosenwald High School; in 1949 married John Davenport (aka "Goo Goo") of Reedville, VA; two daughters: Jacqueline Davenport ("Jackie") and Shirley Davenport Farrow ("Mootney"); moved to Reedsville, VA, affectionately called "across the river" to live with mother-in-law, Ellen Davenport; move did not deter her from visiting her mom and dad daily in Bogey Neck.

Under the pastoral leadership of Rev. B. L. Robinson at the Mt. Olive Baptist Church, accepted the challenge of community service, i.e., the National Association for the Advancement of Colored People (NAACP); had the honor and pleasure to be in the presence of Dr. Martin L. Luther King, Jr., at an event in Hopewell, VA; shook Dr. King's hand (he signed a program); attended the fortieth anniversary of the 1963 March on Washington with sister Helen; resided in Virginia until Shirley completed elementary school and Jackie graduated from Central High School in Heathsville, VA; relocated to Washington, DC, to seek better employment and to join husband, who worked in Washington, DC, during the week and joined the family on weekends; found employment at Georgetown University, advancing to supervisor in the housekeeping division; opportunity to meet with a number of great basketball players who attended Georgetown during her tenure, including Patrick Ewing; retired from Georgetown University in 1995 after thirty years of service; loves traveling; on one of many trips, visited New York City and toured the famous Coney Island with cousin Reilly Jones, met a long-lost cousin, Otis Blackwell, the famous songwriter who wrote many number one hits for famous singers, including Elvis Presley and Jerry Lee Lewis. Otis penned the following songs: 1) "All Shook Up" and "Don't Be Cruel," sung by Elvis Presley, and 2) "Great Balls Of Fire" and "Breathless," sung by Jerry Lee Lewis; currently enjoys working in her church, Rock Creek Baptist Church of Washington, DC., and home church of Mt. Olive Baptist Church; president of the Washington Helping Hand ministry of Mount Olive Baptist Church and has served in this capacity for over forty years. (*Source: Violet Norris Davenport.*)

Jackie Davenport, born in Northumberland County, VA; daughter of John and Violet Davenport of Washington, DC; resides in Upper Marlboro, MD; owner of Davnor Insurance; proud mother of Stephanie Jackson Pace, PhD, who passed in 2010. Stephanie's son, Kendall Pace, a soon-to-be high school graduate at age sixteen, has been accepted at Columbia University in New York and has received a full scholarship. (*Source: Violet Norris Davenport.*)

Shirley Davenport Farrow, born in Northumberland County, VA; daughter of John and Violet Davenport of Washington, DC; married Tyrone Gary Farrow; parents of twins Rashad and Camille Farrow, each attended historically black colleges and university (HBCUs): North Carolina A&T State University, Greensboro, NC, and Virginia Union University, Richmond, VA (graduation: 2010); oldest daughter Chantal passed in 1993; Shirley employed by the Courts/Registrar of Wills Office, Prince George's County, MD. (*Source: Violet Norris Davenport.*)

Mary Beatrice Taylor Middleton, daughter of Anna Smith Blair; oldest grandchild of Travis and Emily (Walters) Smith and raised by them; lived on a farm on Pepple Hill in Harvest Neck, Remo, VA; had to work on the farm, but there was plenty of playtime; twelve years old when grandfather died; grandmother Emily was the center of the house after grandfather's death and taught the children to have faith and trust in God; grandmother was a Christian woman and made sure the family went to church with her; known as Sissy, grandmother was good to everybody in the neighborhood, was honored at church as "mother of the year" for her community service; although grandmother had many children of her own, it did not stop her from helping others until she died; proud mother of eight children; resides in Reedville, VA. (*Source: Mary Taylor Middleton.*)

Synethia Taylor (b. 1954), great-granddaughter of James Taylor (b. 1889) in Northumberland County, VA, and Essie Sorrell Taylor (b. 1894) in Richmond County, VA; granddaughter of Walter Taylor and Anna Smith of Remo, VA, Wicomico district of Northumberland County, VA.; one of eight children; the oldest and only child of Mary Taylor of Remo, VA, and Handy Coleman of Weems, VA (Lancaster County); raised in Bogey Neck by George Otha (1908–1970) and Eula Jane Smith Wallace (1913–1970); former member of Mt. Olive Baptist Church, Wicomico Church, VA; attended Anna T. Jeanes Elementary School, Central High School, and Northumberland Senior High School; continued education in Charleston, WV; received certification in business administration in 1976 from Charleston Opportunities Industrialization Center, Charleston, WV; retired March 2000 from municipal government, Baltimore City, MD; currently employed in corrections for the State of Maryland; resides in Gwynn Oak, MD; certified cruise specialist with Phoenix Travel; mother of three: Karen M. Taylor of Philadelphia, PA, William "Billy" Powell of Institute, WV, and Tisha Powell of Reedville, VA; grandmother of four: Kenny (17), Jalen (11), Jamel (9), and Trinity (6). (*Source: Synethia Taylor.*)

Emily Beatrice Walters Smith (1904–1963); daughter of John Walters (b. ca. 1873) and Emma Johnson Walters (b. ca. 1871); m. Travis Smith (b. 1920); seventeen children; Travis was a farmer, hunter, and waterman and raised a garden, pigs, chickens, cows, and vegetables to feed the family; in his later years, Travis worked with Mr. Miles as an electrician who installed electricity in many of the houses throughout the Northern Neck; Emily cared for the home, cooked, and sewed for the family; she made cakes, puddings, and pies for the family and friends, especially those who visited on the weekend; family was active in Mt. Olive Baptist Church where Emily was a member of the Church Aid ministry. (*Source: Emma Smith Jones.*)

Joyce Cornelia Norris Thomas Wilson (1942) posing with son Alan; the ninth child of Grace Cornelia Walters and Emerson Norris, Sr., of Bogey Neck; remembers first year walking to and from Mila School with Barbara Jones and Deloris "Giggi" Williams; Mrs. Alma Butler was the only teacher and cook in this one-room school; spent the next six years at Anna T. Jeanes Elementary School; attended first three years of high school at Julius Rosenwald in Reedville, VA; transferred to the new Central High School in Heathsville, VA (1958) and graduated (1960); after spending several years in Philadelphia, PA, relocated to Washington, DC; married James W. Thomas of Cherryville, NC, and they became the proud parents of two children, Alan W. Thomas, Jr. and Shanelle M. Thomas Goss; Alan is a corporal in the Prince Georges County Police Department in Prince Georges, MD, married to Felicia Knight Thomas, and they are parents of four sons and one daughter and grandparents of a boy and girl; Shanelle Thomas Goss recently relocated to Greenbelt, MD, from Detroit,

MI, and is employed by Verizon Wireless, mother of four sons and grandmother of one daughter, in 1981, she married Ernest D. Wilson (1935–1996), son of David and Hilda Wilson, whose family lived in Bogey Neck; resided in Detroit after marriage to Ernest; employed by the Society of the Cincinnati, the oldest patriotic organization that has its headquarters at the Anderson House Library and Museum in Washington, DC; envisions returning home to Bogey Neck and living in the family home built by her parents and passing along the way of life to her grandchildren and great grandchildren; Alan and Shanelle spent a lot of summers with Mom and Dad and always speak of the fond memories and happy times they spent with them. (*Source: Joyce Cordelia Norris Thomas Wilson.*)

Emerson Norris, Jr., (b. 1934) grandson of John Walters, son of Grace Walters and Emerson Norris; attended Mila School in Bogey Neck and completed seventh grade at Anna T. Jeanes School; married to Grace Conley; two children: Emerson Morris III (who drowned at age thirty-five) and Yvette Norris Harding Jones; four grandchildren: Emerson Norris IV, Michael Norris, and Jason and Terrell Jones; employed as a Menhaden fisherman with captain out of Reedville, VA; oystered with father on the Wicomico River; shucked oysters at Booth Oyster House in Glebe Point; member of Mt. Olive Baptist Church in Wicomico Church, VA; resides with wife in Heathsville, VA. (*Source: Emerson Norris.*)

Patricia Mae Norris Walton (b. 1948), twelfth child of Grace and Emerson Norris, Sr.; attended Anna T. Jeanes Elementary and Central High Schools; received religious training from godly parents and Mt.

Olive Baptist Church, Wicomico Church, VA; enjoyed singing in the Junior Choir and Sunday school; inspired by Rev. B. L. Robinson, who exposed teenagers to new experiences and educational outings, including a most memorable outing to Richmond, VA, to see Civil Rights Leader Ralph E. Bunch; moved to Washington, DC, after graduation from high school to continue education and seek employment in 1966; attended Strayer Business School and University of Maryland; entered the federal government workforce in 1968 and retired after thirty-five years of service; as a legal secretary for the Redevelopment Land Agency for ten years, shared in the revitalization for housing in the District of Columbia; transferred to the US Treasury Department and worked as a finance research assistant and staff assistant in 1980; enjoyed working for political appointees and meeting Presidents Jimmy Carter, Ronald Reagan, and William Jefferson Clinton; m. Abraham B. Walton, Jr., in 1973, sharing thirty-three years of marriage; active member of Bible Way Church in Washington, DC; chaired performance arts program for the Youth Department; along with husband, co-produced and hosted "Living in the Word," a religious TV program in Prince Georges County, MD, for eight years, awarded best religious production for six years; Abraham passed away in 2006 after an extended illness; continuing active participation in the Bible Way Church as Sunday school teacher, member of Senior Missionary, member of various committees and executive board; continuing to be active in retirement, volunteering at the Bowie Senior Center as an administrative assistant, traveling with the seniors and assisting in community events; member of the Washington Helping Hand Ministry of Mt. Olive Baptist Church, providing financial assistance to home church; resides in Washington, DC. *(Source: Patricia Mae Norris Walton.)*

Carroll Smith (b. 1938), born in Harvest Neck; son of Travis and Emily Smith; grandson of John and Ann V. Walters; attended Northumberland County Public Schools (Mila Bogey Neck, Anna T. Jeanes, and Julius Rosenwald); acquired skills through work experience; began working for Willie and Emaline Blackwell at age thirteen for three years; at age sixteen, worked at McNeal Edward fish factory; employed by Henry Thorndike for forty-five years; in 1958, m. Walice Edwards, daughter of Rev. H. W. Edwards of Browns Store, VA; one daughter, Jarlene Smith Clayton (1955–2006); has resided in family home with wife of fifty-four years; maintains a small farm, raises hogs, and provides lawn services for community residents; often thought of as the "unsung hero," unselfishly volunteers and reaches out to others in the community and church family.

Mt. Olive Baptist Church

Observing the cemetery in need of grooming, often stopped and cut the grass; asked Deacon Jones what could be done with the condition of the cemetery; Deacon Jones called a meeting of Carroll Smith, David Wilson, Elizabeth Savoy, and Hortense Jones; thus, the cemetery committee was born; Deacon Jones appointed Carroll as the chair, and he has remained in this position with the same committee members since the committee's inception in 1973—except for two years when David Wilson served as chair; initiated the building of a monument at the entrance to the old cemetery with the support of the trustee board and Thorndike, his employer, who designed the monument using old bricks from the old church that was destroyed by fire.

Supportive of wife, formerly a member of Morning Star Baptist Church, when she joined Mt. Olive and was appointed by Deacon Jones to serve as superintendent; assisted her whenever needed to implement various church activities.

In addition to serving as trustee, continues to support many churchwide initiatives, delivers meals to members who are "sick and shut in," and performs minor repairs when needed, saving the church the expense of contracting outside services.

Bogey Neck Community

Frequently visits the elderly and other members in the community; provides lawn services and minor home repairs; plants a garden at his homeplace and shares the vegetables with neighbors in Bogey Neck and surrounding communities. (*Source: Carroll and Walice Smith.*)

Emma Jones of Heathsville recently met President Barack and First Lady Michelle Obama.

Emma Smith Jones (b. 1927), daughter of Travis and Emily Beatrice Walters; one of seventeen children; granddaughter of John and Emma Walters; attended Mila and Anna T. Jeanes Elementary Schools and Julius Rosenwald High School; m. Joseph Jones (1946); had eight children, all high school graduates and some finished college; five went into the military; raised one granddaughter, who is a college graduate; celebrated fiftieth wedding anniversary in 1996; worked at Smith Seafood for thirty-one years; husband Joseph made his living as a waterman and oyster shucker and was a great gardener; the family attended Mt. Olive Baptist Church, Wicomico Church, VA, where Joseph served on the deacon board; active in church deaconess ministry, secretary of Church Aid Society, member of the Mass Choir and missionary society and works with senior citizens; in spare time, enjoys traveling; visited Dr. Martin Luther King's home and church in Atlanta, GA, and Dr. King's memorial in Washington, DC; the highlight of her travels was accompanying granddaughter, Tara Jones, to the White House Annual Gala in December 2012 and speaking with President Barack Obama and First Lady Michelle Obama;[123] attended great-grandson's graduation from the US Navy Prep School (2013); enjoys crafts and church activities; husband Joseph passed away in 2004; resides in family home in Mila Neck. (*Source: Emma Walters Jones, interview.*)

William David Smith, one of four children of Travis, Jr., and Inez Roane Smith (James E. Smith, Ethel N. Smith, and Frank O. Smith); graduate of Brookvale High School, Lancaster County, VA; attended Norfolk State College (two years); worked for the city of Detroit, MI, in transportation; retired and currently residing in Michigan; four children: Darnell Smith, Bridgette Smith, Daria Smith, and William E. Holloman. (*Source: William D. Smith.*)

Fannie Mae Smith Kennedy (b. 1943), born in Wicomico Church district, Northumberland County, VA; one of seventeen children of Emily Walters and Travis Smith; granddaughter of John and Ann V.

---

123 *Rappahannock Record*, "Mrs. Jones attends White House Gala," February 14, 2013.

Walters; m. Ivory Kennedy; resides in NJ; attended Anna T. Jeanes Elementary School, Julius Rosenwald High School, and graduate of Central High School in Northumberland County; employed as a teacher's aide in Newark Public School system; enjoys helping family get to know each other; created a "Family History" wall in her home of grandparents, parents, siblings, children, and grandchildren, which serves as a conversation piece when relatives visit. (*Source: Fannie Mae Smith Kennedy.*)

Jacqueline Bromley Short (b. 1950), daughter of Mildred Smith and James Orsie Bromley of Remo, VA; granddaughter of Emily Walters and Travis Smith; attended Anna Jeanes Elementary School in Wicomico Church, VA; fond memories of Mt. Olive Baptist Church and especially being baptized in the river; formerly married to William Short, Sr.; employed by Verizon for thirty-seven years as a senior analyst; two children: William Short, Jr., employed by United Parcel Service, and daughter, Jennora Short employed by Continental Airlines; five grandchildren and one great-granddaughter; resides in Irvington, NJ. (*Source: Jacqueline Bromley Short.*)

Joan Smith Askins (b. 1963), youngest of five girls born in Baltimore, MD, to Oneil and Mary Helen Blackwell; granddaughter of Emily Walters and Travis Smith of Remo, VA; parents and grandparents born in Northumberland County, VA; one year old when mother died; all five girls placed in two foster homes—Debra, Carolyn, and Gail lived with Edith Bowie; she and Catherine lived with Mable Carmabatch until she died; Catherine and Joan were placed in different homes; father remained involved with all of his girls until his death; saw that they attended family gatherings, special events, and attended their graduations from high school; lost contact with sister Catherine after father's funeral and have been searching for her for almost thirty years; it is believed that she relocated out of state with foster mother's sister; went to live with her aunt Thelma Austin after graduation from high school; married Calvin Askins, Sr., at age twenty-one and has two sons: Calvin Askins and Clifton Oneil Askins; employed as a housekeeper in hotels and a funeral parlor; currently owns a house-cleaning service and wedding florist; "my greatest wish is to see my sister, Catherine Smith, again."

Generation 1: William W. Walters, Sr

Generation 2: Children of William W. Walters

Generation 3—Grandchildren of William and Addie Walters; Children of Washington and Maggie Walters (born in Bogey Neck)

1. **Solomon Walters** (b. 1898); first m. Louise Waddy (b. 1905); resided in Mila Neck; oysterman; children: Beatrice Walters Brown (b. 1920), Herbert Walters (b. 1922), Otha Walters (b. 1926), Harry Walters (b. 1928), Shedrick Walters (b. 1930), and Clara Walters Priester (b. 1931); second m. Gladys Fallin in 1938; waterman, farmer, hunter.

2. **Ernest Walters** (1900–1988), m. Emma Kent (1908–2000); attended Mila Neck school; resided in Bogey Neck with parents prior to moving family to Wicomico Church, VA, on Route 200; worked as a waterman; children: Agnes Walters Cottrell (1928–1998), Steven Walters (1934–1976), and Lillie Walters Kearney (b. 1936).

3. **Lena Walters** (b. 1903); m. Isaac Johnson; resided in Baltimore, MD, until death; worked as a domestic. Child: Hortense Walters Jones (b. 1922).

4. **William Henry Walters** (b. 1905); m. Pricilla Tolson in 1928.

5. **Washington Walters, Jr.** (b. 1907).

6. **Sarah Walters** (b. 1908); first m. Joseph Jones; child: Coolidge Jones.

7. **Not named** (1910–1910).

8. **Luther Walters** (b. 1912); m. Genevieve Yerby of Harvest Neck, Wicomico Church district; children: Frederick Walters (1932–2000), Mattie Walters Humphrey (b. 1933), Steward Walters (b. 1937), Sarah Walters Harcum (b. 1936), Jettie F. Walters (b. 1935), James A. Walters (b. 1942), Melvin L. Walters (b. 1944), Lela Walters (b. 1948), and Larry Walters (b. 1955).

9. **Gertrude Walters** (b. 1917).

Generation 4–Great-Grandchildren of William and Addie Walters; Grandchildren of Washington and Maggie Walters

Children of William Solomon and Louise Waddy Walters, Mila Neck, VA:

1. **Harry Walters,** Sr., m. Mattie Walters; children: Harry Walters, Jr., Alfreda Walters, and Angela Walters Davis.

2. **Otha Walters,** m. Hilda Walters.

3. **Herbert Walters,** m. Odell Walters; children: James Walters, Ruth Walters, Michael Walters, Joan Alfreda Walters, John Walters, Sandra Walters Williams, Debbie Walters, and Teresa Walters.

4. **Alice Beatrice Walters Brown,** m. Samuel Brown, resided in Bogey Neck; child: Sandra Brown.

5. **Shedrick Walters,** m. Annie Bell.

6. **Clara Walters Priester** (b. 1931), first m. H. B. Thomas; second m. Arbon Priester (d. 2002); children: Christopher Priester and Brenda Priester; resides in Ft. Lauderdale, FL. [*See biographical sketch.*]

Children of Ernest and Emma Kent Walters, born in Bogey Neck, lived in Wicomico on Rt. 200:

1. **Agnes Walters Cottrell** (1928–1998), attended Northumberland County, VA, Public Schools, resided in Baltimore, MD; m. Emerson Cottrell (1924–1987); children: Carnell Cottrell (b. 1949), Darlene Cottrell Goggins (b. 1951), and Andrea Cottrell (b. 1967).

2. **Steven Walters** (1934–1976); attended Northumberland County Schools, m. Shirley V. Walters (b. 1924).

3. **Lillie Walters Kearney** (b. 1936); m. Robert Kearney (b. 1929); resides in Philadelphia, PA; retired teacher; child: Sonya Kearney (b. 1967).

Children of Luther and Genevieve Walters, born in Harvest Neck, Remo Post Office:

1. **Frederick Walters, Sr.** (1932–2007); m. Emma Moore Walters (1934–2001); children: Viola L. Rich (b. 1952), Robert W. Walters (b. 1954), Alverta D. Walters Rice (b. 1955), Patricia W. Dorsey (b. 1956), and Frederick Walters, Jr. (b. 1960).

2. **Mattie Walters Humphrey** (b. 1933); m. Chester Humphrey (deceased).

3. **Steward Walters** (b. 1937); m. Darlene Walters; children: Sheila Scott, Stewart Nole, Denise Nole, Urcela Walters, Percill Walters, Daren Walters, Norman Walters, and Beatrice Walters.

4. **Sarah Walters Harcum** (b. 1936); m. Norman Harcum (b. 1938); child: Joanne H. Johnson (b. 1956).

5. **Jettie F. Walters** (b. 1935); m. Larry Smith (deceased); children: Rex Walters (b. 1959), Julius Mayo (b. 1960), Charles Mayo (b. 1961), Anthony Mayo (b. 1963), Jeffery Mayo (1964–1989), William Mayo (b. 1966), and Linda Mayo (b. 1967).

6. **James A. Walters** (b. 1942); m. Betty Walters; children: Cynthia Walters and Cherrie Walters.

7. **Melvin L. Walters, Sr**. (b. 1944); m. Phyllis Walker; children: Christopher Walker, Melvin L. Walters, Jr. (b. 1972), and Allen Walters (b. 1981).

8. **Lela Walters Brown** (b. 1948); m. James Brown; child: Wanda Davis Galloway (b. 1967).

9. **Larry J. Walters** (b. 1955), m. Pamela S. Walters; resides in Kansas; children: Rosalyn M. Taylor, Pamela S. Coleman, and Tamika M. Polk

Generation 5–Great-Great Grandchildren of William and Addie Walters; Great-Grandchildren of Washington and Maggie Walters

Grandchildren of Solomon and Louise Waddy:

1. **Harry Walters, Jr.,** son of Harry and Mattie Walters; m. Alecia Walters; resides in Jacksonville, FL; children: Harry Walters

III, Patrick Walters, Desiree Walters, Brandi Walters, Whitney Walters, and Joshua Walters.

2. **Alfreda Walters.**

3. **Angela Walters Davis**, daughter of Harry and Mattie Walters; m. Butch Davis; child: Leslie Davis.

4. **James Walters**, son of Herbert and Odell Walters; m. Lavern Walters.

5. **Ruth Walters**, daughter of Herbert and Odell Walters; m. Jessie Wiggins; children: Cheryl Wiggins, Sherry Wiggins Fenwick, Shirley Wiggins White, Charmaine Wiggins (d.), Jessie Wiggins, Jr., and Jason Wiggins.

6. **Michael Walters**, son of Herbert and Odell Walters; m. Pamela Noel; resides in Virginia.

7. **Joan Alfreda Walters**, daughter Herbert and Odell Walters; resides in Washington, DC; child: Brandon.

8. **John Walters**, son of Herbert and Odell Walters; resides in Germany.

9. **Sandra Walters Williams**, daughter of Herbert and Odell Walters, m. Edward Williams; resides in Baltimore, MD.

10. **Debbie Walters Howard**, daughter of Herbert and Odell Walters; m. Louis Howard; resides in Virginia; child: Morgan.

11. **Teresa Walters Kenner** (b. 2003).

12. **Brenda Priester Fo** (b. 1966), daughter of Clara Walters and Arbon Priester; reared in Ft. Lauderdale, FL; m. Darran Fo (b. 1966); resides in Ft. Lauderdale, FL; children: Travisa Skinner (b. 1987), Trakiya Skinner (b. 1990), Sydnee Fo (b. 2002), and Darran Fo, Jr. (b. 2003).

13. **Christopher Priester** (b. 1971); son of Clara Walters and Arbon Priester; m. Cormic Priester (b. 1976); resides in Ft. Lauderdale, FL; children: Devaughn Priester (b. 1995) and Dillon Priester (b. 2010).

14. **Sandra Brown,** daughter of Beatrice Walters and Samuel Brown; child: Darcell.

Grandchildren of Ernest and Emma Kent Walters, born in Bogey Neck, lived in Wicomico, on Rt. 200:

1. **Carnell Cottrell** (b. 1949), Child of Agnes Walters and Emerson Cottrell, resides in Baltimore, MD; children: Tomika Dates (b. 1968) and Parin Braswell (b. 1971).

2. **Darlene Cottrell Goggins** (1951–2013), child of Agnes Cottrell and Emerson Cottrell; m. Thomas Goggins.

3. **Andrea Cottrell** (b. 1967), child of Agnes Walters and Emerson Cottrell; child: Danielle Lott (b. 1987).

4. **Sonya Kearney** (b. 1967), child of Lillie Walters and Robert Kearney; child: Zuri Kearney.

Grandchildren of Luther and Genevieve Walters, Harvest Neck, Remo Post Office:

1. **Viola L. Walters Rich** (b. 1952), daughter of Frederick and Emma Moore Walters.

2. **Robert W. Walters** (b. 1954), son of Frederick and Emma Moore Walters.

3. **Alverta D. Walters Rice** (b. 1955), daughter of Frederick and Emma Moore Walters.

4. **Patricia W. Walters Dorsey** (b. 1956), daughter of Frederick and Emma Moore Walters.

5. **Frederick Walters, Jr**. (b. 1960), son of Frederick and Emma Moore Walters.

6. **Sheila Scott**, daughter of Steward and Darlene Walters.

7. **Stewart Nole**, son of Steward and Darlene Walters.

8. **Urcela Walters**, daughter of Steward and Darlene Walters.

9. **Percill Walters**, child of Steward and Darlene Walters.

10. **Daren Walters**, son of Steward and Darlene Walters.

11. **Norman Walters**, son of Steward and Darlene Walters.

12. **Beatrice Walters**, daughter of Steward and Darlene Walters.

13. **Joanne H. Johnson** (b. 1956), daughter of Sarah Walters and Norman Harcum; children: Douglas L. Johnson and Christina M. Johnson (b. 1992).

14. **Rex Walters** (b. 1959), son of Jettie F. and Larry Smith.

15. **Julius Mayo** (1960–2002), son of Jettie F. Smith.

16. **Charles Mayo, Sr.** (b. 1961), son of Jettie F. Smith; children: Latoya Mayo, Charles Mayo, Jr., and Charlene Mayo.

17. **Anthony Mayo** (b. 1963), son of Jettie F. Smith.

18. **Jeffery Mayo** (1964–1989), son of Jettie F. Smith.

19. **William Mayo** (b. 1966), son of Jettie F. Smith; child: Shandon Mayo.

20. **Linda Mayo** (b. 1967) daughter of Jettie F. Smith; child: Tiara Ghee.

21. **Cynthia Walters**, daughter of James and Betty Walters.

22. **Cherrie Walters**, daughter of James and Betty Walters.

23. **Christopher Walker**, son of Melvin L. and Phyllis Walker Walters.

24. **Melvin L. Walters, Jr.** (b. 1972), son of Melvin L. and Phyllis Walker Walters.

25. **Allen Walters** (b. 1981), son of Melvin L. and Phyllis Walker Walters.

26. **Wanda Davis Galloway** (b. 1967), daughter of Lela Walters.

27. **Rosalyn M. Taylor**, daughter of Larry and Pamela S. Walters.

28. **Pamela S. Coleman**, daughter of Larry and Pamela S. Walters.

29. **Tamika M. Polk**, daughter of Larry and Pamela S. Walters.

Generation 6—Great-Great-Great-Grandchildren of William and Addie Walters; Great-Great-Grandchildren of Washington and Maggie Walters, Bogey Neck, Wicomico, Northumberland, VA

Great-Grandchildren of Solomon and Louise Waddy Walters:

1. **Harry Walters III**, son of Harry, Jr., and Alesia Walters; m. Nikki Walters; children: Harry Walters IV, Wyatt Walters, and Colten Walters.

2. **Patrick Walters**, son of Harry, Jr., and Alesia Walters; m. Shardie Walters; children: Arron Walters, Isaiah Walters, and Asia Walters.

3. **Desiree Walters**, daughter of Harry, Jr., and Alesia Walters; child: Roderick.

4. **Brandi Walters**, daughter of Harry, Jr., and Alesia Walters.

5. **Whitney Walters**, daughter of Harry, Jr., and Alesia Walters.

6. **Alfreda Walters**, daughter of Harry, Jr., and Alesia Walters.

7. **Joshua Walters**, son of Harry, Jr., and Alesia Walters.

8. **Tia Walters**, adopted daughter of Harry, Jr., and Alesia Walters; child: Centrell.

9. **Dallas Walters**, adopted son of Harry, Jr., and Alesia Walters.

10. **Perris Walters**, adopted son of Harry, Jr., and Alesia Walters.

11. **Terry Walters**, adopted son of Harry, Jr., and Alesia Walters.

12. **Arrianna Walters**, adopted daughter of Harry, Jr., and Alesia Walters.

13. **Leslie Davis**, daughter of Angela and Lester Davis; granddaughter of Alice Beatrice and Samuel Brown.

14. **Darcell Brown Carter**; daughter of Sandra Brown; children: Marchus and Myeel.

15. **Travisa Skinner** (b. 1987), daughter of Brenda Priester Fo.

16. **Trakiya Skinner** (b. 1990), daughter of Brenda Priester Fo.

17. **Sydnee Fo** (b. 2002), daughter of Brenda Priester and Darran Fo.

18. **Darran Fo, Jr.** (b. 2003), son of Brenda Priester and Darran Fo.

19. **Devaughn Priester** (b. 1995), son of Chris and Cormic Priester.

20. **Dillon Priester** (2010), son of Chris and Cormic Priester.

Great-Grandchildren of Ernest and Emma Kent Walters, Wicomico, VA:

1. **Tomika Dates** (b. 1968); daughter of Carnell Cottrell; grandchild of Agnes Walters Cottrell and Emerson Cottrell; m. Marlon Dates; children: Corliss Dates and Toni Dates.

2. **Parin Braswell** (b. 1971); son of Carnell Cottrell; grandson of Agnes Walters Cottrell and Emerson Cottrell.

3. **Danielle Lott** (b. 1987), daughter of Andrea Cottrell; granddaughter of Agnes Walters Cottrell and Emerson Cottrell; child: Madison Neally.

4. **Zuri Kearney** (b. 2004), son of Sonya Kearney, grandson of Lillie Walters and Robert Kearney.

Great-Grandchildren of Luther and Genevieve Walters, Harvest Neck, Remo Post Office:

1. **Jordan Robert Walters** (b. 1979), grandchild of Frederick., and Emma L. Moore Walters, Sr.

2. **Earl L. Smith, Jr**. (b. 1972), grandchild of Frederick, Sr., and Emma L. Moore Walters.

3. **Tunisha Smith** (b. 1978), grandchild of Frederick, Sr., and Emma L. Moore Walters.

4. **Jonathan M. Rice** (b. 1987), grandchild of Frederick, Sr., and Emma L. Moore Walters.

5. **Nathaniel Rice** (b. 1989), grandchild of Frederick, Sr., and Emma L. Moore Walters.

6. **Towanda G. Stankey** (b. 1977), grandchild of Frederick, Sr., and Emma L. Moore Walters.

7. **Melissa Gordon** (b. 1978), grandchild of Frederick, Sr., and Emma L. Moore Walters.

8. **Jarone D. Gordon** (b. 1985), grandchild of Frederick, Sr., and Emma L. Moore Walters.

9. **Tina Scott**, grandchild of Steward and Darlene Walters.

10. **Traves Scott,** grandchild of Steward and Darlene Walters.

11. **Douglas L. Johnson** (b. 1990), grandchild of Sarah Walters and Norman Harcum.

12. **Christina M. Johnson** (b. 1992), grandchild of Sarah Walters and Norman Harcum.

13. **Latoya Mayo** (b. 1986), grandchild of Jettie F. Walters and Larry Smith; child of Charles Mayo, Sr.

14. **Shandon Mayo** (b. 1986), grandchild of Jettie F. Walters and Larry Smith; child of William Mayo.

15. **Charles Mayo, Jr.** (b. 1988), grandchild of Jettie F. Walters and Larry Smith.

16. **Tiara Ghee** (b. 1989), grandchild of Jettie F. Walters and Larry Smith.

17. **William Mayo** (b. 1990), grandchild of Jettie F. Walters and Larry Smith.

18. **Charlene Mayo** (b. 1991), grandchild of Jettie F. Walters and Larry Smith.

19. **Lyria Henderson** (b. 2010), grandchild of Jettie F. Walters and Larry Smith.

20. **Camden Mayo** (b. 2011), grandchild of Jettie F. Walters and Larry Smith.

21. **Teia,** grandchild of James and Betty Walters.

22. **Damieh**, grandchild of James and Betty Walters.

23. **Latiyatt L. Clower** (b. 1998), grandchild of Melvin L. Walters and Phyllis Walker.

24. **Amber L. Walters** (b. 2002), grandchild of Melvin L. Walters and Phyllis Walker.

25. **Christopher Walters** (b. 2002), grandchild of Melvin L. Walters and Phyllis Walker.

26. **Marlin Walters** (b. 2006), grandchild of Melvin L. Walters and Phyllis Walker.

27. **Mikayla Walters** (b. 1985), grandchild of Melvin L. Walters and Phyllis Walker.

28. **Demetrius Davis** (b. 1985), grandchild of Lela Walters and James Brown.

29. **Desaire Davis** (b. 1987), grandchild of Lela Walters and James Brown.

30. **Nikia Davis** (b. 1990), grandchild of Lela Walters and James Brown.

Note: Names unavailable for the nine grandchildren of Larry and Pamela Walters.

Generation 7—Great-Great-Great-Great-Grandchildren of William and Addie Walters; Great-Great-Great-Grandchildren of Washington and Maggie Walters, Bogey Neck, Wicomico Church, VA

Great-Great-Grandchildren of Solomon and Louise Waddy Walters:

1. **Harry Walters IV**, son of Harry III and Nikki Walters; grandson of Harry and Alesia Walters, Jr.; great grandson of Harry and Mattie Walters.

2. **Wyatt Walters**, son of Harry III and Nikki Walters; grandson of Harry and Alesia Walters, Jr.; great-grandson of Harry and Mattie Walters.

3. **Colten Walters**, son of Harry III and Nikki Walters; grandson of Harry and Alesia Walters, Jr.; great-grandson of Harry and Mattie Walters.

4. **Arron Walters**, son of Patrick and Shardie Walters; grandson of Harry and Alesia Walters, Jr.; great-grandson of Harry and Mattie Walters.

5. **Isaiah Walters**, son of Patrick and Shardie Walters; grandson of Harry and Alesia Walters, Jr.; great-grandson of Harry and Mattie Walters.

6. **Asia Walters**, daughter of Patrick and Shardie Walters; granddaughter of Harry and Alesia Walters, Jr.; great-granddaughter of Harry and Mattie Walters.

7. **Roderick Walters**, son of Desiree Walters; grandson of Harry and Alesia Walters, Jr.; grea-grandson of Harry and Mattie Walters.

8. **Centrell Walters**, child of Tia Walters; grandchild of Harry and Alesia Walters, Jr.; great-grandchild of Harry and Mattie Walters.

9. **Travis Lipscomb**, son of Travisa and Garrett Skinner; grandson of Brenda Fo, great-grandson of Clara Walters Priester.

Great-Great-Grandchildren of Ernest and Emma Kent Walters, Wicomico, VA:

1. **Madison Neally** (b. 2012), child of Danielle Lott; grandchild of Andrea Cottrell; great-grandchild of Agnes Walters Cottrell and Emerson Cottrell.

2. **Carless Dates** (b. 1995), child of Tomika Cottrell and Marlon Dates; grandchild of Carnell Cottrell; great-grandchild of Agnes Walters Cottrell and Emerson Cottrell.

3. **Toni Dates** (b. 2002), child of Tomika Cottrell and Marlon Dates; grandchild of Carnell Cottrell; great-grandchild of Agnes Walters Cottrell and Emerson Cottrell.

Great-Great-Grandchildren of Luther and Genevieve Walters, Harvest Neck, Remo Post Office:

1. **Andres Bujanda** (b. 1992), great-grandchild of Frederick, Sr., and Emma L. Moore Walters.

2. **Andrinna Baker** (b. 1994), great-grandchild of Frederick, Sr., and Emma L. Moore Walters.

3. **Brooklyn Walters** (b. 2009), great-grandchild of Frederick, Sr., and Emma L. Moore Walters.

4. **Ahmad Bea** (b. 1997), great-grandchild of Frederick, Sr., and Emma L. Moore Walters.

5. **Rashad Bea** (b. 2000), great-grandchild of Frederick, Sr., and Emma L. Moore Walters.

6. **Ariyanah Hudnall** (b. 2003), great-grandchild of Frederick, Sr., and Emma L. Moore Walters.

7. **Deanna Hudnall, Jr**. (b. 2004), great-grandchild of Frederick, Sr., and Emma L. Moore Walters.

8. **Javone Gordan, Jr**. (b. 2009), great-grandchild of Frederick, Sr., and Emma L. Moore Walters.

9. **Treyvone Gordan** (b. 2009), great-grandchild of Frederick, Sr., and Emma L. Moore Walters.

10. **Michael Hall, Jr.** (b. 1998), great-grandchild of Frederick, Sr., and Emma L. Moore Walters.

11. **Ja'Monte Thompson** (b. 2003), great-grandchild of Frederick, Sr., and Emma L. Moore Walters.

12. **Navaeh Smith** (b. 2001), great-grandchild of Frederick, Sr., and Emma L. Moore Walters.

13. **Makell Wheeler** (b. 2007), great-grandchild of Lela Walters and James Brown.

14. **Devynn N. Wikians** (b. 2010), great-grandchild of Lela Walters and James Brown.

15. **Morgan M. Williams** (b. 2012), great-grandchild of Lela Walters and James Brown.

16. **Ly'Riq Henderson** (b. 2010).

17. **Camden Mayo** (b. 2011).

Generation 8—Great-Great-Great-Great-Great-Grandchildren of William and Addie Walters; Great-Great-Great-Great-Grandchildren of Washington and Maggie Walters.

<u>Great-Great-Great-Grandchildren of Luther and Genevieve Walters, Harvest Neck, Remo Post Office:</u>

1. **Jacorey Journey** (b. 2011), great-great-grandchild of Frederick, Sr., and Emma L. Moore Walters.

BIOGRAPHICAL SKETCHES OF WILLIAM W. AND EVA WALTERS (WASHINGTON AND MAGGIE WALTERS)

Clara Walters Priester (b. 1931), sixth child of Solomon and Louise Waddy Walters of Mila Neck, Wicomico District of Northumberland County, VA; at age three, her mother passed, and she was reared by siblings; had to learn to cook and do household chores and get ready for school; attended Northumberland County, VA, schools (Mila Neck and Anna T. Jeanes) and graduated from Julius Rosenwald High School in 1950; first teachers were Mrs. Lillian P. Sebree and Mrs. Elizabeth Burton Carter; walked to elementary schools and rode bus to Anna T. Jeanes and Julius Rosenwald, driven by "aunt" Emma Walters and Mrs. Claudine Smith. [Photo of Clara and second husband, Arbon Priester.]

Family were fishermen, gardeners, and hunters; bought very little from the store because the family had a garden for vegetables, chickens, hogs, cows, and wild game for meats; usual grocery list was sugar, flour, rice, and corn meal; cooked on a woodstove, drew water from a well, and used tin tub for a bath, with two people sometimes using the same water and outhouse; in late 1950, got electricity and then came radio, television, and telephone; children shared whooping cough, measles, mumps, and chickenpox and were cured with home remedies; a midwife (Aunt Lou) delivered the babies and kept a string around the baby's navel until it fell off; some medicines were Father John, cod liver oil, white rubbing alcohol, liniment, and a drop of oil on sugar for colds.

Church was a "must" and no questions were asked; baptized in the river because there was no baptismal pool; arriving at Mt. Olive Baptist Church on a summer Sunday morning, the windows would be raised, and the deacons would be having devotions—her grandfather Washington Walters and Deacon Daniel Jones would be singing the old Baptist hymns, such as "At the Cross," "Amazing Grace," or "Precious Lord Take My Hand" and then send up one of their long spine-chilling prayers that would shake the building. Mrs. Sampson, a white neighbor, made a suit for my first Easter speech at church.

Upon graduation from high school in 1950, recommended by teacher Miss Homer Beane to work as a babysitter, cook, and housekeeper for Mr. and Mrs. Mack Sydnor, educators in Arlington, VA, for seventy-five dollars a week; moved to Ocean City, NJ, in 1954 and found employment at California Dress Shop owned by Mrs. Clark, making seventy-five dollars a week from June to October (owner moved to Florida during off season); in the early fifties, married H. B. Thomas, who was in the military; lived with HB's family while continuing to work in the dress shop. HB passed away at a very young age. Mrs. Clark was from Ft. Lauderdale, FL, and invited me to go with her; worked in Ocean City, NJ, for a short time; later moved to Ft. Lauderdale to work for Mrs. Clark and it has been home ever since; can never forget the first trip down south and life thereafter.

Train Trip to Florida: I went to Virginia to tell my family that I was moving permanently to Florida and boarded the train the next day. Of course, my family was sad but wished me well. A few days later, I boarded the train from Baltimore. Wearing my long purple coat with a black velvet collar buttoned to my neck, I began an all-night and day trip to Jacksonville, FL; arriving in Jacksonville, all "colored" people were moved to one coach and served by a waiter. I didn't quite understand at first but soon realized that the dining room was for "white" only. The trip from Jacksonville to Ft. Lauderdale was all day, and it got hotter as we traveled south. Looking out the window, I could see the people with no jackets and sleeves rolled up, and by the time the train arrived in Ft. Lauderdale, it was ninety degrees and off came the long purple coat.

Ft. Lauderdale, FL: As I got off the train, I observed signs all around labeled "white" or "colored"—taxis, bathrooms, water fountains, and restaurants. A "colored" lady weighing about two-hundred-fifty pounds grabbed my luggage and escorted me to Las Olas Boulevard to

Mrs. Clark's shop, where I met the staff—some of whom I knew from Ocean City, MD. I stayed at the shop until closing. Mrs. Clark took me to the "colored" section of town where I would be living. We stopped at Mrs. Sylvia who owned a "colored" taxi service and the first "colored" employment service. Mrs. Clark told Mrs. Sylvia to send me to her shop the next morning, and that she wanted the driver (Rabbit) to transport me by nine o'clock. It was obvious that Rabbit was Mrs. Clark's favorite taxi driver. For several weeks, I stayed with Mrs. Sylvia and was transported to work by Rabbit; later, I moved in with Mrs. Sylvia permanently, which was one street behind the shop.

"The Colored Town." I soon realized that the hot climate was for me, and I was enjoying Florida; as time went on, I became acquainted with people (tourists, chauffeurs, maids, natives, snowbirds, etc.). In the summer, some of the residents ("Northern Snowbirds") moved north to their summer resorts in Atlantic City and Ocean City; I made the move with Mrs. Clark.

As I became more acquainted with the people in the "Colored Town," I learned more of its history—some good and some not so good. I soon found a church to my liking and attended every Sunday—New Mt. Olive Baptist Church. The schools, like everything else, were segregated. The "colored" children had to stay out of school to pick beans for the white farmers; therefore, their school year was shortened. "Colored" folk were not allowed on Las Olas "white beach" and across the railroad track unless going to work. I never had any trouble with anyone because I knew why I was in Florida and my job. The "colored" people could take the ferry across to Dania Beach.

Driving back north. Soon it was spring and time to prepare for the trip back north, which involved packing the merchandise to be shipped to Ocean City, NJ. On my way back to New Jersey, I stopped to see my family for a few days, and we were happy to see each other. I remember my first car was a 1956 Chevy, new right out of the showroom, purchased from T. D. McGinnis in Kilmarnock, VA. I can't say that I was thrilled to drive to Florida during those days when things were so segregated, but I had no trouble. After driving a few years between Florida and Ocean City, MD, on Route 301 north, I knew most of the places for "colored only." If I stopped for gas and there was no bathroom, I moved on until I found a "colored" gas station and hotel. I met a lady from Philadelphia who became my driving partner, and we traveled together. Florida in the winter and New Jersey in the summer became my way of life for fifteen years.

My new life. When Mrs. Clark decided to just keep her business in Florida year round, I decided to make Florida my permanent home and continued to work in her shop. In 1964, I found a home in the "white town," where the "colored" people had started buying, and the "white" people had begun to sell and move out. The lady who sold me the house was also named Clara; soon thereafter, I married my second husband, Aubon Priester, and we had two beautiful children, Chris and Brenda; five grandchildren and a three-year-old great-grandson. My children grew up in a neighborhood that looked out for each other's children, attended church, were active in community activities, including the scouts, went to good public schools, and graduated from college with honors.

I retired in 1992 from American Express; my husband passed in 2002. I enjoy my time with my family and friends; I am a member of a group called "Keenagers" for fifty-five and over; I enjoy traveling, bowling, helping the needy, and just having fun. I am grateful for the opportunity to share a part of my life story.

Christopher Priester (b. 1971), born in Ft. Lauderdale, FL; son of Clara Walters and Arbon Priester; grandson of Solomon and Louise Waddy Walters; great-grandson of William W. and Ava V. Walters; attended Ft. Lauderdale public schools; played football in high school; graduate of Florida A&M University (2001); August 2002, appeared on the *Weakest Link* in California; has two boys; resides in Ft. Lauderdale with the rest of his family; involved in community service activities, including coaching youth leagues.

Brenda Priester Fo (b. 1966), daughter of Clara Walters and Arbon Priester, reared in Ft. Lauderdale, FL; active member of Girl Scouts and twice represented the Florida troop—in New Orleans at age twelve and California at age sixteen; attended Ft. Lauderdale High School, a predominately white school, out of district with special permission from the area superintendent; only black on the cheerleader squad; graduated in the top 10 percent of the class; graduate of Florida Atlanta University (1984); married to Darran Fo, Sr.; children: Travisa Skinner (b. 1987), Trakiya Skinner (b. 1990), Sydnee Fo (b. 2002), and Darran Fo, Jr. (b. 2003); Travisa, a 2009 graduate of Florida A&M University and Trakiya, a 2011 graduate of Florida A&M University; both graduated with a BS in criminal justice.

GENEALOGY OF FREDERICK WARNER, SR. (ca. 1847)

Generation 1: Frederick Warner, Sr.—Introduction[124]

Frederick Warner, Sr. (b. ca. 1847) lived in Wicomico Church, VA, with his wife, Sophronia (b. ca. 1850). They were married in 1865. Their post office was Browns Store in 1870. He worked as a laborer. There were three children in the home in 1870: Annah J. (age 4), George H. (age 2), and John F. (age 6 months). Frederick was one of the founders of Mt. Olive Church in 1873. According to descendants and the 1910 census, Frederick and Sophronia were believed to have lived at the north end of Bogey Neck next to the family cemetery. When the Bogey Neck Road was relocated, the road ran across Frederick's property, putting his house on the west side of Bogey Neck Road and the cemetery on the east side. Children: Anna Warner (b. ca. 1866), Mary Warner, Clara

---

124   Federa Census 1880.

Warner, George H. Warner (b. ca. 1868), John F. Warner (b. ca. 1870), Julian Warner, Alfred Warner, Frederick Warner, Jr. (b. ca. 1873), Sylvester Warner (ca. 1884–1937), Lavinia Warner Dameron (b. ca. 1887), Charles Warner (b. ca. 1889), and Louis J. Warner (b. ca. 1892). Their neighbors were: Robert Wallace (B), James Hudson (W), Thomas Jessen (W), Hiriam Cockrell (B), and Hannah Blackwell.

Generation 2—Son of Frederick and Sophronia Warner,[125] children born in Wicomico district, Northumberland County, VA

1. **Anna Warner** (b. ca. 1866).

2. **Mary Warner**

3. **Clara Warner**.

4. **George H. Warner** (b. ca. 1868).

5. **John F. Warner** (b. ca. 1870).

6. **Julian Warner.**

7. **Alfred Warner.**

8. **Frederick Warner, Jr.** (b. ca. 1873); resided with wife, Martha Warner, in Brooklyn Assembly District 11, Kings, NY; employment: church janitor, laborer in navy yard; living in household—children: Granville Warner (b. 1909), Hellen Warner (b. 1910), Clifford Warner (b. 1918), brother: Louis Warner (b. ca. 1892); nephews: George Warner (b. ca. 1899) and Thomas Norris (b. ca. 1899); boarders: Charles Pinn (b. ca. 1892) and Jones Pinn (b. ca. 1898).

9. **Sylvester Warner** (b. ca. 1884–1937); born in Wicomico district, Northumberland County, VA; m. Cornelia Sebree (b. ca. 1888–1976) of Mila Neck; resided in Bogey Neck community,

---

125   Federal Census 1920, 1930.

Wicomico district; served as superintendent of New Chapel Sunday School, a branch of Mt. Olive Baptist Church; active in several other capacities in church, including member of deacon board; children: Reva E. Warner (b. 1912), John F. Warner (b. 1914), Rozena (Rosie) Warner Knox (1915–2006), Sylvester "Billy" Warner (1916–1998), Robert Warner (b. 1924), William J. Warner (1925–2011), Lloyd A. Warner (1928–2013), and Laura A. Warner Wilson (1928–2012).

10. **Lavinia Warner Dameron** (b. ca. 1887), m. Joseph Cephus Dameron (b. ca. 1881) in 1906 in Philadelphia, PA; resided in Wicomico district, Northumberland County, VA; widowed in 1930; second m. Lombard Coleman Jones of Bogey Neck in 1930 at Howland Chapel; children: Howard Dameron (b. 1909), David Dameron (b. 1911), Maude Dameron (b. 1919), Lillian Dameron (b. 1921), and Griffin Dameron (b. 1923).

11. **Charles Warner** (ca. 1892–1988); resided with brother, Frederick Warner in 1920, Brooklyn, NY; m. Hortense Warner (b. ca. 1892) of Wicomico district, Northumberland County, VA; child: Louis Warner, Jr. (1930–1953).

Generation 3—Grandchildren of Frederick and Sophronia Warner.[126]

Children of Frederick, Jr., and Martha Warner, Brooklyn, NY:

1. **Granville Warner** (b. 1909).
2. **Hellen Warner** (b. 1910).

---

126   Federal Census 1940.

3. **Clifford Warner** (b. 1911).
4. **Lorenzo Warner** (b. 1914).
5. **Charles Warner** (b. 1918).

Children of Sylvester Warner, Sr., and Cornelia Sebree Warner, Bogey Neck, Wicomico district, Northumberland County, VA:

6. **Reva E. Warner Smith** (b. 1912); m. George Allen Smith;children: Christine Warner (1931–1989) and Lucille Warner.
7. **John F. Warner** (b. 1914); m. Bertha; resided in Brooklyn, NY; retired in Bogey Neck community; buried in family cemetery in Bogey Neck. Child: raised niece, Lucille Warner.
8. **Rozena Warner Knox** (1915–2006); m. Booker Knox, Sr. (1913–1940) of Accomack County, VA; resided in Baltimore, MD; spent last years in Bogey Neck in the family home; buried in family cemetery in Bogey Neck; children: James Knox (b. 1936), Booker Knox "Junior" (b. 1938), Gloria Knox Bell (b. 1939), and Odell Knox.
9. **Sylvester "Billy" Warner** (1916–1998); resided in Brooklyn, NY, on Herkimer Street; retired and returned to Bogey Neck with wife, Ruth; served in US Army, World War II; buried in family cemetery in Bogey Neck; children: Sylvester Warner III, Deborah Warner Peace, Cathy Warner, and Sheila Warner.
10. **William J. Warner, Sr.** (1925–2011); m. Julia Taylor (1925–2011) of Remo, VA, and moved to Brooklyn, NY; returned to Virginia and lived with in-laws; moved to Bogey Neck; children:

Julia M. Warner (b. 1948), William J. Warner, Jr. (b. 1954), and Denise "Denia" Warner John-Charles (b. 1955).

11. **Lloyd Warner** (1928–2013); first m. Mary Reeves (1920–1995); resided in New York and retired in Bogey Neck; second m. to Irene Handy of Mila Neck; resided in Bogey Neck at time of death; buried in family cemetery.[*See biographical sketch.*]

12. **Laura Warner Wilson** (1928–2012); m. Henry Wilson; resided in Brooklyn, NY; returned to Bogey and resided in family home until death; buried in family cemetery in Bogey Neck; children: Henry Wilson, Jr., and Jerome Wilson. [*See biographical sketch.*]

Children of Lavania Warner and Joseph Cephus Dameron:

13. **Howard Dameron** (b. 1909); m. Beulah Branch; resided in Windsor, NC.

14. **David Dameron** (1911–1945); m. Edith Spence; served in US Navy; resided in Wicomico Church, VA; died in Columbia, SC, buried in family cemetery in Northumberland County, VA; children: Richard Dameron (b. 1932), Joseph Dameron (b. 1924), Howard Dameron (b. 1937), and Barbara Ann Dameron Davis (b. 1942).

15. **Maude Dameron** (b. 1914).

16. **Otelia Dameron Pope** (1916–1983); m. Rev. Carter N. Pope (1916–1993) of Wicomico Church, VA; resided in Brooklyn, NY.

17. **Louis Dameron** (1917–2004); served in WWII; m. Cheynee Dora Daniel; buried in Enfield, NC; five children: Duane Carlton Dameron, (other names unavailable).

18. **Lillian Dameron** (b. 1912).

19. **Griffin Dameron** (b. 1923).

20. **Sophronia Dameron** (1926–1988); resided in Brooklyn, NY; died in Brooklyn, buried in Rosehill Cemetery, Linden, NJ.

Son of Louis, Sr., and Hortense Warner, Brooklyn, NY:

21. **Louis Warner, Jr.** (1930–1953).

Generation 4—Great-Grandchildren of Frederick and Sophronia Warner[127]

Grandchildren of Sylvester, Sr., and Cornelia Sebree Warner, Bogey Neck community, Wicomico district:

1. **Christine Warner Landon Veney** (1931–1989), daughter of Reva Warner Smith; raised by grandparents; first m. to Fred Landon; second m. to Albert Veney; children: Clifford Landon, Revia Veney, Gary Veney (d. 2009), Albert Veney, Jr., Shirley Veney, and Carolyn Veney.

2. **Lucille Warner**, daughter of Reva E. Warner Smith; child: Leah Reaves.

3. **James Knox** (b. 1936), son of Rozena Warner and Booker Knox, Sr.; born in Baltimore, MD; resides in Baltimore, MD.

4. **Booker Knox** (b. 1938) son of Rozena Warner and Booker Knox, Sr.; born in Baltimore, MD; resided in California until his death.

---

127 Federal Census; oral history.

5. **Gloria Knox** (b. 1939), daughter of Rozena Warner and Booker Knox, Sr.; born in Baltimore, MD; resides in Baltimore, MD.

6. **Odell Knox,** son of Rozena Warner and Booker Knox, Jr.; m. Bernadette Tolson; resides in York, PA; children: Liszette Knox (b. 1963, Denita Knox (b. 1965), and Anthony Odell Knox (b. 1966).

7. **Sylvester Warner III**, son of Sylvester, Jr., and Ruth Warner; born in Brooklyn, NY; resides in Virginia.

8. **Deborah Warner Peace**. daughter of Sylvester, Jr., and Ruth Warner; born and resides in Brooklyn, NY.

9. **Cathy Warner**, daughter of Sylvester, Jr., and Ruth Warner; born in Brooklyn, NY.

10. **Sheila Warner** (deceased), daughter of Sylvester, Jr., and Ruth Warner; born in Brooklyn, NY.

11. **Julia M. Warner** (b. 1948), daughter of William, Sr., and Julia Taylor Warner; born in New York; raised in Bogey Neck; resides in New York.

12. **William J. Warner, Jr**. (b. 1954), son of William, Sr., and Julia Taylor Warner; born in Remo, VA; raised in Bogey Neck; enlisted in US Air Force; m. Shirley Taylor; child: Stephanie Warner Smith; Tameika Gordon (mother, Gladys Taylor of Reedville). [*See biographical sketch.*]

13. **Denise "Denia" Warner John-Charles** (b. 1955), daughter of William, Sr., and Julia Taylor Warner; born and raised in Bogey Neck; remained in Bogey Neck until graduation from high school; resides in New York.

<u>Grandchildren of Lavinia Warner and Joseph Vephus Dameron, Wicomico district, Northumberland County, VA; children of David and Edith Spence Dameron:</u>

14. **Richard Dameron** (b. ca. 1932).
15. **Joseph Dameron** (b. ca. 1934–deceased).
16. **Howard Dameron** (b. 1937–deceased).
17. **Barbara Ann Dameron Davis** (b. 1942), resides in Hampton, VA.

Generation 5—Great-Great-Grandchildren of Frederick and Sophronia Warner, Great-Grandchildren of Sylvester, Sr., and Cornelia Sebree Warner, Bogey Neck[128]

1. **Clifford Landon** (b. 1948), son of Christine and Fred Landon; grandson of Reva Warner Smith; raised by grandparents; children: Dawn Landon Mason and Pamela Landon Sterrett.
2. **Carolyn Veney** (b. 1958), daughter of Christine and Albert Veney; granddaughter of Reva Warner Smith.
3. **Shirley Veney** (b. 1956), daughter of Christine and Albert Veney; granddaughter of Reva Warner Smith.
4. **Albert Veney, Jr**. (b. 1953), son of Christine and Albert Veney; grandson of Reva Warner Smith.
5. **Gary Veney** (1950–2009), son of Christine and Albert Veney; grandson of Reva Warner Smith.
6. **Revia Veney** (b. 1949), daughter of Christine and Albert Veney; granddaughter of Reva Warner Smith.

---

128 Oral history.

7. **Leah Reeves**, daughter of Lucille Warner Smith; granddaughter of Reva Warner Smith.

8. **Liszette Knox** (b. 1963), daughter of Odell and Bernadette Tolson Knox; granddaughter of Rozena and Booker Knox, Sr.; children: Ciarra Walker (b. 1986) and Aszira Knox (b. 2009).

9. **Denita Knox** (b. 1965), daughter of Odell and Bernadette Tolson Knox; granddaughter of Rozena and Booker Knox, Sr.; child: Anthony Knox.

10. **Anthony Knox** (b. 1966), son of Odell and Bernadette Tolson Knox; granddaughter of Rozena and Booker Knox, Sr.

11. **Tameika Gordon** (b. 1975), daughter of William J. Warner, Jr.; granddaughter of William, Sr., and Julia Warner; children: Chris Gordon and Cerron Gordon.

12. **William Antoine Warner**, (b. 1982), son of Denise "Denia" Warner-John Charles; grandson of William, Sr., and Julia Warner; child: Kalina Warner.

13. **Stefanie Denise Warner Smith** (b. 1984), daughter of William J. Warner, Jr., and Shirley Taylor Warner; granddaughter of William, Sr., and Julia Warner.

Generation 6—Great-Great-Great-Grandchildren of Frederick and Sophronia Warner, Great-Great-Grandchildren of Sylvester, Sr., and Cornelia Sebree Warner, Bogey Neck[129]

1. **Dawn Landon Mason** (b. 1967), daughter of Clifford and Portia Courtney Landon; granddaughter of Christine and Fred Landon; great-granddaughter of Reva Knox Smith; m. Damian

---

129 Oral history.

Mason; children: Nehemiah Mason (b. 2006) and Neia Mason (b. 2005).

2. **Pamela Landon Sterrett** (b. 1969), daughter of Clifford and Portia Courtney Landon; granddaughter of Christine and Fred Landon; great-granddaughter of Reva Knox; m. James Sterrett; children: Jaché (b. 1997) and Jaden (b. 2007).

3. **Ciarra Walker,** daughter of Liszette Knox; granddaughter of Odell and Bernadette Tolson Knox; great-granddaughter of Rozena and Booker Knox,, Sr; child: Marquise D. Walker.

4. **Aszira Knox,** daughter of Liszette Knox; granddaughter of Odell and Bernadette Tolson Knox; great-granddaughter of Rozena and Booker Knox, Sr..

5. **Anthony Fuston,** son of Denita Knox; grandson of Odell and Bernadette Tolson Knox; great-grandson of Rozena and Booker Knox, Sr.

6. **Chris Gordon,** son of Tameika Gordon; grandson of William J. Warner, Jr., and Shirley Taylor; great-grandson of William, Sr., and Julia Taylor Warner.

7. **Cerron Gordon,** son of Tameika Gordon; grandson of William J. Warner, Jr., and Shirley Taylor; great-grandson of William, Sr., and Julia Taylor Warner.

8. **Kalina Warner,** daughter of William Antoine and Karen Warner; granddaughter of William J. Warner, Jr., and Shirley Taylor; great-granddaughter of William, Sr. and Julia Taylor Warner.

Generation 7—Great-Great-Great-Great-Grandchildren of Frederick and Sophronia Warner, Great-Great-Great-Grandchildren of Sylvester, Sr., and Cornelia Sebree Warner, Bogey Neck

1. **Nehemiah Mason** (b. 2006); son of Dawn Landon Mason; grandson of Clifford and Courtney Landon; great-grandson of Christine Warner Veney; great-great-grandson of Reva Warner Smith.

2. **Neia Mason** (b. 2005); son of Dawn Landon Mason; grandson of Clifford and Courtney Landon; great-grandson of Christine Warner Veney; great-great-grandson of Reva Warner Smith.

3. **Marquis D. Walker,** son of Ciarra Walker; grandson of Liszette Knox; great-grandson of Odell and Bernadette Tolson; great-great-grandson of Rozena Knox and Booker Knox, Sr.

BIOGRAPHICAL SKETCH—Descendants of Frederick and Sophronia Warner

Laura Alice Warner Wilson (1928–2012), born in Bogey Neck; granddaughter of Frederick and Sophronia Warner; youngest daughter of Sylvester and Cornelia Warner; twin brother, Lloyd Warner; attended Mila and Anna T. Jeanes Elementary School; graduated from Rosenwald High School in 1946; moved to New York after high school and pursued a career in nursing; m. Henry Wilson; employed by the Manhattan State Hospital; returned to Bogey Neck and lived in the family home until death; two sons. (*Source: Obituary.*)

Lloyd Warner (1928–2013), youngest son of Sylvester and Cornelia Warner; of Bogey Neck; twin sister, Laura (Puddin); attended Mila and Anna T. Jeanes Elementary Schools; twelve years old when father passed in 1940; helped Mama with gardening and made the fires in the morning so that house was warm when Mama got up for work; enjoyed playing ball with Coolidge and William Jones and a bunch of other childhood friends; after graduation from high school in 1946, worked at the fish factory for a short period of time; moved to New York and got a job on the waterfront as a longshoreman; sent money home every week to help his mama out; helped twin sister finish nursing program; m. Mary Reeves, a school teacher; lived in Brooklyn, NY; a close friend of Otis Blackwell, who wrote music for Elvis Presley; did well in New York financially; ordained deacon at Capernaum Baptist Church (1986); joined and served as vice president of the male chorus at the New Hope Baptist Church in New York; built home in Bogey Neck on family property, paid for it before retiring after forty years and returning home; became active in Mt. Olive Baptist Church, serving on the deacon board and singing with the men's chorus; organized a church softball team for kids, served as assistant coach, and played against other churches, using the school fields; received a plaque in recognition for work with the softball program.

After Mary's death, m. Irene Handy; enjoyed playing golf until poor eyesight impaired his game; played guitar and sang the old hymns (his favorites: "'Tis the Old Ship of Zion" and "Somewhere Listening"); other pleasures included visiting different churches in the community, teaching Sunday school and vacation Bible school, and being with family and friends (*Source: Lloyd Warner, interview 2012 and obituary, June 1, 2013.*)

William Warner, Jr. (1954), born in New York; son of William, Sr., and Julia Taylor Warner of Wicomico, VA; family moved to Virginia when he was one year old and lived with grandparents in Remo before moving to Bogey Neck; two sisters, Julia and Denia; attended Rehoboth Elementary School for grades one through six, Wicomico Elementary School for grade seven (one of five African American children, along with sister Denia), Northumberland Middle School grades seven and eight, graduate of Northumberland High School, class of 1973; upon graduation from high school, lived with Aunt Rosie in Baltimore for six months. Enlisted in the US Air Force (1974); tour of duty included Bolling Air Force Base in DC (seven years) serving as Presidential Honor Guard. Transferred to Araxos air base, Greece, for a one-year remote tour. Transferred to Zaragosa, Spain, in 1982. While there, served as academic instructor for young airmen, preparing to become commissioned officers and traveled to Turkey, Belgium, Germany, and Italy. Returned to the United States and was stationed at Whiteman Air Force Base in Missouri as first sergeant for Security Police Career Field. A highlight of his career while at Whiteman AFB was being selected as one of two initial first sergeants for the B2 bomber; was promoted to senior master sergeant and transferred to Seymour Johnson AFB in Goldsboro, NC, in 1994. Retired from the Air Force in 1998 and currently employed with the State of North Carolina in the field of corrections as lieutenant, anticipating a promotion to captain.

Married to the former Shirley Taylor of South Carolina, and they have one daughter, Stefanie Warner Smith. William has a daughter, Tameika Gordon (mother, Gladys Taylor of Reedville, VA). [*Source: William Warner, Jr.*]

GENEALOGY OF JAMES WILSON, Jr. (ca. 1816)

Generation 1: James Wilson—Introduction[130]
James Wilson, Jr. (b. ca. 1816), lived in the seventh district, Northumberland County, VA (1850); m. Nancy Wilson (b. ca. 1821); worked as a laborer; children: Mary Wilson (b. ca. 1842), Nancy Wilson (b. ca. 1843), John Wilson (b. ca. 1844), Polly Wilson (b. ca. 1846), and William Wilson (b. ca. 1850)

Generation 2—Children of James and Nancy Wilson
1. **Mary Wilson** (b. ca. 1842).
2. **Nancy Wilson** (b. ca. 1843).
3. **John Wilson** (b. ca. 1844).
4. **William Wilson** (b. ca. 1850); Mulatto; ancestors traced to District 7 of Northumberland County, VA (1850 federal census). Children: Anna Wilson (b. ca. 1877) and William Wilson (b. ca. 1880); farmer.[131]

---

130   Federal Census 1850.
131   Federal Census 1880, 1900, 1910.

Generation 3—Grandchildren of James and Nancy Wilson, Children of William and Clara Wilson[132]

1. **Anna Wilson** (b. ca. 1877).
2. **William "Willie" Thomas Wilson** (ca. 1880–1940); born in Cople, Westmoreland County, VA; m. Julia A. Corbin Wilson of Mila Neck, VA (ca. 1889–1945); purchased thirty-six acres in Bogey Neck and lived there (1912–1940); employed as a cook on a steamer operated by Virginia Fisheries; registered for WWI draft (1918); buried on family property in Bogey Neck; children: Maude Wilson (1909–1979), William Corbin Wilson (1911–1958), Robert Henry Wilson (1914–2001), Frederick Lucius Wilson (1914–1997), David Carroll Wilson (1916–1991), Mary Alice Wilson (b. 1919), and Sarah Wilson (1923–1988).

Generation 4—Great-Grandchildren of James and Nancy Wilson; Grandchildren of William and Clara Wilson; children of William (Willie) Thomas Wilson, born in Bogey Neck, Wicomico, VA[133]

1. **Maude Wilson Norris** (1909–1979).
2. **William Corbin Wilson** (1911–1958).
3. **Robert Henry Wilson** (1914–2001); m. Mazie Beatrice.
4. **Frederick Lucius Wilson** (1914–1997); m. Emma Lee; children: Kantania Wilson and Corbin Wilson.
5. **David Carroll Wilson** (1916–1991); m. first wife, Hilda Bank (1918–1879) of Browns Store, VA, in 1937; resided in Bogey Neck; moved house to Route 200 in Wicomico Church; child:

---

132 Federal Census 1900, 1910, 1920, 1930.
133 Federal Census 1920; oral history.

Ernest D. Wilson (1936–1996); second wife, Geraldine Caster (1923–1998).

6. **Mary Alice Wilson Yerby** (1919–1988), m. Dennis Yerby (d. 1955), resided in Bogey Neck; child: Dennis Leon Yerby (1937–1989).

7. **Sarah Wilson Campbell** (1923–1988), m. Robert Campbell; resided in New York; returned to Bogey Neck after retirement; buried in Mt. Olive Church cemetery.

PHOTO: (1945) Left to right: David Carroll Wilson and William Corbin Wilson, sons of William and Julia Wilson

Generation 5—Great-Great-Grandchildren of William and Elizabeth Wilson; Great-Grandchildren of William Thomas (Willie) and Clara Wilson[134]

---

134   Oral history.

1. **Kantania Wilson**, daughter of Frederick Wilson; resides in Bogey Neck.

2. **Corbin Wilson**, son of Frederick Wilson; resides in Lancaster County, VA.

3. **Ernest Wilson, Sr**. (1935–1996), son of David and Hilda Spence Wilson; first wife, Vernell Cruse; second wife, Joyce Norris, Jr.; children: Dafney Wilson, Connie Wilson, and Ernest Wilson, Jr. (Ernest and Vernell Cruse Wilson).

4. **Dennis Leon Yerby**, (1937–1989), son of Alice and Dennis Yerby; m. Doris Keeve; resided in New York until his death; children: Chauncey Lionel Yerby and Clifton Oneal Yerby.

Generation 6—Great-Great-Great-Grandchildren of William and Elizabeth Wilson; Great-Great-Grandchildren of William Thomas (Willie) and Clara Wilson; Great-Grandchildren of Willie T. and Julia Wilson

Children of Dennis Leon and Doris Keeve Yerby, grandchildren of Alice Wilson and Dennis Yerby:

1. **Chauncey Lionel Yerby.**
2. **Clifton Oneal Yerby.**

Children of Ernest and Vernell Cruse Wilson, grandchildren of David and Hilton Banks Wilson:

3. **Dafney Wilson.**
4. **Connie Wilson.**
5. **Ernest Wilson, Jr.**

Generation 7—Great-Great-Great-Great-Grandchildren of William and Elizabeth Wilson; Great-Great-Great-Grandchildren of William Thomas (Willie) and Cl and Julia Wilson; Great-Grandchildren of Alice Wilson and Dennis Yerby.

Grandchildren of Dennis Leon and Doris Keeve Yerby:

1. Jamilla
2. Andra
3. Jamella
4. Demeek
5. Nortrell
6. Corey
7. Nowella
8. Yolanda
9. Jareé
10. Teon

CHAPTER VIII–EULOGY OF MY FATHER

Daniel Olin Jones
"Servant, Well Done" (2 Timothy 4:6–7)
By Rev. Ronald Turner[135]
December 30, 1986
(Notes)

This text embodies the evidence of the imminent martyrdom of Paul. In it, we hear that great apostle, that great example of Christian fidelity, as he speaks while contemplating his situation as he is at the point of being sacrificed. He compares himself to the disciplined athlete. The words that he speaks, he speaks of himself; however, these same words could be equally well said of Deacon Daniel Jones.

Deacon is a word that at its basic core means servant. Deacon Jones was a great servant of the Lord, and as could be said of Paul, the very same can be said of Deacon Jones.

For I am now ready to be offered; the time of my departure is at hand. I have fought the good fight, I have finished

---

135 Ronald Turner, 9th pastor of Mt. Olive Baptist Church, Wicomico Church, VA.

*my course, I have kept the faith; henceforth, there is laid
up for me a crown of righteousness, which the Lord, the
righteous judge, shall give me at that day and not to me
only, but unto all of them also that loved his appearing.*

I. I've fought a good fight.

Deacon Jones's life could be compared to an athlete in the arena
in competition who has done his best.

His training as a trustee began in 1931 when he was elected to
the board of trustees. He has been active as a trustee for fifty-
five years. He performed so well, that in 1937, when the church
was looking for a heavyweight contender, Deacon Jones was
sought after and ordained as a deacon in 1937. His performance
as a deacon, as a servant of the Lord, helper to the pastor, and a
spiritual guide to the church has been unsurpassed.

There is not a deacon who knew him that did not respect his
wisdom, as well as the way he walked and the way he talked.
And though he had the capability to aspire to the ministry and
though he had the competence to be a preacher, he blossomed
where God had planted him. But I declare to you that he was a
preacher—a preacher, a teacher, a leader, a father, a brother, a
friend, and a counselor.

He guided this church, by the help of God, through the storm-
tossed seas. When times grew rough, he did not quit or give up.
He did not go home and sit down. Each time he was knocked

down, he begged of God to lift him up and make him strong. He endured the backbiting and backstabbing, the hassles, the heartaches, and the pains that many right here brought upon him because he knew on whom he could depend. He knew that Jesus must not bear the cross alone. He realized that he had a cross to bear. The songwriters sum it up well for us:

If you can't stand a little disappointment,
If you can stand being talked about sometime,
If you think you should always be up,
Never be down; remember no cross, you
Don't get no crown.

Deacon Jones has fought a good fight and like Paul he could say, "I've finished my course."

II. A long time ago:

    a. The year was 1922. Deacon Jones decided to make Jesus his choice—his mind was fixed, and his heart made up. September of 1922, he was baptized, and Jesus started him on his journey.

    b. This race was a long one to run. It took seventy-nine years for him to complete the journey.

    c. It wasn't an easy course to run:

There have been hills and mountains to climb. The road has been tedious at times. There have been some sorrows and disappointments and sickness, but there has also been a lot of love, joy, peace, and happiness along the way. But even when the race became extremely difficult to run, Deacon Jones didn't take any shortcuts. He did not quit. He did not quit prematurely. Windless and exhausted, he ran on to see what the end would be.

He ran over discouragement, frustration, disillusionment, and despair. He ran past hopelessness and despair. He ran past the obstacles—both physical and mental.

He ran past the roaring twenties, the frilling thirties, the fabulous forties, the nifty fifties, the solemn sixties, the set-back seventies, and the energized eighties. He ran *all* the way to the finish line.

III. And like Paul, Deacon Jones kept the faith.

Faith seems like such an easy thing to have when everything is going right. When only a little journey is to be made, it is easy to muster up enough faith to make the journey. When no problems confront an individual, it seems like we can go on endlessly. However, when life is more than thirty days, situations and circumstances can and do arise in our lives that will try, test, and prove our faith.

For sixty-four years, Deacon Jones has been on the battlefield for the Lord. For sixty-four years, he has been a soldier in the army for the Lord. Sixty-four years he has been holding up the blood-stained banner for the Lord. Sixty-four years ago he promised the Lord that he would serve him until he died. And for sixty-four years, his faith in God has never failed him.

He knew that "from everlasting to everlasting thou art God." Consequently, his faith carried him in the happy and sad times. When it looked as if he could not find his way, his faith guided him all along the way.

No wonder he could sing "My faith looks up to thee, thou lamb of Calvary, Savior divine." Deacon Jones kept the faith:

-through the darkness and through the night, and
-when folks appreciated him, and when they didn't.

"*I have fought a good fight, I have kept the faith, I have finished my course*" So, what's left now? Is it all over?

IV. No, it's not over at all. There is something left.

Deacon, now that you've fought the good fight, now that you have kept the faith, now that you have finished your course, it is time to move on up a little higher. I told you that if you lived right, you would see me again. I told you that when I left, I was going to be busy preparing some things for you. Now, it is time to move on up a little higher.

Come on and get your crown that I have prepared for you— not any ole kind of crown but a crown of righteousness.

And then there is something that I want to tell you as I give you this crown. It's only three words, but they mean everything: "Servant, well done."

Chapter IX — Tragedy Strikes In Bogey Neck

The Bogey Neck community has been faced with a number of unfortunate events over the years. Whenever families were faced with a tragedy, the residents of Bogey Neck and members of surrounding communities were there for them.

- Oscar Ross, a logger, died when a tree fell on him. He was survived by his wife, Eula Jones Ross of Bogey Neck, and one son, Darrell "Bassel" Ross.

- In the midforties, Daniel Olin Jones saw smoke coming from Celeste and Cleveland Thompson's house on Bogey Neck Road. As he ran toward the house, he heard children screaming. When he arrived, he saw the four-year-old at the open window and yelled to her to jump, but she didn't; it was already too late to rescue the children; the four-year-old girl and an infant died in the fire. The house was adjacent to the properties of William H. Ball and Joseph Warren Jones. The Thompsons found housing in the Harvest Neck Community. Clothing and household needs were provided by the neighbors. Children: Robert Henry (died 2003), Cleveland (died 2006), David (resides in Mississippi),

Barbara (resides in Wicomico Church, VA), Yvonne (resides in Camden, NJ), Myrtle (resides in Kilmarnock, VA), Melvin (resides in Wicomico Church, VA), Joyce (resides in Wicomico Church, VA), and Wayne (d. 2006).

- Dennis Yerby, son of Alfred and Lela Yerby of Mila Neck, drowned in Delaware in 1955 while fishing on a Menhaden commercial fishing vessel. At the time of his death, Dennis had resided in Bogey Neck since 1939 with wife Alice Wilson Yerby (a native of Bogey Neck) and son Dennis Leon Yerby. Also living with the family was Dennis's sister, Margaret Yerby Haynie.

- Cecil and Viola Taylor's family house was destroyed by fire in the 1960s. The family's five-acre tract of land was purchased in 1939. The house sat on a tract of land between the Warner family cemetery and near Barrett's Creek. After Cecil's death, Viola and the children remained in the home until the fire. After several moves, Viola and the children moved in the home of Cora and the late Adolphous Wallace. Christine Taylor, daughter of Cecil and Viola Taylor, is currently living in the home with her daughter.

- Two cousins, William Thomas Jones and Coolidge Jones, were playing with sticks in the field. Minutes after William's mother yelled, "Put the sticks down before you punch your eyes out," William ran to the house, screaming, with a stick in his eye. William was rushed to Dr. Morgan E. Norris's office for treatment. Dr. Norris referred William to the hospital in Richmond. Unfortunately, William lost his eye.

- Cornelia Sebree Warner's home built in 1912 was destroyed by fire in the 1950s. A new home was built on the property, where Cornelia lived the remainder of her life.

- Sarestine "Ressie" Taylor (1964–1993) fell out of a car in front of her house on Bogey Neck Road. She was the daughter of Christine Taylor and granddaughter of Cecil and Viola Coursey Taylor.

- Emerson Norris III drowned (at age thirty-five) while working on a sailboat. Emerson III was the son of Emerson, Jr., and Grace Conley Norris of Heathsville; grandson of Grace Walters and Emerson Norris, Sr.; two sons: Emerson IV and Michael.

- Raymond Norris (1950–1969) died while on active duty in the US Marine Corp; son of Grace Walters and Emerson Norris, grandson of John W. and Emma J. Walters of Bogey Neck.

- A tornado destroyed Violet Norris Davenport's and Edward Norris's trailers, sending pieces down Bogey Neck Road. No one was injured.

Chapter X—A Tribute To The Matriarchs

"The measure of a woman's character is not what she gets from her ancestors but what she leaves her descendants." —Unknown

The second- and third-generation women of Bogey Neck were highly respected wives and mothers who played a vital role in the home, church, and community. Their contributions to the families and community continue to live on through the lives of their descendants and in the memories of others who were fortunate to have known them. As affectionate and caring individuals, they worked hard in the home and outside of the home. The following is a tribute to these outstanding women.

Mary L Jackson Jones, (ca. 1875–1954); believed to have been born in Browns Store located in the Wicomico Church district; two known siblings were Julia Beane of White Stone and Walter Lee, a merchant seaman in Newport News, VA; m. Joseph Warren. Jones in 1893 and lived in Bogey Neck until her death;

fourteen children: Paul, Arthur (d. at birth), Clarence, Eula, Kennard, Glesner, Gladys, Joseph, Daniel, Onard, Logan, Miriam, Elaine, and Ellis; worked as a maid for Otis Harding family on Edge Hill plantation and on Billy Rowe's family plantation; during summers, worked in New York as a maid to get school clothes for the children; active in Mt. Olive Church— choir, Willing Workers Circle, Missionary Society's representative to first Northern Neck Women's Education and Missionary Society (1912)—first in Bogey Neck to subscribe to newspaper, and neighbors depended on her for the weather forecast; known for her raisins and dumplings, which she prepared on Sunday and served when friends and neighbors visited; cooked at Anna T. Jeanes School; loved to travel and read.[136]

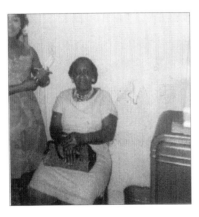

Cornelia Sebree Warner (ca. 1888–1976), born in Mila Neck, VA; daughter of John, Jr., and Sally Sebree, granddaughter of John, Sr., and Sally Pride Sebree; attended Mila Neck School; nine siblings: John Sebree III, Elizabeth "Lizzie" Sebree Parker, Maggie Sebree Carter; William Sebree, Northern Sebree, Henrietta Sebree Howard Tolson, Laura Alice Sebree, and Gertrude "Gertie" Sebree Johnson.

In 1910, married Sylvester Warner (ca. 1884–1937); moved to Bogey Neck in 1912; seven children: Reva, John F., Rozena, Sylvester "Billy," William J., and twins, Lloyd and Laura.

---

136   Oral history.

Worked as a crabber on the Wicomico River, Tippers and Barrett's Creeks; lived in Bogey Neck thirty years after the death of husband; sold crabs to Robert Northern; with the support of children and grandchildren, maintained her home in Bogey Neck and cared for the garden and livestock; walked to visit niece Vera Jones every morning during crabbing season; built home on family property after the original family home burned.

Very active in Mt. Olive Church serving on deaconess board, member of Missionary Society and the food committee for the annual second Sunday in August revival dinner; a memorial window placed in church by family "In Honor of Cornelia Warner." (*Obituary and church anniversary program.*)

Julia Lela Yerby (ca. 1892–1999); died twenty-six days after the celebration of her 107th birthday on May 1, 1999; daughter of Isaac and Sally Johnson Taylor of Remo, VA; used limited formal education and life experiences to survive; married Alfred Yerby, who died at an early age; had to take on the role of mother and father to raise fourteen children (seven boys and seven girls); used self-taught skills of cooking, canning, quilting, sewing, and gardening to care for her children; passed talents and skills to her children as they grew into adulthood; resourcefulness was a way of life and wasted nothing—i.e., made quilts from fabric scraps; used pictures in catalog book as patterns to make children's clothes.

Lela was always considered a part of the Bogey Neck family; daughter, Ceddra, married James Edward Jones, the great grandson of Stafford B. Jones; called "granny" by family and "Miss Lela" by the others; in later years, lived in Bogey Neck with her daughter, Ceddra Yerby Jones, who cared for her until her death; had an amazing memory, and whenever I visited her after she reached the age of one hundred, she would greet me with, "Hello, Mary," and we would engage in conversation.

Growing up in a religious home, she had strong Christian values; an involved member of Mt. Olive Baptist Church all of her adult life; took children to Sunday school and church and made sure they were involved; remembered by family as "a unique woman of wisdom."

A tribute by the children:

"We are grateful to God for our beautiful mother. Her characteristics and influence have been passed on to her fourteen children, 116 grandchildren, ninety-four great-grandchildren, forty-nine great-great-grandchildren, and one great-great-great-grandchild. She was a beacon of light, our ray of hope, and our inspiration at family gatherings. She was our teacher when life's lessons were hard. She was our joy, who gave us love when we did wrong. She was everything to us, and we were everything to her." (*Obituary and family.*)

Vera Sebree Jones (1907–2003), born in Mila Neck, Remo, VA; great granddaughter of John Sebree, Sr., and Peggy Pride, granddaughter of John Sebree (b. ca. 1850) and Sally Ball Sebree; daughter of John Sebree III (ca. 1884–1937) and Mahalia Smith Sebree (ca. 1884–1922); grandfather believed to have been named Charles Sebra and that his name was changed after slavery; family reared on twelve acres waterfront property, which grandfather left to his two sons, John and William, on the Wicomico River; attended Mila Neck school, teacher was Aunt Lillian Pollard. Sebree; dropped out of school at age thirteen to help father care for six siblings after mother's death; washed, ironed, cleaned house, cooked, and saw that the children got off to school; worked while siblings were in school, doing housekeeping and laundry for neighboring white families to "help make ends meet" (favorite saying); m. Daniel Olin. Jones of Bogey Neck, moved to Bogey Neck (1933) and shared fifty-three years together; five children: William Thomas, David Samuel, Daniel Rudolph, Mary Mahalia, and John Irvin.

Known as a hard worker who often said, "Hard work ain't killed nobody"; crabbed for years on the Wicomico River, Tippers and Barrett's Creeks and was considered one of the best; in later years, stopped crabbing to become a crab picker, quickly perfecting the skill and taking pride in being a good crab picker; worked one day a week for crab house owner, Robert Northern, cleaning his house and washing his clothes for many years ($2 for cleaning and $1.25 for washing clothes); in addition to working five and six days a week, she took pride in maintaining an immaculate home, cooking the family hot meals, canning, and gardening; the outside of the house had to look equally as good—grass cut, hedges trimmed, house and roof painted, shutters on the windows, white ceramic chickens across the front (along with a bird bath), white fencing, round-graveled driveway, a lamppost, and a sidewalk.

Canned vegetables and fruit for the winter; pantry was always filled with not just canned fruits and vegetables but stocked with such items as toilet paper, paper towels, sugar, flour, salt, pepper, soaps, etc.; another favorite saying, "You don't know what the winter will bring"; among other good traits, she was an excellent money manager and would negotiate any purchase until satisfied.

Loved traveling with friends (Ms. Emma Smith, Ms. Roberta McGlone, and cousin Alice Handy); trips included Spain, Miami, California, Atlanta, North Carolina, Bahamas, and frequent visits with children wherever they lived in the United States; spent hours knitting with cousin Alice and selling products—dusters made out of coat hangers and yarn, doorknob covers for Christmas, toilet paper covers, and potholders, to name a few items in the inventory; at Christmastime during the late forties and early fifties, made wreaths and gathered holly and mistletoe to sell door-to-door in Baltimore, MD, accompanied by sister, Versie Pope, and brother-in-law, Lawrence Pope, who drove the truck; she made more than enough money for her children's Christmas gifts.

Vera is remembered as a hard worker who took pride in everything she did and for her dedication to her church and community; a caring person who was always helping somebody in need; last, but not least, she knew how to make a dollar work for her. (*Source:* My Father's Journey, *by Mary Jones Day, 2009.*)

Grace Cornelia Walters Norris (1911–1986); born in Bogey Neck, Wicomico Church, VA; daughter of John and Emma Walter; granddaughter of William W. and Ann V. Walters; nine siblings were reared in Bogey Neck; father was a fisherman; mother was a housekeeper; member of Mt. Olive Baptist Church, serving as a deaconess and with the Church Aid ministry for many years. [Photo: age nineteen].

Married Emerson Norris, a farmer, painter, waterman, and barber; Emerson raised black-eyed peas and other vegetables; during the Depression, Emerson provided food to neighbors; did the food shopping for family at Joe Delano's store; an order included ten or twelve pork chops, twenty-five pounds of flour, and one can of molasses; raised eggs and traded for food.

Every day Grace made the family hot meals, which always included two to three pans of biscuits, meat, and potatoes; daughter Helen said, "I remember my mother made tea cakes when I was a child. She would make enough to fill two water pails full and serve them with snow ice cream" [See recipe in Chapter XII.]; helped husband on the farm and coordinated appointments in the barbershop; a quiet-mannered woman, walked softly but could carry the big stick when necessary; moved barbershop out of the pantry in the house to the smokehouse in the backyard when she grew tired of cleaning up hair.

Family lived in the house on ten acres purchased by William Walters from Sam Walker's estate (1904); in early 1960, built a new home on 6.75 acres, adjacent to father's homeplace, purchased from Alice Whaley in 1938 for $225 at 6 percent interest; property remains in family; old homeplace was occupied by Alonzo and Hannah Norris; family voluntarily razed the house after Alonzo and Hannah moved. (*Source: the children.*)

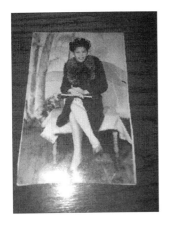

Ceddra Kistel Yerby Jones (1924) Seventh of fourteen children of William Alfred Yerby and Lela Taylor Yerby of Remo community; entered the workforce at the Wicomico Church, VA; at the tender age of nine or ten, scrubbed floors for white families in the Remo community; at age thirteen, worked as tomato peeler after giving age of sixteen in order to work; got away with giving the wrong age because records were not kept, and laws were not strict in verifying age of the workers; continued to peel tomatoes for five cents a bushel for green tomatoes and three cents for ripe tomatoes; was a fast peeler with small hands but could peel more than average buckets a day; salary increased to one dollar; spent five cents of earnings to buy lunch: three cents for ginger snaps, two cents for a piece of cheese and a soda.

Lived with Mrs. Susan Scofield (who had lost her husband) "across the river" in Fairport, VA; had a side job of babysitting on weekends for James and Minnie Carter in Lillian and had to walk from Fairport to Lillian; rode bus to Rosenwald High School; at age fourteen, cut greens in a big field, put in bushel baskets, and weighed; cutting greens required going early in the morning to cut while the dew was still on the greens and while the greens were fresh and tender.

Moved back home with mother but soon left again for a short time to live with Daniel and Vera Jones (Uncle Flossie and Aunt Vee) of Bogey Neck to babysit the twins (David and Daniel); returned to doing odd jobs—scrubbing floors, working at the tomato factory, washing dishes, and once again babysitting; earned seventy-five cents for babysitting two little white boys who taught her how to roller skate on the paved road and to ride a bicycle; saved up a week's earnings and bought first pair of roller skates for seventy-five cents at the store in Remo; worked for the Stephens family to help with the newborn baby for one dollar a week; left the Stephens family and worked for the Joe Delano family for one dollar a week cleaning, washing, hanging out clothes; while working for the Delanos, a job opened up at the Mila School located on the corner of Bogey Neck Road for a cook paying eighteen dollars a month; the teacher, Mrs. Lillian Pollard Sebree, and supervisor, Mrs. L. B. Cheatham, applied for money to pay a cook for the children and recommended her; made donuts for the children and to sell at ball games to raise money for the school; excited to earn eighteen dollars a month and to make the children happy; became pregnant with first child, William Alfred, at age eighteen, while working at the school; continued to work at the school until it closed for the summer (1942); gave birth and stayed home to take care of baby for a while before going to work at Raymond Haynie's fish factory.

Moved to Baltimore to live with sister Annie Mae and later moved to Philadelphia to live with sister Olyne; never been to a city other than Richmond, so it was definitely an eye-opener; worked in a laundromat for a year in Philadelphia, PA; continued babysitting and cleaning houses; Ed (James Edward Jones), the father of firstborn, drafted in the army (1942); Ed returned home from the armed forces (1945). Married Ed in Wilmington, DE (1946); lived with Ed's parents (Louis and Fragia Jones) in Mila Neck; went back to work at the tomato and fish factories; second child, Katherine (Snooks, b. 1947) and third child Carolyn (b. 1950); family moved in new home in Bogey Neck built by Lawrence and Bernard Pope (1954); family later blessed with the birth of three sons, James, Jr. (Jimmy), Michael, and Mark.

Worked for Smith Seafood Company as a crab picker for thirty-plus years; known as one of the fastest workers in all the jobs. Husband passed away (1992); stopped working to care for mother, Lela Yerby, who passed away (1999) at the age of 107; began working with the Northumberland County Social Services Department as a caregiver for Fred Conley (2000), and at age eighty-nine, continues to work in this position.

Joined Mt. Olive Baptist Church at age fourteen and remains a faithful and dedicated member—singing in the choir, working in the food pantry; honored as the church's "Mother of the Year"; through it all—losing father at a young age and losing husband, son, mother, grandson, sisters, and brothers—has remained strong and held family together; loves to work in the yard, cutting the lawn, trimming trees, and tending flower gardens; loves to cook large meals for family and friends; bakes thirty or more cakes, rice pudding, and bread pudding for the annual Bogey Neck picnic; entrusted by God with great gifts and remains encouraged rather than complain; has given children, grandchildren, great-grandchildren, and great-great-grandchildren a strong foundation for life and stresses trust and faith in God. (*Source*: *Ceddra Yerby Jones and children.*)

Hortense Walters Jones (1922–2013), born in Wicomico Church, VA; only child of Lena Walters Johnson; reared by grandparents Washington and Maggie Carter Walters, who were land owners in Bogey Neck; attended Mila Neck School and Hygeia School in Burgess and graduated from Julius Rosenwald High School in Lillian, VA, class of 1940; m. Ellis Jones in 1941; three children: Elwood, Barbara, and Warren; mentored neighborhood children; long-term substitute teacher at Anna T. Jeanes and Booker T. Washington schools; attended local and statewide church conventions; longtime involvement in Mt. Olive Baptist Church (president of Church Aid Ministry, church clerk, member of senior choir, director of vacation Bible school, Sunday school teacher, Youth Council Sponsor, Centennial Committee, architect committee); called upon to help write obituaries for loved ones of Bogey Neck neighbors; often talked about her high school classmates and graduation (senior class motto: *"Our sails are set for the voyage of life"*); involved in organizing her thirty-fifth high school class reunion; today, bedridden in her home of seventy years; blessed to have her daughter, Barbara, as her primary caretaker and the support of her two sons, Elwood and Warren; receiving medical in-home care daily; enjoys daily visits from family and friends; celebrated ninety-first birthday with family and friends, hosted by her children. (*Source: Barbara Jones.*)

Mertice Elaine Williams (1920–2007); born in her lifelong community, Bogey Neck; youngest child of fourteen children of Joseph and Mary L. Jones; attended Mila Neck school; baptized by sixth pastor, Rev. John J. Nickens, at Mt. Olive Baptist Church, where she was active for over seventy years. Following in the footsteps of her mother, she sang in the senior choir; m. Leon Williams and had five children: Milfret, Deloris, Maurice, Duval, and Christopher.

Elaine, a caring, nurturing, and loving woman, enjoyed a simple life revolving around her children and Bogey Neck community; had a passion for keeping a neat home, canning, sharing baked pies with family and neighbors; often forgetting her own physical handicap, a crippling leg, walked throughout the neighborhood, caring for family and neighbors who needed help; enjoyed visiting her children and spending time with her seven grandchildren, eight great-grandchildren, and three great-great-grandchildren; loved her two daughters-in-law as daughters (Cora Roy and Rena Jones) and two dear women that she treated as daughters (Loretta Fills and Arnisha Boyer); had two devoted friends of many years (Priscilla Sutton and Evelyn Conaway).

During her many trips away from Bogey Neck, often referred to herself as a "country girl" and would say to her children, "There's no place like home," and returned to the comforts of her beautiful little bungalow with the many improvements done by her son-in-law Johnny Gordon and son Maurice and decorated by her daughter, Deloris; lived in her home alone until illness impacted her independence, and she welcomed the invitation to live with her son Christopher and his family in Richmond, VA, until hospitalization was needed. Elaine will be remembered for her nurturing and unselfish nature.

Chapter XI—Military Service Of Bogey Neck Descendants

"Ask not what your country can do for you; ask what you can do for your country." —John F. Kennedy

Generation I (Head of Households	Name	Branch
Walters, William	Bromley, Louis	Army
Walters, William	Brown, Teresa	Air Force
Jones, Stafford	Brown, Dorian	Army
Jones, Stafford	Cheatham, Lenora Jones	
Jones, Stafford	Day, Robert E., Jr.	Air Force
Jones, Stafford	Dorsey, Brita	Air Force
Jones, Stafford	Jones, Clarence (Bert)	Army
Jones, Stafford	Jones, Clarence Carter	Army
Jones, Stafford	Jones, David S.	Army
Jones, Stafford	Jones, Elwood, Jr.	Marine
Jones, Stafford	Jones, Elwood, Sr.	Army
Jones, Stafford	Jones, Grafton	Navy
Jones, Stafford	Jones, James E., Jr.	Army
Jones, Stafford	Jones, James E., Sr.	Army
Jones, Stafford	Jones, John	Army
Jones, Stafford	Jones, Jonathan	Army
Jones, Stafford	Jones, Leonard	Army

Jones, Stafford	Jones, Louis Thomas	Navy
Jones, Stafford	Jones, Lionel	Army
Jones, Stafford	Jones, Mark A.	Army
Jones, Stafford	Jones, Michael	Army
Walters, John	Jones, Morris	Army
Jones, Stafford	Jones, Reid	Army
Walters, John	Jones, Sherman	Army
Jones, Stafford	Jones, Stafford	Union Army
Walters, John	Jones, Walter	Army
Jones, Stafford	Jones, Warren	Army
Jones, Stafford	Moody, Edward, Jr.	Army
Jones, Stafford	Moody, Gregory	Army
Walters, William	Bromley, James A.	Army
Walters, William	Norris, Emerson III	Army SP4
Walters, William	Norris, Raymond	Marine Corp
Walters, William	Smith, James Earl	Army
Walters, William	Smith, Jasmine	Marine Corp
Walters, William	Smith, Elvin Smith	Marine Corp
Walters, William	Smith, Oneil	Navy
Warner, Sylvester	Warner, Stefanie	Army
Warner, Frederick	Warner, Sylvester, Jr.	Army
Warner, Sylvester	Warner, Sylvester, Sr.	Army
Warner, Sylvester	Warner, William, Jr.	Air Force
Warner, Sylvester	Warner, William, Sr.	Navy

Chapter XII — Recipes Of Bogey Neck Cooks[137]

"One cannot think well, sleep well, love well, if one has not dined well." —Virginia Woolf

---

BLUEBERRY LOAF—Christine Taylor

1 c. all-purpose flour	½ c. chopped nuts
3 c. whole wheat pastry flour	2 eggs
¾ c. sugar	1 tbsp. vanilla
1 tbsp. baking powder	1 tbsp. salt
1 tbsp. shredded lemon peel	½ c. milk
⅓ c. melted butter or margarine	
1 c. fresh or unthawed blueberries	

Preheat oven to 350°. In mixing bowl, beat butter, sugar, vanilla, and eggs. Combine flour, baking powder, and salt. Stir into egg mixture alternately with milk. Fold in lemon peel, nuts, and blueberries. Pour into greased 8 x 4½ inch loaf pan. Bake for 60 or 70 minutes or until bread tests done. Cool in pan for 10 minutes. Yields one loaf.

---

137   *The Northern Neck Cooks 1998*, sponsored by Northumberland County Community Center Organization, Wicomico Church, VA.

Sweet Potato Pie—Elaine Jones Williams

5 large potatoes (mashed)

2 eggs   1 c. whole milk

2 c, sugar   ¼ tsp. salt

3 tsp. vanilla   1 tsp. nutmeg

1 tsp. lemon flavoring   1 stick butter

1 (12 oz.) can evaporated milk

Preheat oven to 350°. Mix ingredients in order, blending well. Potatoes should be warm to hot when adding ingredients. Pour in unbaked pie crust. Cook for 45 to 50 minutes.

Tea Cakes — Grace Walters Norris

1 c. butter (other shortening
will not have the same taste)

3 eggs   1 c. sugar

1½ tsp. vanilla   3½ c. sifted flour
flavoring

½ tsp. baking   1 tsp. baking powder
soda

Cream together butter, sugar, and eggs. Add vanilla. Sift dry ingredients and add by hand. If necessary, more flour may be used to make dough stable enough to knead. Place dough on a floured board and roll out fairly thick. *Do not* roll the dough out thin. Cut out dough with biscuit cutter. Place cookies on a greased sheet. Do not let sides touch. These tea cakes will be crisp. Bake at 400° until browned.

Contributed by Helen Ball, daughter of Grace Walters Norris

Coconut Cake — Vera Sebree Jones

3 c. sugar	2 tbsp. butter-flavored Crisco
3 c. flour	¼ tsp. salt
5 large eggs	2 tsp. vanilla extract
½ tsp. baking powder	1 tsp. lemon extract
3 c. homogenized milk	2 sticks butter

Preheat oven to 325°. Cream butter, Crisco, and sugar. Add one egg at a time and beat well. Sift flour 3 times and add 1 cup at a time. Add salt and baking powder. Add vanilla, lemon, and milk. Beat well with electric mixer for 2 minutes. Bake for 1½ hours.

Icing: 1 box 10X sugar, 2 tbsp. homogenized milk, 1 tsp. fresh lemon.

SOUR CREAM POUND CAKE

Julia Taylor Warner

3 sticks butter (room temp)   3 c. flour
3 c. sugar   1 c. sour cream
1 tsp. vanilla extract   6 eggs

Preheat oven 325°. Cream butter and sugar until light and fluffy—about one minute. Add eggs, one at a time, blending well after each addition. Add flour, alternating with sour cream and beginning and ending with flour. Mix well until smooth. Add vanilla and blend well. Pour batter into a greased and floured ten-inch tube pan. Bake one hour twenty-five minutes or until cake tester inserted in center comes out clean. Cool in pan ten minutes before inverting onto cake plate.

OLD-FASHIONED PORK SAUSAGE — Ceddra Jones

Canned Patties

1. Cut up lean and fat trimmed from parts of the hog shoulder, ribs, and ham.
2. Put meat through a grinder.
3. Add seasoning (sage, salt, and pepper) according to the amount of ground meat.
4. Let sit overnight.
5. Make into sausage cakes and cook in oven.
6. Put cooked sausage in glass jars (save the liquid).
7. Pour liquid over the sausage and screw top on tight.
8. Turn jars upside down on back of stove and let grease melt.
9. Turn upright and store.

Stuffed Patties

1. Use cheesecloth to make small bags for stuffing sausage.
2. Stuff bag, leaving about two inches at the top to tie with a string in a loop.
3. Pour scalding hot water over bag.
4. Roll bag in sausage liquid.
5. Roll in corn meal.
6. Hang in smokehouse or inside house to preserve.
7. When ready to eat, slice sausage into patties. Fry or bake in oven.

Chapter XIII — The Annual Bogey Neck Picnic

"Family faces are magic mirrors. Looking at people who belong to us, we see the past, present and future." Gail Lumet Buckley

For thirty-three years, descendants of the first families who settled in Bogey Neck more than a century ago have continued to gather for their annual community reunion on the second Saturday in August. An event that started with relatives and a few families from neighboring communities has grown from about fifty people to as many as three hundred.

The idea to hold a Bogey Neck picnic originated on a hot Saturday afternoon August 8, 1981, with Stanley Norris, Elwood Lavern Jones, and Mary Jones Day sitting on the back porch of Ellis and Hortense Joneses' home. On the second Saturday in August, the Bogey Neck relatives came home for the church's annual revival service. We usually met at my Uncle Ellis's house to catch up on what had happened since our last gathering. This time, however, we agreed that we were bored and needed to do something other than sit on the porch, stand in the yard talking, or watch the cars go by. We had a lot in common: we grew up in the same neighborhood, went to the same schools, worshipped at the same church, did quite well in our careers, and had parents who were still alive and for whom Bogey Neck was still home.

We remember the Bogey Neck Road community as one big happy family, and we always find our way back home. Our great-grandparents were the pioneers; our grandparents were the first to settle in Bogey Neck; our parents never left; and we keep coming back. We laughed about the games we played when we were growing up, the outhouses, the hog pens, the day that somebody got the first TV, and the whole neighborhood watched, the fact that we thought we had arrived when we got the party-line telephone, and the moment when we got our driver's licenses. The conversation shifted back to "let's have a picnic next year," and of course, Stanley and Elwood said in unison, "And, Mary, you plan it."

Not being one to run away from taking orders from the boys and never afraid to take charge, I started the ball rolling. It was on that day, August 9, 1980, that the Bogey Neck idea was born.

I called the meeting to order. The first order of business was to discuss the idea with our fathers—Emerson Norris and Ellis and Daniel Jones—whom we named the "Bogey Neck commissioners" and Emerson Norris, the mayor. The commissioners jumped at the idea of bringing the children, their families, and other relatives back home. The planning began with giving out assignments:

1) *Location and date.* The picnic will be in the field between Ellis and Daniel's houses on the second Saturday in August. (We moved from the porch to the field.)

2) *Announcements.* Mary will get flyers printed to be distributed to each household.

3) *Setup.* The commissioners (Ellis, Daniel, and Emerson) will get the field ready, order a "Johnny-on-the-spot," and arrange for tables and chairs.

4) *Food.* Each family will bring a picnic basket with enough food to feed their families and friends; the food will be shared on one table.

5) *Parking.* Elwood and Stanley will take care of parking details. (Fields were designated. As the year progressed, so did the planning—and enthusiasm—by telephone.)

By the time we arrived home on that second Saturday in 1981, the grass was cut in the field and every lawn on the road, and the makeshift tent was up—four poles in the ground and a blue canvas tied overhead with rope. The impromptu facility was in place at the end of the field. On the morning of the picnic, Ellis pulled out the old rusty grill he had stored in a shed (it had a piece of tin in the bottom to keep the coal from falling out) and washed and cleaned it to cook the hot dogs. "Mayor" Emerson Norris provided the hard crabs (still a favorite of the day) as one of the items on the menu. The commissioners arranged the seating, with tables and chairs borrowed from the church and neighbors' backyards.

Vera and Hortense Jones provided white linen tablecloths. Each Bogey Neck family showed up with food, and families from neighboring communities (Mila Neck, Harvest Neck, Wicomico) also contributed covered dishes. By the time we put the food together, we had a great variety: apple cobbler, assorted cakes, rice pudding, baked beans, fried chicken, potato salad, and sliced tomatoes. I bought the hot dogs and made the hamburgers, and Emerson Norris donated the hard-shell crabs. David Jones was in charge of the drinks (Kool-Aid and water).

I was the MC for the program (and continue to be). The program included greetings by me and an observance of a moment of silence for the deceased, followed by a prayer and blessing of the food by Deacon Daniel Jones. Following the devotion, everyone walked around the food tables and helped themselves to some down-home cooking. The children amused themselves with their own made-up games, which usually just consisted of chasing each other or playing dodge ball, tag, or hide-and-seek. Ironically, our teenagers complained that there was "nothing to do," so they strolled down Bogey Neck Road. The adult attraction was a game of horseshoes, which was always such a popular sport in the neighborhood. Players stood in line to challenge the winner.

There was no closing time for our first neighborhood picnic. After cleaning up, by dark we were still just standing under the tent, talking about old times and telling jokes. After everyone left, the neighborhood dogs began their picnic—cleaning up the scraps of food that were left on the ground.

This neighborhood reunion, "Bogey Neck Day," continues to be the highlight of the community. The commissioners are no longer with us, but the descendants are carrying on, along with others who come every year and help to make this a great event. The difference today is that there are at least three big tents—one or two always donated by the local undertaker, Berry Waddy. Friday night, while the cooks are getting the grills ready and preparing the food, onlookers gather under the tent or around the grills. Elwood Lavern Jones, Stanley Norris, and John Irvin Jones, sons of the original commissioners, coordinate the Saturday activities. Elwood has assumed the role of "Mayor." John spends the night in his truck so he can watch the meats that have to cook all night. Michael Jones, chief chef for the chicken and fish, drives from Georgia each year to assume his role. All the cooks gather early Saturday morning before sunup, fire up the grills, and start the cooking.

At approximately 8:30 a.m., Ceddra Yerby Jones sends the breakfast of bacon, sausage, fried potatoes, and fried potato pancakes across the road to the cooks. When the tents and tables are in place, the ladies (Erna Jones, Bessie Bromley, Barbara Jones, and Dawn Jones) prepare the tables with coverings and work with the cooks on the logistics for setting up the food—interesting dynamics, indeed. Everybody looks forward to eating Elsie Norris's coconut and chocolate cakes; Ceddra Jones prepares an assortment of about thirty cakes and delivers them in time for dessert; Louis Bromley carries out parking details, post signs, and, with the help of volunteers, directs traffic. Ulysees Jones often provides the music. Volunteers prepare the vegetables, salads, and other side dishes. Local merchants and friends from other neighborhoods contribute. Others show up and fall in line wherever needed, whether it is serving at the buffet tables, preparing plates for the elderly, or bringing the meats from the grills to the servers. As always, I coordinate the program and other details as directed by the commissioners.

Today, the entire Bogey Neck Road and the surrounding communities—black and white, old and young—assemble in the same field by four o'clock in the afternoon. The participation has grown from less than one hundred people in 1981 to about 250 in 2012. Compared to the days of the early settlers—when their only means of transportation was on foot or the horse and buggy—people travel to the picnic by foot, car, boat, bus, motorcycles, and airplane. In 2011 and 2012, the attendees represented the District of Columbia and nineteen states: Maryland, Virginia, Texas, Pennsylvania, Oklahoma, New York, New Jersey, North Carolina, Michigan, South Carolina, Mississippi, Kentucky, Kansas, Illinois, Georgia, Florida, Colorado, California, and Virginia. Neighbors share their yards and fields for parking.

The men have taken over cooking all of the meats on two or three huge grills under the trees, preparing fried chicken, barbecued chicken, fried fish, ribs, pulled pork, fried hard- and soft-shell crabs, ham, hot dogs, and hamburgers. The side dishes and desserts are prepared by neighbors and include tossed salad, coleslaw, potato salad, green beans, cabbage, baked beans, corn pudding, sliced tomatoes, macaroni and cheese, deviled eggs, macaroni salads, fresh fruit salad, and rolls. The dessert table is filled with a variety of cakes, pies, puddings, cookies, and watermelon.

With the growing popularity of this annual neighborhood event, we honor the three men—Daniel Olin Jones, Emerson Norris, and Ellis Dubois Jones—who supported the idea and helped to organize the picnic each year until their deaths. This occasion truly reflects the close relationship that Bogey Neck families have with each other and the evidence that through this tradition we can truly say that "the roots are still growing."

Bogey Picnic Photos[138]

138   Photos contributed by Warren Dubois Jones.

APPENDIX A — TIMELINE

"If you [don't] know history, then [you don't] know anything. You [are] a leaf that [doesn't] know it [is] part of a tree."
—Michael Crichton

Date	Events
1648	Northumberland County formed
1813	Wicomico Church Post Office opened; Thomas Brown, first postmaster
1826	Stafford Jones born, head of first generation of African American family in Bogey Neck
1826	Betsey Ball born, head of first generation African American family in Bogey Neck
1837	Frederick Warner born, head of first African American family in Bogey Neck
1840	Robert Wallace born, head of first generation of African American family in Bogey Neck
1845	William Walters born, head of first generation of African American family in Bogey Neck
1849	William "Willie" T. Wilson born, head of first generation of African American family in Bogey Neck

1870	Browns Store Post Office opened; John Robertson, first postmaster
1873	1,545 acres in Snowden Park divided into five tracts among Harding children
1873	Mt. Olive Baptist Church organized
1882	Mt. Olivet School opened
1888	Mila Neck School opened
1900	First African American family moved to Bogey Neck
1901	Northern Neck Industrial Academy in Richmond County opened for blacks
1913	Remo Post Office opened; Joseph P. Delano, first postmaster
1916	Northumberland County training school opened
1917	Dr. Morgan E. Norris set up medical practice in Lancaster County, VA
1919	Northumberland County training school renamed Julius Rosenwald
1938	Northern Neck Industrial Academy closed
1939	Mila Neck School closed
1939	Mila School–Bogey Neck opened
1942	Anna T. Jeanes School opened
1949	Mila School–Bogey Neck closed
1954	Julius Rosenwald closed
1959	First graduating class from Central High School

APPENDIX B—DESCENDANT CHART[139]

"Your descendants shall gather your fruits." —Virgil

[G = Generation]

G 1 Head of Household	G II	G III	G IV	G V	G VI	G VII	G VIII	Total
Ball, Betsey	4	15	8	10				**37**
Davenport, Mary	6							**6**
Jones, Stafford	8							**8**
Raleigh Jones		5	1	5	7	1		**19**
Joseph Jones		14	25	29	46	8	1	**123**
Lombard Jones		2	6	19	41	49	11	**128**
Wallace, Robert	5	6	2	8	16	13		**50**
Walters, William	10							**10**
John Walters		10	31	75	134	61	1	**312**
W. Washington Walters		9	18	47	54	29	1	**158**
Warner, Frederick	11	21	17	13	8	3		**73**
Wilson, William	4	2	7	4	5	10		**32**
Fallin, James	4	2						**6**
	52	86	115	210	311	174	14	962

---

139 Federal Census records and oral history.

APPENDIX C—CHURCH PARTICIPATION— GENERATIONS 1–3

"Then he said to his disciples, 'The harvest is plentiful, but the laborers are few.'"—Matthew 9:37 (ESV)

Head of Household	Name	Service
Jones, Stafford	Jackson, Julia	Helping Hand Ministry
Jones, Stafford	Jones, Daniel	Treasurer, Deacon Board chair, Sunday School Supt., Trustee Board, Centennial Committee, Cemetery Club, Boy Scouts; Northern Neck Deacon's Union
Jones, Stafford	Jones, Ellis	Boy Scout Leader, Architect & Planning Board, Trustee Board chair, Men's Chorus, church site committee; signee for church loan
Jones, Stafford	Jones, Joseph	Choir Director, Sunday School Superintendent, Church Clerk
Jones, Stafford	Jones, Kennard	Usher Board President, Men's Chorus
Jones, Stafford	Jones, Mary L.	Missionary Society (Representative to first Northern Neck Women's Education and Missionary Society, 1912), Choir
Jones, Stafford	Jones, Raleigh	Deacon, Sunday School Supt., church organizer

Jones, Stafford	Jones, Vera	Church Aid President, Deaconess
Jones, Stafford	Palmer, Miriam	Helping Hand Ministry-Baltimore
Jones, Stafford	Williams, Elaine Jones	Choir
Wallace, Robert	Wallace, Robert	Treasurer
Walters, William	Jones, Hortense W.	Youth Council Sponsor, Choir program chair, Church Aid, Centennial Committee, Treasurer
Walters, William	Norris, Emerson	Trustee Board Treasurer, Memorial-Four Porch Columns, church site committee, signee for church loan
Walters, William	Norris, Grace	Church Aid, President
Walters, William	Jones, Ellis	Treasurer. Deacon Board chair, Sunday School Supt., Trustee Board, Centennial Committee, Cemetery Club, Boy Scouts
Walters, William	Jones, Hortense W.	Choir, Clerk, Church Aid Pres., Centennial Committee, Vacation Bible School
Walters, William	Walter, Washington	Deacon, church organizer
Walters, William	Walters, Ernest	Trustee Board, signee for church loan
Walters, William	Walters, Luther	Memorial door
Walters, William	Walters, Wilbert	Trustee Board, Treasurer
Warner, Frederick	Warner, Cornelia	Memorial Window, Deaconess
Warner, Frederick	Warner, Frederick	Deacon, Founder, Trustee

Warner, Frederick	Warner, Louis	Helping Working Club-founder (NY)
Warner, Frederick	Warner, Sylvester	Deacon, Trustee, Sunday School Supt.
Warner, Frederick	Warner, William	Men's Chorus, Usher, Choir President
Warner, Frederick	Warner, Julia	Choir Treasurer, Missionary Society,
Warner, Frederick	Warner, Lloyd	Men's Chorus, Deacon, Youth Baseball Coach
Wilson, William	Wilson, David	Trustee, Cemetery Club, signee for church loan

Appendix D—Family Cemeteries

"And if I go and prepare a place for you, I will come again, and receive you unto myself; that where I am, there ye may be also."
—John 14:3

For many years, it was a tradition to bury loved ones in family cemeteries. The body was prepared by the undertaker and brought back to the home for viewing and remained there until the "Home Going" service. Hiram Thrift, a white undertaker, located in Wicomico Church area, was probably one of the earliest undertakers for Bogey Neck. He transported the "colored" bodies by horse and wagon, once driven by Opie Norris. Thrift's wife, Mrs. Mary Thrift, was a florist. Mr. Quentin Campbell, the first African American funeral director in the area, provided funeral services during the first half of the twentieth century. Today, funeral services are provided by Campbell Funeral Home under the direction of Brenda Campbell in Kilmarnock, VA, and Berry O. Waddy, director of Berry O. Waddy Funeral Home, Lancaster, VA.

Appendix E—Bogey Neck Family Cemeteries[140]

The year in parentheses represents the date of death.

Warner

Frederick Warner (unknown), Sophronia Warner (unknown), Sylvester Warner (1937), Cornelia Sebree Warner (1976), Sylvester "Billy" Warner, Jr. (1998), Rozena Warner Knox (2006), *Laura Warner Wilson* (2012), *Mary Warner*

(1995), Lloyd Warner (2013), Christine Warner Landon Veney (1989), Lewis Warner (unknown), Ruth Warner (unknown), John Warner (unknown), Bertha Warner (unknown)

Photo by Warren Dubois. Jones

Jones (Joseph)
*Paul Jones (1928), Susan Carter Jones (*unknown), *unknown* graves

---

140 Family documents, oral history.

Jones (Raleigh)

Raleigh Dolman Jones, Sr. (1944), Hannah Jones (unknown), unknown graves

Walters (John)

Howard Walters (unknown), Stewart Walters (unknown)

Wallace

Adolphus Wallace (1930), Cora Braxton Wallace (1974), Elizabeth Wallace Washington (1966), George Otha Wallace (1970), Jane Eula Smith Wallace (1970), Robert Wallace (1974), Beatrice Hazel Wallace Jones (1967), Beatrice Butler Wallace (1993)

Wilson

William "Willie" Wilson (1940), Julia Wilson, unknown graves

Jones-Williams

Mary "Aunt Mae" Jones (1937), unknown graves

This monument, constructed with bricks from the old church that was destroyed by fire in 1982, sits at the entrance of the old Mt. Olive Church cemetery. Trustee Carroll Smith, with the support of the trustee board, coordinated the project. Henry Thorndike drafted the plans.

Mt. Olive Baptist Church Cemetery

Location of cemeteries: **Old Church Site**, Mt. Olive Road, west corner on Mt. Olive Road, below a slope behind site, gated area northeast of the old church; adjacent to site of where Mt. Olivet School was located; **New Church Site**, Route 200, adjacent to new church.

Ball, Stanley Burnell (2009)	Norris, Norma G. (1993)	**Neighbors in Bogey Neck**
Bromley, James A. (2012)*	Norris, Maude Wilson (1994)	Corsey, James (unknown)
Bromley, Mildred Smith (1998)	Norris, Raymond Glascoe (1968)*	Corsey, William Leonard, Jr. (1989)*
Campbell, Sarah Wilson (unknown)	Smith, Lewis M., Jr. (2009)	Corsey, William, Jr. (1990*)
Jackson, Miriam Jones (2006)*	Walters, Emma Kent (2000)	Jessup, Merita (1999)
Jones, Alice C. (1970)	Walters, Ernest James (1988)	Norris, Alonzo (1987)*
Jones, Daniel Olin (1986)	Walters, Frederick, Sr. (2007)	Norris, Hannah (1996)*
Jones, Daniel Rudolph (1975)	Walters, Genevieve Yerby (1995)	Taylor, Cecil (1959)*
Jones, Ellis D. (2004)	Walters, Otha (1994)	Taylor, Maria (1975)*
Jones, Emily Smith (1963)	Walters, Solomon (1962)	Taylor, Roosevelt (1971)*
Jones, James Edward (1992)	Walters, Steven (1976)	
Jones, Joseph E., Sr. (2004)	Walters, Wilbert P. (2006)	Taylor, Serestine "Ressie" (1993)
Jones, Joseph W. (1941)*	Warner, Julia (2011)	Taylor, Viola (1977)*
Jones, Leonard Sky Joe (2006)	Warner, William James (2011)	Taylor, Walter H. "Sonny" (2004)*
Jones, Louis T., Sr. (1987)	Williams, Elaine Jones (2007)	Taylor, Wilbert (1990)

Jones, Mary L. (1958)*	Williams, Leon Mason (1967)*	Waddy, Lola Taylor (unknown)
Jones, Morris Allen (2005)	Wilson, Ernest D. (1996)	Walters, Emma Lee (2000)
Jones, Onard (1993)	Wilson, Frederick (1997)	Walters, Wilbert P., Jr. (2009)
Jones, Sherman P. (1977)	Wilson, Hilda D. (1979)	Wright, Lola Taylor (1996)*
Jones, Vera Sebree (2003)	Wilson, Robert Henry (2001)	
Jones, Walter (1931)*	Wilson, David C. (1991)	
Jones, William H. (1990)	Alice Wilson*	
Noel, Jean Smith (unknown)	Yerby, Dennis Leon (1989)*	
Norris, Emerson, Sr. (1992)		
Norris, Grace Walters (1986)		
Norris, Jennis P. (1952)*		
Norris, Kermit (1963)		
*Old cemetery		

Appendix F—A. G. W. Christopher General Store—1915 Ledgers

Walter Kennard Jones, Raleigh Doleman Jones,
Lombard Coleman Jones,
William W. Ball, Adolphus Wallace

150

Raligh Jones 1915

	1914 Bill			70
" " "			80
Mar. 1	1 Pair Shoes			250
8 1 " Pants			100
June 7	Bal. on Shoes			57
24 1 Shoes chop			200
July 5	Paid by Cash	2 57	
22 1 Shirt Tied	2 00		200
Aug. 7	Paid by cash	5 00	
" 20	70 mdse		1 29
" 25 " "			1 66
Sept. 14	1 Hat Medicine			2 35
" 20	70 mdse		18
" 25 " "			104
Oct. 2	Paid by cash	2 35	
" 4 " "	1 49	
" 1	Bal on sugar			18
" 9 " " Shoes & mo			85
" 1	1 Bot Medicine			67
16 1 " Soda			85
Nov. 6	Paid by cash	1 80	
" 12	1 Pair Pants			200
" 20	Paid by Cash	2 00	
Dec. 17	1 Pair Shoes & Squares	50		300
" 24	1 Bot M.S.			86
				2433

Lombert Louis 1915

1 Sack Feed		2 00
1 Bbl. Flour		7 50
1½ yds Cloth		35
1 Bbl. Gasoline		—
1 Bot. Medicine & Horse		60
Harness & Rake		1 49
to Hay		60
		50
Paid by cash	5 00	
10 Tobacco		1 45
Pipe & Pipe		30
Paid by cash	3 00	
½ lb. Mdse.		19
" "		60
Paid in full	7 50	
Meat & Flour		46
1 F. Shirt		2 00

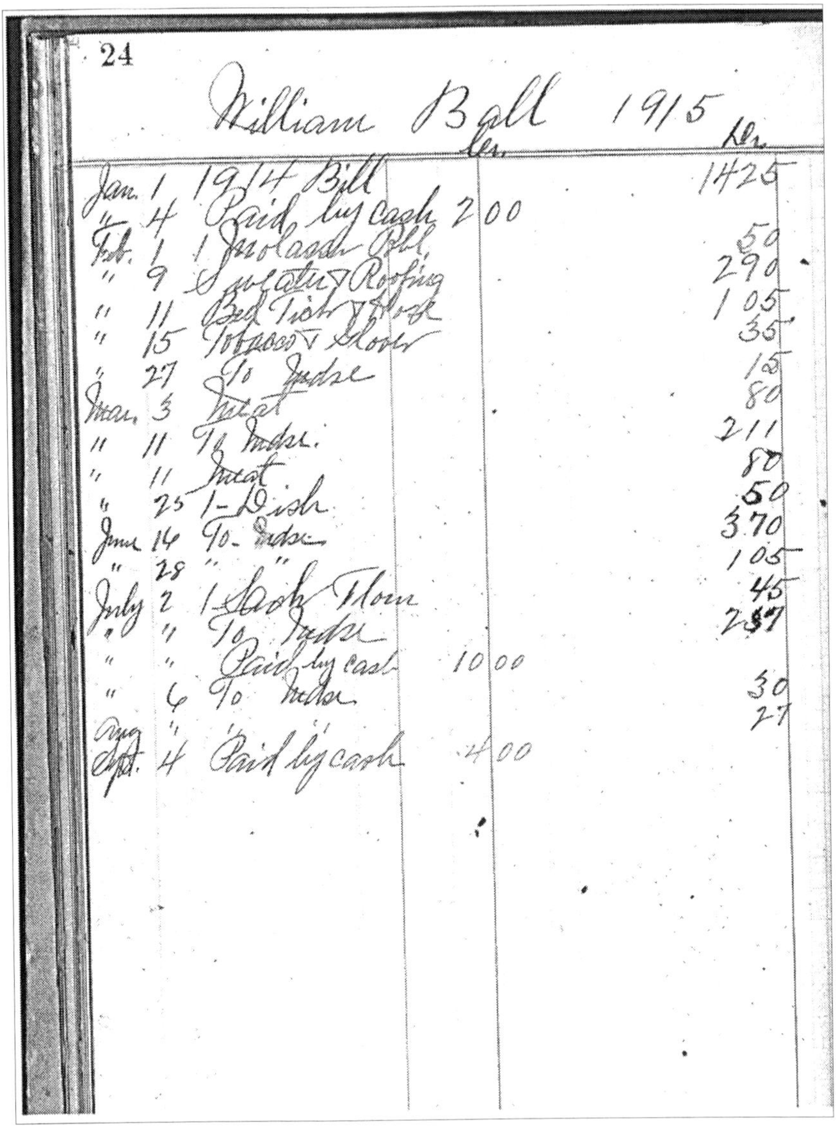

24

William Ball 1915

			Cr.	Dr.
Jan.	1	1914 Bill		14 25
"	4	Paid by cash	2 00	
Feb.	1	1 Molasses Bbl		50
"	9	Sweater & Roofing		2 90
"	11	Bed Tick & Hose		1 05
"	15	Tobacco & Gloves		35
"	27	To Mdse		15
Mar.	3	Meat		80
"	11	To Mdse.		2 11
"	11	Meat		80
"	25	1-Dish		50
June	14	To Mdse		3 70
"	28	" "		1 05
July	2	1 Sack Flour		45
"	"	To Mdse		2 37
"	"	Paid by cash	10 00	
"	6	To Mdse		30
Aug.	"	" "		27
Sept.	4	Paid by cash	4 00	

108

Adolphus Wallace 1915   Dr.

Jan. 1	1914 Bill	5 00
" 8	Shots ▽ Draws	1 30
" 27	To mdse	1 25
Feb. 4	1 Pair Pants	2 00
" 8	1 Bur. Meal	1 10
" 15	1 Bbl. Flour	7 50
" 20	Meal ▽ mdse	2 00
Mar. 6	To mdse	2 41
" 27	Meat ▽ g. P.	21
" "	Groceries	1 57
May 1	To mdse	2 00
May 3	Paid by cash 634	
" 27	1 Shirt	3 00
Aug 5	Corn ▽ Vaseline	30
Sept 1	Balon Shirt	2 00
" 25	70 – Sugar	65
Dec. 4	Paid by cash 400	
" 10	Balance of Boots	3 00
		35 29

313

Appendix G—Family Tree Worksheet[141]

"A family tree can wither if nobody tends its roots." —Unknown

The template below is what I used to record the genealogical data in this book. The census was my source for the period between 1850 and 1940. Selected descendants from each family coordinated the data for their respective families up through 2013.

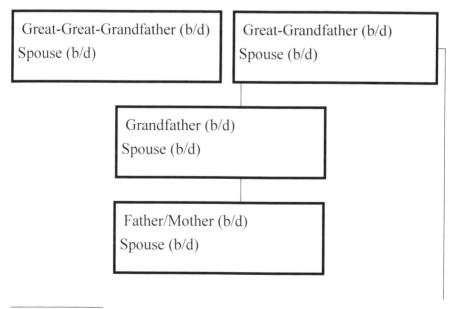

---

141 Worksheet created to collect genealogy data.

CHILDREN

Name	Birth/Death	Spouse	Birth/Death
Ex. *Mary Lee Smith*	1939-	Jay Smith	1937-1972

GRANDCHILDREN

Name	Birth/Death	Parent(s)	Spouse (b/d)
Ex. John Smith Jones	1959-1981	Mary Smith	Ellie Jones

Father/Mother (b/d)
Spouse (b/d)

GREAT-GRANDCHILDREN

Name	Birth/Death	Parent	Spouse

GREAT-GREAT-GRANDCHILDREN

Name	Birth/Death	Parent	Spouse

GREAT-GREAT-GREAT-GRANDCHILDREN

Name	Birth/Death	Parent	Spouse

Epilogue

Tracing the roots of Bogey Neck families has been a very interesting and rewarding experience. When I decided to embark on this project, I had no idea where I was going and how to get there. I am happy to have completed eleven months of research and to have written the history of the first African American families on Bogey Neck Road in Northumberland County, VA.

Although many of the living descendants no longer reside in Bogey Neck, it is a place that they still call home. Bogey Neck is probably one of the least known places in the northern neck of Virginia. It is my desire that sharing the history of this little road will inspire the next generations to continue to record the history of Bogey Neck Road and its people. I have met people that I would have never known had I not written this book. My personal contact has been through telephone conversations, interviews, e-mails, and regular mail. Some family members have said that they have connected with kinfolk for the first time.

The first African American settlers on Bogey Neck Road deserve to be recognized for their family values, perseverance, and contributions to building a stable community. In spite of many hardships, they were survivors. The heads of these households were hard workers and did what they could do to prepare their children for life's challenges. They shared much in common: they owned property (five acres or more); ten of eleven could read and write; they provided for their families; they worked hard as watermen, farmers, carpenters, cooks, servants, and laborers; they were involved in church; and they valued a strong family unit. The wives and mothers stayed home to care for the children and take care of the home. Additionally, they often took on jobs outside of the home, such as servant, cook, or washwoman to help provide for the family.

There are more than nine hundred descendants who have been identified from this rural two-mile dead end road located in Northumberland County, VA. They can be found living across America and abroad. They are educated at all levels and have pursued many different careers. Representatives from all of the generations of descendants have served their country in all branches of the military.

I sincerely hope that my efforts to connect the original African American families from Bogey Neck will inspire others to record their history for many generations to come.

Feel free to contact me with your comments. My e-mail address is mmjd40@gmail.com.

BIBLIOGRAPHY

Commonwealth of Virginia Personal Property Book 1910, issued by the auditor of Public Accounts, Richmond, VA.

Day, Mary J., *My Father's Journey,* Book Surge Publisher, 2009.

Deed Book TT, Northumberland County, VA.

Deed Books 93-152, Northumberland County, VA.

Deed Book 173, p .432-433, Northumberland County, VA.

General Index of Wills for Northumberland County, VA, Book #1.

Jett, Carolyn H. "History…Education," *The Northern Neck Echo* newspaper, March 1, 1984.

Jett, Carolyn H. "Three Hundred Years of Education," *Northern Neck of Virginia Historical Society,* Vol. XLVII, 2010 p, 75.

Land Records Books (1861-1869), Northumberland County, VA.

Land Records Books (0-1931), Northumberland County, VA.

Land Records Books (1885-2010), Northumberland County, VA.

Marriage License 1928-1935, Northumberland County, VA.

Marriage License 1866-1972, Northumberland County, VA.

Marriage Register Colored 1866-1917, Northumberland County, VA.

Marriage Register Colored 1917-1957, Northumberland County, VA.

Marriage Register A 1957-1988, Northumberland County, VA.

Miller, Mary R., *Places-Names of the Northern Neck of Virginia, from John Smith's 1606 map to present,* Virginia State Library, Richmond, VA, 1983.

Mount Olive Baptist Church, the One Hundredth Anniversary 1873-1973, Fifth Anniversary of the Pastor, Wicomico Church, VA, 1973.

Mount Olive Baptist Church, 133rd Church Anniversary, 53rd Homecoming Souvenir Booklet, Wicomico Church, VA, September 24, 2006.

Norris, James E. C., *Fight On My Soul, Iowa:* The Write Place Publishing Company, 2009.

"Northumberland Post Office," *Northern Neck of Virginia Historical Magazine,* Vol. XLVIII, The Northern Neck of Virginia Historical Society; Montross, Westmoreland County, VA, December 1998.

Remo General Store, A. G. W. Christopher's Ledger pages; Northumberland County Historical Society, Remo, VA, 1915.

Northumberland County Directory (1971). Prepared, published, and distributed by the Chamber of Commerce of Northumberland County, VA, March 1971.

Personal Property Tax Book (1920), Northumberland County, VA.

Personal Property Tax Book (1930)—Counties and Towns, Northumberland County, issued by the Department of Taxation, Richmond, VA.

Personal Property Tax Book (1940), Northumberland County, issued by the Department of Taxation, Richmond, VA.

Personal Property Book (1950), Northumberland County, issued by the Department of Taxation, Richmond, VA.

Stump, Bruce, "Man Is Last in State to Make Oyster Tong Shafts," *Daily Times* of Salisbury, MD, April 16, www.celmarvanow.com.

The Shepherd's Fold: Cemetery Records of Northumberland County, Virginia Churches," compiled by The Genealogical Society of the Northern Neck of Virginia, 2012.

Will Book, p. 672, Northumberland County, VA.

"As the tree grew, the generation grew. I hope that all the people who read this book will realize how the men and women of Bogey Neck— mothers and fathers, cousins, aunts, uncles, friends and family—helped to influence and mold me into the man that I am today. As a young man leaving this small community and going out into the world, I was equipped with a foundation that could withstand whatever the world threw at me. This foundation was created by the men who worked hard to provide for their families and the strong black women who worked by their sides to help make ends meet. It takes a village to raise a child, and Bogey Neck Road was my village. Thank God for this small community that still means so much to me and a place I still call home." —**Mark Alonzo Jones** *(great-great-grandson of Stafford B. Jones)*

About the Author

MARY MAHALIA JONES DAY (1940); great granddaughter of Stafford B. Jones (ca.1826) who fought with Union Army in the Civil War and Susan Warner (ca.1840) of Wicomico Church, VA; granddaughter of Joseph Warren Jones (ca. 1867–1940) and Mary L. Jackson Jones (ca.1887–1958) of Bogey Neck, a two-mile dead end road in the Wicomico Church district of Northumberland County, VA; one of five children and the only daughter of Daniel Olin Jones (1907–1986) of Bogey Neck and Vera Sebree Jones (1909–2003) of Mila Neck, VA; attended Mila Bogey Neck and Anna T. Jeanes elementary schools, Julius Rosenwald High School and graduate of Central HS class of 1959; B.S. degree in Business Education (1963) from Hampton University, Hampton, VA; Master's Degree in School Administration, Supervision and Curriculum (1976) from Loyola College, Baltimore, MD; retired June 2010 from Howard County Public School System, Howard County, MD after forty seven years in education as a teacher, counselor and high school administrator; former member of Mt. Olive Baptist Church, Wicomico Church, VA; currently a member of First Baptist Church of Guilford, Howard County, MD; member of Delta

Sigma Theta Sorority, Inc.; Author of "My Father's Journey – The Life Lessons of Deacon Daniel Olin Jones"; resides with husband, Robert E. Day Sr., in Columbia, MD; two sons –Robert Eugene Day, Jr. a graduate of United States Air Force Academy and Timothy Alan Day, a graduate of North Carolina A & T University; grandmother of four – Ryan Alexander Day, Rachel Michelle Day, Andrew Sterrett Day, and Emmanuel Timothy Day; step granddaughter, Chasity Pittman.